American Literature and the Long Downturn

American Literature and the Long Downturn

Neoliberal Apocalypse

DAN SINYKIN

OXFORD
UNIVERSITY PRESS

OXFORD
UNIVERSITY PRESS

Great Clarendon Street, Oxford, OX2 6DP,
United Kingdom

Oxford University Press is a department of the University of Oxford.
It furthers the University's objective of excellence in research, scholarship,
and education by publishing worldwide. Oxford is a registered trade mark of
Oxford University Press in the UK and in certain other countries

First Edition published in 2020

Published in the United States of America by Oxford University Press
198 Madison Avenue, New York, NY 10016, United States of America

British Library Cataloguing in Publication Data
Data available

Library of Congress Control Number: 2019946127

ISBN 978–0–19–885270–4

DOI: 10.1093/oso/9780198852704.001.0001

for my parents

Acknowledgments

I want to thank Kevin Attell, Jeremy Braddock, Cathy Caruth, and Dagmawi Woubshet for guiding me from the beginning. To find such fabulous mentors was an incredible stroke of luck.

At Cornell, Joel Anderson, Adhaar Desai, Luke Donohue, Megan Kruer, and Adin Lears were constant friends, who, over many dinners and drinks, talked ideas and told me when I was wrong. Liz Blake, Michaela Brangan, Jacob Brogan, Carl Gelderloos, Diana Hamilton, James Ingoldsby, Thom May, Anna McCormick, and everyone in the Big Fat Postwar American Novel Reading Group brought to scholarly life camaraderie and joy. I learned much from the Theory Reading Group in all its instantiations and want to thank, especially, Liron Mor and Johannes Wankhammer. This book began during evening conversations with Nathan Taylor on the porch of 118 Sears Street, where I first formulated most of these ideas.

At Grinnell, the students of "Neoliberal Apocalypse" helped me think through the central questions of this book at a crucial stage. Steve Andrews gave me the push I needed to get back to work on this.

I spent a happy year at the College of Wooster rewriting and thank Anthony Tognazzini for our rich conversations. Leslie Wingard provided important feedback on the first chapter. Laura Finch and Bertie Wooster made life extraordinary.

At Notre Dame, Matt Wilkens was generous with his time, thought, and counsel. CJ Jones was always up for an energetic conversation about theory over dinner. Francisco Robles and Brandon Menke made me feel at home in South Bend.

As I moved between institutions, Post45 provided an intellectual home. I am especially grateful to Sarah Chihaya, Annie McClanahan, and Richard Jean So.

It is frightening to meet one's academic dopplegänger. Fortunately for me, mine for this book is the brilliant Jessica Hurley with whom studying contemporary apocalypticism became a communal project. Jonathan

Eburne was a dream editor for the special issue of *ASAP/Journal*, "Apocalypse," that Jess and I co-edited.

This book is much better than it would have been otherwise thanks to Eric Cheyfitz, Wai Chee Dimock, and Don Pease, who read portions along the way and offered crucial feedback. I am indebted to the anonymous readers for Oxford University Press, my editor, Jacqueline Norton, and my copyeditor, Tim Beck, who pointed me in the right directions.

Kevin McNellis has read more of this book more times than anyone. We often disagree, and that has made this book much more rigorous. Thanks to Marissa Brostoff, Cory Cochrane, Mike Littell, Nicole Novak, and Ben Ratzlaff.

Thanks to my family: my brothers, Andy and Alex, and my parents, Stu and Carol.

Masha Vlasova is my world, which, despite the darkness surrounding us, is now full of light.

Some of this book was previously published and I gratefully acknowledge permission to republish here. Most of this material has been extensively revised. An excerpt from the introduction appeared in *The Washington Post* as "This is the Philip Roth Novel that Explains Philip Roth." An excerpt from Chapter 1 appeared in *Dissent* as "The Apocalyptic Baldwin." Excerpts from Chapter 2 appeared in *Los Angeles Review of Books* as "Charles Manson and the Apocalypse to Come" and "Trump and the End Times." An earlier version of Chapter 3 appeared in *American Literary History* as "Evening in America: *Blood Meridian* and the Origins and Ends of Imperial Capitalism." The editors there sharpened my arguments, polished my prose, and clarified my vision. The excerpt from "September 1, 1939," © 1940 and renewed © 1968 by W. H. Auden, from *Selected Poems* by W. H. Auden, edited by Edward Mendelson, is used by permission of Vintage Books, an imprint of the Knopf Doubleday Publishing Group, a division of Penguin Random House LLC. All rights reserved.

Contents

Introduction

Apocalypse shapes the experience of millions of Americans. Not because they face imminent cataclysm, however true this is, but because apocalypse is a story they tell themselves. It offers a way out of an otherwise irredeemably unjust world. Adherence to it obscures that it *is* a story, rather than a description of reality. And it is old. Since its origins among Jewish writers in the first centuries BCE, apocalypse has recurred as a tempting form through which to express a sense of hopelessness. Why has it appeared with such force in the United States now? What does it mean?

This book argues that to find the meaning of our apocalyptic times we need to look at the economics of the last five decades, from the end of the postwar boom. Scholars across disciplines recognize this as a coherent period. After historian Robert Brenner, I call it the long downturn.[1]

The long downturn led to the betrayal of civil rights by the government's failure to pursue economic justice. African Americans felt this betrayal as rat-infested housing in rotting inner cities, the replacement of lost jobs with informal economies, and mass incarceration. The long downturn led to stagflation and oil crises in the 1970s, the bankruptcy of New York City in 1975, and the rise of global finance and multinational conglomerates that challenged, not least in the minds of white evangelicals, US sovereignty. The long downturn led to decades of wage stagnation, and the explosion of public and personal debt. The long downturn witnessed the erosion of mechanisms, such as labor unions and civic organizations, through which, in the past, people ameliorated immiseration. This is how the long downturn came to feel like the end of the

[1] See Robert Brenner's *The Economics of Global Turbulence: The Advanced Capitalist Economies from Long Boom to Long Downturn, 1945–2005.*

American Literature and the Long Downturn: Neoliberal Apocalypse. Dan Sinykin, Oxford University Press (2020). © Daniel Sinykin.
DOI: 10.1093/oso/9780198852704.001.0001

world. This is how the long downturn ripened minds to forge, from an old form in new times, what I call neoliberal apocalypse.[2]

Apocalypse tends to make totalizing claims. The cataclysm comes for all of us. But there is no universal "we" who experiences "our" times as apocalyptic. Given the inequalities produced by the long downturn, diverse groups turned to apocalypse for different reasons. African Americans, white nationalists, and evangelicals took up the form. Writers used it to respond to imperial violence in American borderlands and the growing ubiquity of addiction. It is seductive as an expression of the experience of climate change. These are the lives and literature, the experiences and crises, presented in this book.

Apocalypse is a political literary form. During the long downturn, writers adopted it in an attempt to resolve what felt like insurmountable crises for political agency. Out of hopelessness, they wrote literary essays and novels. They invested literature with powers it would prove to lack. But the attempts are an indispensable archive that reveal the textures of life, and the meanings of literature, under neoliberalism.

In this introduction, I make the case for understanding this diverse literature as participating in a common form. A shared critique of America, from across a range of political ideologies, unites the texts I study. I argue on behalf of importing the concept of the long downturn to literary studies. I defend neoliberalism as a concept for making sense of what is happening in contemporary literature. I sketch apocalypse as a

[2] Faced with the crises of the long downturn, the populace could respond with reform, revolution, apocalypse, or an embrace of the status quo. Reform, revolution, and apocalypse have stood in tension throughout the period. Readers might recognize the positions with regard to climate change: regulate emissions; overthrow capitalism; wait until we all sink into the sea. Literature of the long downturn is not without its revolutionary moments. Consider militant 1970s feminism, certain elements within the Black Arts Movement, or Oakland-based Commune Editions. Exemplary is the poetic pamphlet "#Misanthropocene: 24 Theses" by Joshua Clover and Juliana Spahr, co-editors (along with Jasper Bernes) of Commune Editions, which published it. At once a prose poem and a political pamphlet, the lyric speech or political address of "#Misanthropocene" is organized around repeating a misanthropic "fuck you" to all in a historical moment whose dominant affect, for the speakers and audience of the poem/pamphlet, is identified as "west melancholy." Clover and Spahr echo Fredric Jameson's observation that because of the "sheer scale" of contemporary capitalism, "our minds feel small and inert" (4). Whereas once it felt as though "every fragment seemed to bear within it the whole," now "the whole being too large for the mind to see stands before us always as a fragment" (ibid.). The situation thus defined, the speakers could turn—like the figures studied in this book—in hopelessness at the impossible scope of the problem, to apocalypse. Instead, the twentieth thesis announces: "This is how the misanthropocene ends. We go to war against it" (8). The final five theses give instructions for revolutionary insurrection.

form with a long history to account for what it offers today's writers. I describe my methodology. I set us on a path toward understanding how neoliberal apocalypse organizes contemporary American literature and contemporary American lives.

America

Neoliberal apocalypticists dissent from a common understanding of America. They critique myths that sustain American nationalism: meritocracy, progress, exceptionalism. Rather than aim to restore the nation to foundational principles, they see the American project as doomed. James Baldwin, for example, who produced one of the great nationalist documents of the civil rights era in *The Fire Next Time*, arrived within a decade at a position from which he believed the only possibility for America was for it to burn to the ground.[3] This political position, as we will see, follows from apocalyptic form. I consider Baldwin's trajectory in Chapter 1.

Here, to illustrate, I offer the oeuvre of Philip Roth. Roth's lauded, late-career American Trilogy—*American Pastoral*, *I Married a Communist*, and *The Human Stain*—conveys an allegorical vision of America on the verge of succumbing to its "indigenous American berserk." The berserk, in *American Pastoral*, is the indignant fury of all-American Swede Levov's terrorist daughter Merry, who, in 1968, bombs a post office and kills a bystander. 1968, that year of riot and revolution, was marked by outbursts against a United States poised to pivot from boom to downturn, saddled with a war it could not afford and with dispossessed and disproportionately black populations at home it could not employ and would, instead, incarcerate. Coleman Silk, protagonist of *The Human Stain*, tries to escape blackness by passing as Jewish, only to be disgraced by American puritanism and killed, the narrator believes, by an unhinged Vietnam vet—the ghosts of 1968 lingering to murder America. As Sean McCann argues, Roth's trilogy "suggests that the very pursuit of

[3] Kevin Quashie rightly foregrounds how different Baldwin's nationalism is from that of the Black Arts Movement. Baldwin "speaks to the volatility of the sixties and the ravages of racism through an aesthetic of interiority. This is the quiet of Baldwin's nationalism, that his investigation exhibits vulnerability, multiplicity, confusion, and intimacy" (89).

the pastoral dream of democratic community demands the coercion and repression, and produces the resentment, that will ultimately destroy it" (191).[4]

Roth followed the trilogy with *The Dying Animal.* It is a short novel that culminates in New York City on New Year's Eve, 1999, a night of fear that Y2K—a potentially devastating computer bug—would bring America from the height of the dot-com boom into darkness. David Kepesh, the protagonist, is a cultural critic, part-time professor, and self-described "great propagandist for fucking" (105). On the first day of class, he picks out the students he wants to sleep with but waits to approach them until the semester ends to avoid claims of sexual harassment.

Kepesh, at 62, falls for his 24-year-old student, Consuela Castillo. They have an affair, but this time it's different. He is jealous. He obsesses. He becomes attached. She breaks his heart. But then, several years later, on—dramatically—New Year's Eve, 1999, she returns to him. She is dying of breast cancer and wants him to console her. He does.

Together, they watch the "brilliance flaring across the time zones" on TV (144). Kepesh thinks that the world is watching "the mockery of the Armageddon that we'd been awaiting in our backyard shelters since August 6, 1945" (ibid.). He ventriloquizes a world beyond fear of nuclear apocalypse: "the disaster of the end will now never arrive" (145). Speaking in the voice of the conglomerate global media, Kepesh thinks, "no bombs go off, no blood is shed—the next bang you hear will be the boom of prosperity and the explosion of markets" (ibid.). Nuclear fears have receded and given way to the optimism of the Washington Consensus. The aging Kepesh observes the obsolescence of his generation and its

[4] McCann compares Roth's apocalyptic disenchantment to "earlier writers, like Whitman or Stein or Wright or Ellison, who were more enticed by the image of presidential leadership, [and who] had found precisely such a solution to the problems of pain and loss in an idealized image of the nation-state" (190). For Roth, however, "no invocation of the solemn dignity of the nation or of the sovereign will of the people can be called on to justify and thus dispatch the bottom truth of coercion and violence" (190–1). McCann's narrative aligns with my claim that writers of the long downturn, in their apocalypticism, turned away from the nationalism that allowed earlier writers to seek resolution in the image of presidential power. Michael Szalay provides further evidence of the compatibility of pre-downturn writers with the state. In Hip Figures (2012), Szalay argues that boom-era writers, including Normal Mailer, John Updike, William Styron, and Ralph Ellison, "invoked hip . . . to consolidate the voting constituencies of postwar liberalism" (3). The same cannot be said for the downturn-era writers examined in this book.

fears in the glow of the bright lights of the indomitable New Economy at the end of history.

But from the midst of the dot-com bubble, Kepesh harbors doubts about the future, seeing "the slightest lucidity about the misery made ordinary by our era sedated by the grandiose stimulation of the grandest illusion" (ibid.). It is a simple bit of ideology critique, leading him to his conclusion: "Watching this hyped-up production of staged pandemonium, I have a sense of the monied world eagerly entering the prosperous dark ages. A night of human happiness to usher in barbarism.com" (ibid.). Capital, raging for more, will, like imperial Rome, fall at the hands of its self-created enemies ("barbarism.com"), leaving capitalists ("the monied world") "prosperous," though, if we take Roth's allusion to history seriously, capitalism will have given way to "the dark ages," a new feudalism.[5]

Roth wrote *The Dying Animal* during the dot-com bubble's deflation, in the early months of the new millennium. The economic growth of the late 1990s, fueled by investor confidence in the promise of the internet,[6] turned out to be a momentary reprieve from decades of slow growth. For Roth, the bursting of the bubble was an occasion to punctuate his apocalyptic American trilogy with an exclamation on the cataclysm of American capitalism. That Roth could assume that misery had been made ordinary by our era shows how much had changed from the beginning of his career, in 1959, when the postwar boom was incorporating and whitening Jews, bringing them into the mainstream, to which Roth responded by publishing *Goodbye, Columbus*. The era that, for Roth, made misery ordinary was the one that followed the boom: the long downturn.

[5] Kepesh's casual sense that the world is rushing toward a new feudalism is formalized in the predictions of Wolfgang Streeck, who anticipates that capitalism will fail to overcome the long downturn and will enter "a long period of systemic disintegration, in which social structures become unstable and unreliable" (36). He writes, "Life in a society of this kind demands constant improvisation, forcing individuals to substitute strategy for structure, and offers rich opportunities to oligarchs and warlords while imposing uncertainty and insecurity on all others, in some ways like the long interregnum that began in the fifth century CE and is now called the Dark Age" (36–7).

[6] Robert Gordon describes the dot-com bubble as "a brief revival during 1996–2004 that most analysts attribute to the influence of the invention of the web, search engines, and e-commerce, as well as to the sharp spike of investment in information and communication technology (ICT) equipment" (523).

The Long Downturn

During the two decades that followed World War II, the United States experienced an economic boom with few if any historical parallels.[7] But between 1965 and 1973, economic growth slowed, inflation ballooned, and Richard Nixon, under pressure, unpegged the dollar from the gold standard, which led to the collapse of the Bretton Woods Agreement, the international system of fixed exchange rates, "which had sustained and regulated the post-war expansion" (Arrighi 3).[8]

Growth has been slow since.[9] Many of the maladies of our moment that have, especially since the financial crisis of 2007–8, become familiar have their roots in these decades of slowed growth: wage stagnation, the decline of unions, mass incarceration, the rise of the finance sector, economic instability. Wealth inequality has reached levels unseen in nearly a century.[10] These decades have also seen the expansion of debt. When the financial crisis of 2008 arrived, "US households held $13

[7] Giovanni Arrighi suggests that 1848–73 may have been "not all that different" from 1950–75 (307). Robert Brenner argues for a similarity between the prosperity of the postwar boom and that of the years "between 1890 and 1913" (xxvi).

[8] For the reasons identified by Arrighi, cultural critic Joshua Clover marks 1973 as the "swivel, with the collapse of industrial profits signaling the onset of what should rightly be called the Long Crisis" (9).

[9] Economist Robert Gordon, in *The Rise and Fall of American Growth*, points to 1970 as the "distinct break point between faster and slower growth" (522). Gordon argues that growth has been slow in the United States for almost fifty years, and will only be worse in the next fifty. Robert Brenner defines "the long downturn" as "the extraordinarily extended phase of reduced economic dynamism and declining economic performance, persisting through the end of the old millennium and into the new" (xix). Key indicators for this decrease of dynamism and performance are the "rate of profit" and productivity growth (Brenner 6). Economists offer competing theses to explain the falling rate of profit and slowing growth. Gordon argues that technological innovations stopped having the expansive force to spur growth that they had from 1870 to 1970. Brenner argues that Germany and Japan quickly caught up with the United States in terms of productive capacity in the postwar years, triggering a glut of surplus manufactured goods that drove down prices, which led to declining rates of profit and slowed growth. Both theses are contestable. Both are embedded in debates among economists. That said, the reason for the downturn matters less for this book than the downturn itself. In my account of the downturn, I lean on Brenner, along with Gordon, Giovanni Arrighi, Greta Krippner, Thomas Piketty, and Wolfgang Streeck, among others.

[10] French economist Thomas Piketty, in *Capital in the Twenty-First Century*, devotes himself to the study of wealth inequality, which, he argues, expands when capital investments (in, say, the stock market) grow faster than the economy as a whole. Since this has been the case for almost fifty years in the United States, with the intensifying factors of wage stagnation for most and soaring incomes for CEOs, Americans have "regained—indeed, slightly exceeded—the level [of wealth inequality] attained in the [extremely unequal] second decade of the previous century" (15).

trillion in debt, more than thirty times what they held in the mid-1970s" (McClanahan, *Dead* 1). Slow growth, growing inequality, rising debt: sociologist Wolfgang Streeck calls these "the three apocalyptic horsemen of contemporary capitalism" (17–18).

A closer look at how these changes transpired will offer an outline for this book. As growth slowed in the 1970s, the government "struggled to meet expanded commitments with increasingly limited resources," leading to a "distributional conflict" between "various social groups" (Krippner 16–17). Policymakers had to decide whether to privilege "industry or housing, large corporations or small businesses, urban areas or farmers" (Krippner 24). On one hand, there were "urban riots in the rotting core of inner cities," and on the other, there was "middle-class frustration with credit shortages" (Krippner 59). In plain terms, policymakers faced a choice between favoring capital and further enriching the rich, or favoring labor, the underemployed, and the unemployed, thereby alleviating poverty. They failed to choose, defaulting to capital, and inducing inflation. Meanwhile, manufacturing jobs were outsourced, domestic jobs shifted to the service sector, unemployment rose, and capital clamped down on labor, soon with the assistance of President Ronald Reagan—what Joshua Clover describes as "recompositions of class and global division of labor that progressively undermine[d] the possibilities for militant labor organization in the west," leading to a turn away from the strike as the central tactic for resisting capital, and toward the riot (9–10).

When policymakers finally addressed distributional conflicts by deregulating credit and banking in the late 1970s and 1980s, they ushered in an era of financialization (Krippner 140). Finance proved a potent tactic by which corporations could supplement the lost profitability of manufacturing, and many former manufacturing giants created or expanded financial wings.

Under Reagan, the United States attempted to stimulate growth through large tax cuts, which Paul Volcker, head of the Federal Reserve, paired with high interest rates. This combination led to soaring public debt for the United States, while foreign money flooded in, which propped up the state and gave the ever-more-unfettered US investment banks a surplus of money capital that needed to be invested somewhere (Brenner 190–1). Investment banks found appropriately sized borrowers in nation-states. When these nation-states went bankrupt, pressed by various factors, including the persistence of slow growth at home and high interest rates in the United States, the lending banks, with the help of the International Monetary Fund, imposed structural adjustment plans, forcing policies of widespread privatization of public goods, deregulation, and the opening of markets, all of which worked to siphon money from the poor to the wealthy. Marxist geographer David Harvey calls these techniques of class restoration "accumulation by dispossession," identifying them as part of the history of imperialism (160–5). In short, the 1980s witnessed the rise of the finance sector and the eruption of public debt.

If the 1970s brought inflation and the 1980s public debt, the 1990s brought household debt. The deregulation of credit gave consumers greater access to credit than ever before. Policymakers were surprised by the ceaseless demand for credit, despite how high the price rose (Krippner 83). This demand would only continue to increase over time, leading Annie McClanahan to ask, "what explains the growing *demand* for credit, especially given that it was more available but less affordable than ever?" (*Dead* 10). The answer, as McClanahan points out, is simple. From the 1970s on, wages stagnated, the social safety net was disassembled, and yet prices continued to rise (*Dead* 10–11). Consumers were not going into debt to support "discretionary" spending, they went into debt so that they "were able to continue to survive" (*Dead* 11).

The long downturn, decade by decade, brought inflation, public debt, private debt, and their corollaries, the decimation of labor, the subjugation of nation-states to US investment banks, and the intensification of precarity. These phases—inflation|labor; public debt|subjugation of nation-states by finance; private debt|domestic precarity—comprise the loose chronological structure for this book. Chapters 1 and 2 explore how African Americans and whites thought about and fought against the racial politics and economic crises of the 1970s. Chapters 3 and 4 take up public debt, finance, and imperial capitalism, especially with regard to the United States and Mexico. Chapter 5 investigates the debt economy and the private pain of the 1990s. Though it might have seemed abstract, the economics of the long downturn worked its way, mediated by deleterious effects, apocalyptic narrative, and neoliberalism, into the most intimate experiences of everyday life, including the fear that there would be no tomorrow.

Neoliberalism

Neoliberalism[11] is the long downturn's dominant ideology. Friedrich Hayek, Milton Friedman, and others involved in the Mont Pèlerin Society developed neoliberalism in their writing and advocacy. They believed that the spontaneous, impersonal, and anonymous "mechanism of the market" would best organize society, and thus must be safeguarded by the state (Hayek 73). They came to this belief in reaction against Keynesianism and social planning, which, they felt, if continued, would lead to totalitarianism as "a necessary outcome" (Hayek 59). Hayek claimed that economic freedom—the free market—was required for political freedom (67). The proper role of the state was limited to providing the conditions that would make "the best possible use of the forces of competition as a means of coordinating human efforts," which included maintaining a monopoly on violence (85).[12] In his frequent popular columns, Friedman promoted market fundamentalism, deregulation, human capital, individual responsibility, and entrepreneurialism. These practices and epistemologies proved expedient for those in power. Under Margaret Thatcher, neoliberalism took the slogan, *there is no alternative*, which became one of its tenets.

[11] The scholarship on neoliberalism is expansive and divisive. To get a sense of its breadth, one might read *Undoing the Demos* by Wendy Brown, *The Great Persuasion* by Angus Burgin, *The Birth of Biopolitics* by Michel Foucault, *A Brief History of Neoliberalism* by David Harvey, and *Globalists* by Quinn Slobodian.

[12] Reader's Digest, the most widely read periodical in the United States at the time, published an abridged version of *The Road to Serfdom* just before Hayek came to the country on a speaking tour. A couple years later, Hayek founded the Mont Pèlerin Society, "an international gathering place for leading philosophers, economists, journalists, politicians, and philanthropists who supported the market mechanism" (Burgin 8). In *The Great Persuasion*, historian Angus Burgin tells how Mont Pèlerin was "a point of origin for the elaborate network of policy institutes that inspired and advised the resurgent Anglo-American conservative leadership of the late twentieth century" (8). Among the first members of the Mont Pèlerin Society was the young economist Milton Friedman, who would double down on Hayek's most radical positions and become a powerful public intellectual, advising presidents and writing hundreds of opinion pieces, often for The Wall Street Journal or Newsweek. Friedman insisted on the free working of the market as "a necessary condition for political freedom" and advocated a smaller role for the state than Hayek allowed (4). In practice, Friedman opposed a minimum wage, social security, public housing, national parks, trade restrictions, and regulations (35–6).

Neoliberalism is a contemporary technique by which capitalism coopts and defuses critique by claiming that any dissent is addressed within its ineluctable logic, a tendency that theorists of neoliberalism too often abet.[13] A seductive way to respond to a lack of alternatives is to imagine total annihilation.[14] One meaning of *neoliberal apocalypse* is this response to the closing down of other worlds. Mitchum Huehls argues that writers in the twenty-first century have learned another way: to eschew critique, to refuse to contend with neoliberalism in terms of ideology, and, instead, to oppose it by reconfiguring the world. He sees this literature as "marked thematically by the economic supersession of the cultural, a deep suspicion of ideologies of all stripes, a commitment to presence, and an increased prominence given to things," and, so, as "devoted to literary forms that are neither reflexive nor recursive, that favor networks over oppositions, and that successfully produce meaning without conventional forms of reference" (32). But Huehls is too credulous about neoliberalism's claims to having remade the world. Because he accepts these claims as true, he refuses ideology as impotent, rejecting Marxism, which he considers the major version of critique, and advocates in its place ontological politics based in the work of sociologist Bruno Latour. I agree that neoliberalism *feels* to many monolithic and insuperable, and generates responses like neoliberal apocalypse and, as he argues, an ontological literature.[15] But I remain unconvinced that we

[13] My critique of theories of neoliberalism was first inspired by Sarah Brouillette's "Neoliberalism and the Demise of the Literary."

[14] On the left, Thatcher's there is no alternative became, through the paraphrasing of a slightly different Fredric Jameson quote, it's easier to imagine the end of the world than the end of capitalism. Mark Fisher took up this shibboleth and its implications for contemporary experience in *Capitalist Realism* (2009). Leigh Claire La Berge and Alison Shonkwiler extended Fisher's project to contemporary fiction, nonfiction, television, and film in *Reading Capitalist Realism* (2014). In search of escapes from neoliberalism's foreclosure of any future other than its own, novelists, poets, and scholars have turned to speculative modes. See Aimee Bahng's *Migrant Futures*, a book that "might be considered a 'starter archive' of attempts to imagine if not the end of capitalism, then an alternative to it, by way of those who may find themselves mired in capitalism or displaced by it, but who continue to speculate beyond its logics" (xi). For an account of speculative modes in contemporary poetry, see Ronda, "The Social Forms of Speculative Poetics."

[15] Along with apocalyptic despair and new ontological possibilities, another response to contemporary economics, and specifically to the attempts by nation-states to incorporate authors into creative economies, has been to articulate "complicity with and distance from various facets of the placement of art in instrumental service to the economy," as detailed by Sarah Brouillette in *Literature and the Creative Economy* (1).

should look for successful politics from our literature[16]—an argument I make throughout this book—and that neoliberalism, despite its force and ubiquity, is inevitable or that it has attained, as many of its theorists claim, the status of common sense.[17]

Neoliberals took advantage of the long downturn to institute their ideas. (This against Wendy Brown's claim that neoliberalism was "gestated by Keynesianism, fascism, Nazism, state planning, and social democracy" and "was not born from crises of capitalist accumulation" (59).) Friedman himself narrated the history of neoliberalism as interlocked with economic crisis, writing in the 1982 preface to *Capitalism and Freedom* that, when he first published the book in 1962, he and other neoliberals were "a small beleaguered minority," but in twenty years their ideas had become "almost conventional among the broader public" (xi–xii). He credits the change to the downturn: Lyndon Johnson's "great reform programs" "turning to ashes," the persistence of "high taxes," and inflation (xiii). His "basic function" as a public intellectual, as he understood it, was to develop and promote his vision of the world so that when a crisis occurred, that vision would go from being "politically impossible" to being "politically inevitable" (xiv). There is

[16] Sarah Brouillette puts it best: "we must at least consider the question of why, when work [that critiques capitalism] is so widely circulated and embraced by people within the literary milieu, the incorporative force of capitalism nevertheless motors on? To neglect this question, to ignore the delimitation of literary activity and exposure, to write as if literature is straightforwardly 'an active power in the making of worlds . . . a site of processes of worlding and an agent that participates and intervenes in these processes' (Cheah 2), is to fail to recognize its actual dominant character and the contingencies and mediations that define it. Whose 'worlding' does it shape? In whose thought does it intervene?" (UNESCO 5).

[17] Annie McClanahan argues that "for millions of people across the United States, to say nothing of globally, the realization of ends has always been economic, and we . . . have to think about the ways this dependence is not the consequence of workers' 'commonsense' beliefs" ("Serious" 121). She argues that what theorists mean when they say neoliberalism has become commonsense is that it has become commonsense for the class to which the theorists themselves belong, which often means that of tenured university professors. Wendy Brown has contributed more than any other theorist to the notion that neoliberalism has become common sense and that its dictates are inescapable. Leigh Claire La Berge and Quinn Slobodian argue that Brown "grants more autonomy to the market and closure to political struggle than neoliberals do themselves" (607). In a decisive argument against Brown's positions, McClanahan observes that the influence of human capital—the idea that all one's decisions are in fact economic—only appears novel from a certain privileged class position and that neoliberalism has traction because, "more and more people are finding themselves permanently and newly in the class of people for whom everything on which life depends is profoundly economic, precisely insofar as it is uncertain, precarious, and without guarantee"—and these people often include theorists of neoliberalism themselves ("Serious" 121).

no alternative. Keynesianism and totalitarianism gestated neoliberalism, but it was born from crisis.

Apocalypse

Neoliberalism is contemporary. Apocalypse is ancient. It formed out of centuries of failed Jewish prophecy that promised self-determination in the Promised Land. The crucial year is 167 BCE. The Seleucid empire, an offshoot of Alexander the Great's conquests, came to occupy Judea in 200 BCE, and, thirty-three years later, a vicious king, Antiochus IV, pressured Jews to assimilate to Greek culture. Many did, especially urban elites. Hellenized Jews assumed power in Jerusalem and Antiochus made the practice of Judaism punishable by death, rededicating the Jewish Temple to Zeus, and, to the horror of traditional Jews, desecrating the Temple with the slaughter of a pig.

For several hundred years, Jews had been listening to prophets like Jeremiah who promised that if they only stopped erring, God would restore peace and prosperity. By the time Antiochus arrived, the message was tired. Behaving well did not seem to help the Jews, who felt on the verge of annihilation, so, while the Maccabees took up arms,[18] others took up a form that had just begun flickering to life and crystallized it.

Apocalypse took agency out of their hands in anticipation of divine intervention, when God or his angels would destroy the Seleucid empire. A new Jewish sect moved down from Jerusalem to a valley on the north shore of the Dead Sea, declared itself the true Israel, and awaited the end of the world. This was the Qumran community, which produced the Dead Sea scrolls, a vast body of texts discovered in caves beginning in 1947. Qumran was not alone. Antiochus inspired a craze for eschatology and new apocalyptic writing, none more well known than the Book of Daniel. After Daniel escapes the lion's den, the book takes a dramatic

[18] Traditional Jews from the surrounding countryside, instigated by the priest Mattathias and led by Judas Maccabeus, formed a militia and fought a guerilla war against the Hellenized Jews and imperial Seleucids. The Maccabees bloodily battled their way into Jerusalem and, victorious, ritually cleansed the Temple. Meanwhile, other traditional Jews responded to Antiochus not with blood but with words, and their legacy is vastly more influential.

turn toward divine violence and final judgment. These latter chapters were written between 167 and 164 BCE, in the midst of the Maccabean insurrection, as an alternative vision of anti-imperial salvation. The flourishing of this apocalypticism set the stage for the unlikely ascendance, two hundred years later, of a carpenter from Nazareth who strongly hinted that he was the one we had been waiting for.

The Jesus of the Gospels was an apocalyptic figure, self-identifying as the Book of Daniel's messianic "Son of Man," who claimed the end was nigh, that it would arrive before the generation to which he spoke passed away. He would return to save them from the oppressive imperialism of the Romans. When, after more than fifty years, despite the intensifications of Rome's persecutions, he failed to come, one of his followers, a man named John, who had been exiled to an island called Patmos, received a vision of Christ's imminent return as a warrior who would fill the world with bloodshed. After the annihilation of evil, after the final judgment, a new Jerusalem would descend from heaven as paradise on earth, a return to Eden, complete with the tree of life. Suffused with violence and arcane symbols, John's report, the Book of Revelation, the last book of the Christian Bible, is the most influential account of the apocalypse.

What I mean by apocalypse is the tradition begun by the books of Daniel and Revelation.[19] The texts in this tradition tend to share several features. They present the apocalypse as imminent, miraculous, collective, terrestrial, and total (Cohn 15). The apocalypse will come soon, enacted by an inevitable force beyond human control, and will be experienced as an utter transformation of life on earth. Such texts appear as consolation for groups "undergoing crisis" (McGinn 7). They entail "a profound pessimism about the present that is seen as a time of crisis involving moral degeneration, persecution of the good, and the triumph of the wicked" and "belief in an imminent divine judgment of the wicked and vindication of the just" (ibid.). Apocalypse is literature written in resistance to imperialism. As such, it is, unlike

[19] For comprehensive accounts of the rich tradition of apocalyptic writing from 300 BCE to the present, see John J. Collins, *The Apocalyptic Imagination*; Bernard McGinn, *Apocalyptic Spirituality*; Norman Cohn, *The Pursuit of the Millennium*; Michael Barkun, *Disaster and the Millennium*; and Paul Boyer, *When Time Shall Be No More*.

the prophetic tradition from which it emerged, attuned to an international, rather than national, scale.[20]

The form has a long history in the Americas. Columbus and the Puritans both expected that their arrival in the Americas would accelerate Christ's return.[21] Western New York in the 1840s became a hotbed of apocalyptic revivalism, out of which came the Church of Jesus Christ of Latter-day Saints, the Jehovah's Witnesses, and the Seventh-day Adventists. The horrifying violence of the US Civil War inspired widespread apocalypticism.[22] It has come and gone with tides of real and perceived crises.

A consideration of the preeminent study of literature and the apocalypse, Frank Kermode's *The Sense of an Ending*, will show the force of the

[20] These shared features amount to nothing so comprehensive as a genre. We would not want to try to squeeze James Baldwin's *No Name in the Street*, Leslie Marmon Silko's *Almanac of the Dead*, and Jerry B. Jenkins and Timothy LaHaye's *Left Behind* series—all texts I consider in this book—into a single genre. Studies that attempt to delimit apocalyptic writings as such stretch credulity. Regardless of one's theory of genre, whether that of Northrop Frye or Pierre Bourdieu, apocalypse is an uneasy fit. I understand it, instead, as a loose form joined together under a single term by family resemblances. Following Caroline Levine, I take "form" to mean "an arrangement of elements—an ordering, patterning, or shaping" (3). This meaning of form, though broad, highlights how apocalypticism shapes texts, history, and experience according a particular plot and a worldview that spans ideologies and millennia. Levine's concept of form also emphasizes a form's affordances: in this instance, how apocalypse, however diverse its instantiations, affords hope for the hopeless in a time of perceived crisis.

[21] Thomas O. Beebee and Lois Parkinson Zamora both look back to Columbus and the Puritans in their strong comparative studies of apocalyptic literature in the Americas. Beebee's *Millennial Literatures of the Americas, 1492–2002* includes a sustained analysis of Columbus's apocalyptic letters. To address his concerns, Beebee coins the neologism "eschatechnology" ("juxtaposing three concepts: technological devices (UFOs, assault weapons); a disciplinary regime or 'technology of the self' (decency, honest banking, the 'right to buy'); and divine intervention in the form of the end of the world (Rapture, the Second Coming") (3). Zamora's focus is formalist. She writes about a selection of contemporary US and Latin American writers, arguing that "their self-conscious use of the imagery and narrative forms of biblical apocalypse affects" how these texts negotiate intradiagetic "ends" and extradiegetic "endings," when the reader reaches the last page (2).

[22] A handful of studies have detailed the apocalyptic literature that recurs across US literary history, though their frequent inclusions of Moby-Dick, A Connecticut Yankee in King Arthur's Court, Absalom, Absalom!, The Day of the Locust, and Invisible Man suggests how liberal these studies are in their sense of what counts as apocalypse. See David Ketterer, *New Worlds for Old*; John Lardas, *The Bop Apocalypse*; Zbigniew Lewicki, *The Bang and the Whimper*; Lakshmi Mani, *The Apocalyptic Vision in Nineteenth Century American Fiction*; John R. May, *Toward a New Earth*; Timothy Parrish, *From the Civil War to the Apocalypse*; Douglas Robinson *American Apocalypses*; Elizabeth K. Rosen, *Apocalyptic Transformation*; and David J. Leigh, *Apocalyptic Patterns in Twentieth-Century Fiction*. In the introduction to a special issue of ASAP/Journal, called "Apocalypse," that we co-edited, Jessica Hurley and I called for "a revaluation of apocalypse in its many aspects: as an aesthetic, a form, a genre, a practice, a structure of feeling, and an orientation" (453). The essays in the issue are evidence that such a revaluation is well underway.

resurgence of the apocalypse during the long downturn. Kermode posited apocalypse as the model for how fiction, by providing ends that are consonant with origins—whether via the New Jerusalem, a wedding, or the consummation of a tragedy—satisfies readers' needs for a shape, pattern, or organization to experience (5). Because we are always in the middle of things, Kermode argues, we "need fictive concords with origins and ends, such as give meaning to lives and poems" (7). Plot is the tool to accomplish this goal, "an organization that humanizes time by giving it form" (45). Given the most concordant plot as a paradigm—apocalypse—writers can diverge as much as they want. For a given set of readers, the academics and elites who Kermode calls the "clerisy," the greater the divergence, the greater the refusal of "easy satisfactions," the greater the book (19). James Joyce's *Ulysses* is a good example: it adopts the model of Homer's *Odyssey*, with its trajectory of exile and return, but endlessly diverts from and denies the satisfactions of Homer's paradigm, making it appealing to the clerisy.

From the perspective of 1965, when he first presented *The Sense of an Ending* as a series of lectures, Kermode believed that, although "the End has perhaps lost its naïve *imminence*, its shadow still lies on the crises of our fictions; we may speak of it as *immanent*" (6). Literary writers no longer anticipated imminent cataclysm as an event in the world; instead, they incorporated cataclysm into the psyches of their narrators and characters and into the form of their writing itself. Kermode describes immanence in fiction as characterized by a sense of "eternal transition," when "transition itself becomes an age" (101).[23] For the late modernism exemplified, for Kermode, by Samuel Beckett, Jack Kerouac, and Alain Robbe-Grillet, history is "that which ought to be ignored" (115). Though desiring the certainty of apocalypse, writers only found "vain temporality, mad, multiform antithetical influx" (115). Instead of the end of the world, we have Beckett's "the end is in the beginning and yet you go on," Kerouac's endless pursuit of "the mad ones," Robbe-Grillet's submergence of plot beneath perspective in the *nouveau roman*. Kermode's sense of the transitional yet ahistorical literature of his moment is

[23] For an excellent recent account of the literature of the 1950s as transitional, see Matthew Wilkens, *Revolution*, who, in a clarifying act of categorization, describes an array of major texts from the period as "encyclopedic allegories of the process of revolutionary change itself" (3).

predicated on the culture of the postwar boom: dominated, as many scholars have observed, by anxiety about technology, conformity, and urbanization amid relatively evenly distributed increases in wealth.[24] The consensus among economists in 1965 was that growth would continue indefinitely as it had been.[25] That was about to change; the end was about to get imminent again—apocalypse would become again central to the history and narration of the present.

This is not to say that there were not apocalyptic writings during the postwar boom. Most obviously, writers including Peter George, John Hersey, and Walter Miller wrote about nuclear war. But, as Jacques Derrida argues in "No Apocalypse, Not Now," nuclear war breaks from the tradition of apocalyptic writing because total nuclear war would be totally destructive, leaving no remainder from which to experience revelation. The literary critic's task, as taken up by Daniel Grausam in *On Endings* (2011), is to imagine how the threat of total catastrophe alters literary form.[26] Nuclear technology also motivated post-apocalyptic fiction, which functions by a different set of conventions than those that govern the apocalyptic tradition, and fall outside my purview.[27]

If, per Derrida, nuclear war remains "fabulously textual," apprehensible as a "fable" that casts its shadow back on us, then nuclear infrastructures organize, in a less-remembered Derridean insight, "not only the army, diplomacy, politics, but the whole of the human *socius* today, everything that is named by the old words culture, civilization" (23). Jessica Hurley turns our attention from the proleptic fable of a world-ending blast to the environmental injustice of everyday life in the nuclear age. Hundreds of nuclear tests and their deleterious effects on disproportionately subaltern peoples, along with nuclear infrastructures themselves, remain difficult to perceive, Hurley notes, because of "secrecy, misinformation, and bureaucratic boringness designed to deflect attention" (*Infrastructures* 8). She shows how novelists—including several

[24] For an overview of this scholarship, see Morris Dickstein's introduction to *Leopards in the Temple*.

[25] See Robert J. Gordon, *The Limit to Growth*.

[26] See also Joseph Dewey, *In a Dark Time*.

[27] For an account of post-apocalyptic literature, see James Berger, *After the End*; and Heather Hicks, *The Post-Apocalyptic Novel in the Twenty-First Century*.

I attend to in this study—have found in apocalypse a form through which to make nuclear infrastructures visible. She shows how they transfigure through apocalyptic plots the future foreclosed by these infrastructures into newly imaginable, livable, and just presents (*Infrastructures* 5). Her argument is a necessary complement to this one. Nuclear infrastructures and the long downturn together shape the contours of the foreclosed futures and reimagined worlds of neoliberal apocalypse.

Methodology

Marxist cultural critic Fredric Jameson's *Postmodernism* remains the canonical account of economics and US literature since 1945,[28] though scholars have grown increasingly dissatisfied with "postmodernism" as an organizing concept.[29] Jameson periodizes based on Ernest Mandel's dubious "late capitalism." Jameson himself equivocates for several pages

[28] In the introduction to their useful compendium, The Routledge Companion to Literature and Economics (2018), Michelle Chihara and Matt Seybold write that, in 2015, Routledge senior editor Polly Dodson noticed "an uptick in panels, papers, and plenaries explicitly engaging finance and economics" (3). Many of these have since become books, some of them addressing contemporary literature, with particular attention to the twenty-first century: Aimee Bahng, *Migrant Futures*; Sarah Brouillette, *Literature and the Creative Economy* and *UNESCO and the Fate of the Literary*; Mitchum Huehls, *After Critique*; Theodore Martin, *Contemporary Drift*; Annie McClanahan, *Dead Pledges*; Stephen Schryer, *Maximum Feasible Participation*; and Rachel Greenwald Smith, *Affect and American Literature in the Age of Neoliberalism*. Huehls and Smith gathered work by leading scholars for their essay collection, *Neoliberalism and Contemporary Culture*. Important studies on economics and literature that focus on other periods include Ian Baucom, *Specters of the Atlantic*; Catherine Gallagher, *Nobody's Story* and *The Body Economic*; Jean-Joseph Goux, *Symbolic Economies*; Anna Kornbluh, *Realizing Capital*; Walter Benn Michaels, *The Gold Standard and the Logic of Naturalism*; Mark Osteen and Martha Woodhouse, eds, *The New Economic Criticism*; Mary Poovey, *Genres of the Credit Economy*; and Marc Shell, *The Economy of Literature and Money, Language, and Thought*.

[29] Jason Gladstone, Andrew Hoberek, and Daniel Worden's *Postmodern/Postwar* and "After" serves as a book-length "conversation" about the recent trend of questioning "whether postmodernism was ever a significant aspect of postwar American literary culture" (2). Hoberek dismantles the notion that there ever was a hegemonic literary postmodernism while still positing, and positioning contemporary literature against, a "postmodern project" ("After" 239). In a later essay, he writes that "the history of postmodernist criticism . . . was arguably always more an expression of desire for a literary historical category like modernism than the analysis of a coherent movement in its own right" ("Postmodernism and Modernization" 343). He details the postmodern project, the postmodern desire, extending and revising the thesis from his monograph, *The Twilight of the Middle Class*, as "both mapping middle-class proletarianization and elaborating imagined solutions to this problem" (ibid.). Mark McGurl, meanwhile, provides an influential new schema as a wholesale replacement for postmodernism in The Program Era. Scholars often use "the contemporary" to describe the period after

of his preface, making clear his ambivalence about the category (xviii–xxii). Yet his theses—that the ubiquity of commodification led postmodern artists to abandon any pretense of separation from mass culture; and that an incommensurability between contemporary capitalism and individual comprehension had broken our ability to think historically—continue to enable insightful readings of cultural objects. Jameson is more modest than many give him credit for, acknowledging that he is "very far from feeling that all cultural production today is 'postmodern,'" the scare quotes indicating his skepticism about a term that has stuck closely to his name (6). And his distaste for contemporary US fiction means he seldom writes about it, leaving that work to others.[30, 31]

postmodernism or as an alternative. See Amy Hungerford, "On the Period Formerly Known as Contemporary" and Emily Hyde and Sarah Wasserman, "The Contemporary."

[30] Jameson discovered Giovanni Arrighi's work in 1994. His subsequent essay—"Culture and Finance Capital"—an update to Postmodernism using Arrighi's instead of Mandel's periodization, offers an account of the relationship between finance and culture that Jameson bases on a mistaken sense that finance functions as an autonomous sector of the economy, detached from production. "Culture and Finance Capital," with its misunderstanding of finance and its wishful thesis that culture and finance are mediated through the magic of homology, is a strange lapse for a thinker otherwise rigorous in thinking through mediation. For all the power of Jameson's work, he fails to offer a satisfying literary history of the long downturn. For the implications for contemporary poetics of such mystifications of finance's autonomy, see Christian P. Haines, "Financialisation." Joshua Clover offers one revision of Jameson. Drawing from Arrighi, Brenner, Jameson, and David Harvey, Clover argues that "the postmodern novel's narrative instability and its frequent substitution of sprawl for story" is an instance of "an organizing trope" of the literature of the long downturn: "the conversion of the temporal to the spatial" ("Autumn" 43). John Ashbery's poetry and Thomas Pynchon's fiction are, for Clover, exemplary here.

[31] Matthew Wilkens has written a sophisticated account of late modernism in which he recognizes the ahistorical, transitional qualities of the literature of that moment as a response "to the collapse of an older order—namely, the systems of industrial capitalism, durable social hierarchies, restricted democracy, modernist experimentalism, and the like—before any adequate new arrangement has emerged to take its place" (2). Wilkens identifies allegory and encyclopedism as forms particularly suited to such moments. Andrew Hoberek's *The Twilight of the Middle Class* offers a literary history of the postwar boom. Until Hoberek's book, the prevailing view of postwar US literature held that it had eschewed a concern with economics in favor of psychology. Marx had been the preoccupation of the Great Depression; Freud was on the minds of writers during the boom. Kermode offered an account of late modernism compatible with this, as ahistorical and entrapped in a sense of eternal transition; arguably, though Kermode does not say so, this ahistorical entrapment could be read as a response to the placid conformity of the boom years. Hoberek places economics at the center of literary concerns during the postwar boom. According to Hoberek, fiction of the boom years "is characterized by its increasingly tenuous efforts to create via style a preserve of autonomy that would distinguish the artist from the organization man" (110). As Mark McGurl's *The Program Era* (2011) shows, the prototypical artist was already on his way to becoming an exemplary organization man—as member of the English department. *American Literature and the Long Downturn* picks up where *The Twilight of the Middle Class* left off: from anxieties of autonomy in the boom years to crises of hopelessness in the long downturn. Two recent

Because the long downturn is more adequate than late capitalism as an account of recent economic history, the form I identify as central to it—neoliberal apocalypse—opens literary history to insights unavailable to *Postmodernism*. But these insights depend on methods I inherit from Jameson, above all, mediation. Mediation is the name Jameson gives to the critical practice of establishing a relationship between "the formal analysis of a work of art and its social ground" (39). Here, "its social ground" is misleading. Jameson recognizes that history and society are not givens that a text reflects, but spaces of contestation that texts enter, at once depending on extant conventions to be intelligible and presenting narratives that might shift what's possible in literature and in the world. Mediation is the practice of explicating that struggle, which entails—and this is what Jameson means by the term political unconscious—revealing how a text is unaware of, or mystifies, or represses its struggle's full contours. For Jameson, this struggle took regular form as "a symbolic act, whereby social contradictions, insurmountable in their own terms, find a purely formal resolution in the aesthetic realm" (79). Producing imaginary solutions to real world problems is one function neoliberal apocalypse serves, and one explanation for its popularity.

I find Caroline Levine's formalism salutary. Levine argues that literature and society both manifest as forms, which is to say as "an arrangement of elements—an ordering, patterning, or shaping" (3). With this understanding of form in hand, "the troubling gap between the form of the literary text and its content and context dissolves" (2). Form, for

monographs likewise consider the importance of economics for making sense of contemporary American literature: Jasper Bernes's *The Work of Art in the Age of Deindustrialization* and Leigh Claire *La Berge's Scandals and Abstractions*. Bernes reads artworks of the period as "laboratories in which the emergent social relations, techniques, and ideologies of the future economy and future conditions of labor develop, in most cases, against the intention and conception of the artists and writers themselves" (6). Ultimately, he argues "the critique of labor posed by experimental writers and artists of the postwar period became a significant force behind the restructuring of capitalism" (18). La Berge, following Arrighi and Krippner, takes 1979 to the early 2000s as her period, and focuses on financialization. She offers "a literary history of what happens to narrative form" under finance (3). What happens, she argues, is that novels assimilate "the financial autobiography and financial journalism" into their structure (8). A new "financial masculinity" predominates narrative (11). Finance organizes our experiences of time through its promise of a value-enhanced future (30–2). And finance becomes conceptually coherent and efficacious, La Berge argues, thanks to its representation in "literary and cultural fields," where these fields include the swathe of writing on finance that she names "financial print culture" (21).

Levine, performs similar work to mediation for Jameson, opening a contact zone for literature and society, literature and life. Her conception of form enables her to introduce the idea that forms have affordances, certain tasks that, because of how they impose order, they accomplish. Neoliberal apocalypse resolves social contradictions, yes, and it also, in its encounter with social forms imposed by the long downturn that feel hopeless—like mass incarceration or networks of global finance or debt peonage—affords a sense of hope. The tragedy of neoliberal apocalypse is that the sense of hope it affords is betrayed by the long downturn, lending itself to the contemporary structure of feeling that Lauren Berlant calls "cruel optimism."[32]

Literature, then, entails symbolic acts and the enactment of forms with certain affordances, and it is, also, a commodity vying for distinction within a literary market. Editorial and marketing decisions by figures in and adjacent to the publishing industry, including the author—negotiating between the desire for aesthetic autonomy, cultural capital, and profit—play a role in determining the social significance of a literary work. It matters that Little, Brown and Company publicized *Infinite Jest* as a novel that promised infinite pleasure, in contradiction to the novel's aims. I did archival research, especially for Chapters 3, 4, and 5, that allows me to read a text's formal choices and symbolic acts against its life as a commodity. Throughout, I consider what a text says, what it does, and what these decisions mean for literature and apocalypse under neoliberalism.[33]

The Structure of This Book

American Literature and the Long Downturn builds chronologically. Each chapter introduces an aspect of contemporary apocalypticism that then remains, like individual notes that should, by the end, harmonize in a chord. At first, the failed promises and cultural upheaval of the 1960s weighed heavily on figures as diverse as James Baldwin, Hal

[32] See Lauren Berlant, *Cruel Optimism*.

[33] I learned to attend to a text's embeddedness in institutions like creative writing, prizes, and the publishing industry from Pierre Bourdieu, James English, Mark McGurl, and Sarah Brouillette.

Lindsey, and Charles Manson. Baldwin joined an eclectic group of black artists, including Toni Cade Bambara, Amiri Baraka, Audre Lorde, Sun Ra, and Ishmael Reed who found, in Malcolm X's apocalypticism, an aesthetic form that solved a problem of political agency in the wake of the civil rights movement. They put it to diverse purposes. Some wanted to accelerate the end, others to withdraw and foster alternative visions of a redeemed future within the black community. But civil rights incited an oppositional furor among those whites who Richard Nixon called his "silent majority." Nixon encouraged his silent majority to see the racial other as a threat to white well-being in an economically constrained America. Two cultures of whiteness, and two apocalyptic discourses, emerged: white supremacy and Christian evangelicalism.

Looking at the 1970s through the darkness of the 2008 financial crisis, we see that much of what would become violently obvious was already nascent. Evangelicals transfigured anxieties over globalization, finance, and wealth inequality into a wounded white masculinity that attempts a sexist recuperation of manliness. Baldwin foresaw the warehousing of black lives that is mass incarceration and the central role finance would play in the United States. His observation that "American investments cannot be considered safe wherever the population cannot be considered tractable" could serve as a précis for Cormac McCarthy's *Blood Meridian*. Writing from capitalist crisis, McCarthy depicts a constitutive violence that capitalism has unleashed, but cannot control. His book brings us into the full flowering of financialization as an imperial practice and to the rising institutionalization of neoliberalism. As *Blood Meridian* went through page proofs and typescripts in the early 1980s, Mexico collapsed into a debt crisis orchestrated by Wall Street financiers, only to be restructured according to the dictates of neoliberalism, the setting for Leslie Marmon Silko's *Almanac of the Dead*, which picks up where McCarthy left off, describing characters struggling to survive amid the wreckage of finance and neoliberalism in the borderlands between the United States and Mexico. Against this neoliberal dystopia, Silko imagines the novel's eponymous almanac as an enigmatic indigenous object that incites the apocalypse and prepares a life after neoliberalism.

As a teenager growing up in the Minneapolis suburbs in the 1990s, I believed the economy was strong, that liberal democracy, after the Cold War, was the final governmental form, and that the future was a place of unlimited growth. But this self-congratulation obscured the persistence of the long downturn and capitalism's structural limits. Finance was an engine for creating personal debt and harvesting profits from America's debtors. Neoliberalism collapsed the *citizen* into the *consumer*. David Foster Wallace's *Infinite Jest* satirizes this America. It reveals addiction as a general condition within the debt economy. In anticipation of collective self-destruction, it hopes to save its readers from the pains of addiction and loneliness, but proves incapable of resolving the tension between the personal (addiction) and the structural (the economy), and so, instead, spills out toward infinity.

These aspects of neoliberal apocalypse—horror at the nation's commitment to a racist, exclusionary economic system; resentment about threats to white supremacy; apprehension that the nation has unleashed a violence that will consume it; claustrophobia within the limited scripts of neoliberalism; suffocation under the weight of debt—together form the discordant chord that hums under American life in the twenty-first century. For many of us, for different reasons, it feels like the end is coming soon. Here is how we came to this, and what it has meant for literature.

1
James Baldwin's Apocalypse

At the end of *No Name in the Street*, James Baldwin anticipates his book's poor reception in the United States because of its harsh judgments of the country. In his own defense, he writes:

> A person does not lightly elect to oppose his society. One would much rather be at home among one's compatriots than be mocked and detested by them. And there is a level on which the mockery of the people, even their hatred, is moving because it is so blind: it is terrible to watch people cling to their captivity and insist on their own destruction. I think black people have always felt this about America, and Americans, and have always seen, spinning above the thoughtless American head, the shape of the wrath to come. (474)

The wrath to come. Baldwin borrows this phrase from the King James Bible, Paul's letter to the Thessalonians 1:10, a passage discussing Christ's return and the final judgment. Baldwin's vision of damnation is a striking departure from the rallying cry that ends *The Fire Next Time*, where he dreams that "we may be able, handful [of relatively conscious blacks and whites] that we are, to end the racial nightmare, and achieve our country, and change the history of the world" (347). Whereas in *Fire* Baldwin uses "we" to include himself as part of an interracial nation, in *No Name* he distances himself from the "people"—by which he means white Americans—who have proved themselves, in the decade between, unwilling to pursue his dream, preferring "their captivity" within the confines of racial discord, bound by the chains of their imagined supremacy. Baldwin's old "we" signaled a collective call-to-arms; now his anticipation of mockery forgoes the possibility of being heard, resigned instead to witnessing the apocalypse.

American Literature and the Long Downturn: Neoliberal Apocalypse. Dan Sinykin, Oxford University Press (2020).
DOI: 10.1093/oso/9780198852704.001.0001

The difference is that between Jeremiah and John of Patmos. Jeremiah was a Hebrew prophet from the sixth and seventh centuries BCE who lambasted his fellow Israelites for their sins, but called them to return to their principles and fulfill their destiny as a nation. He lends his name and his form to the jeremiad, a classic American genre, of which Baldwin's *The Fire Next Time* exemplifies the African American variation.[1] John of Patmos was a first-century CE Jewish follower of Jesus who, from exile on the island of Patmos off the coast of Turkey, wrote the Book of Revelation, an indictment of the Roman empire, envisioning its destruction as the end of the world and the inauguration of a Christian paradise. From Jeremiah to John, as from *The Fire Next Time* to *No Name in the Street*, the focus shifts from an interrogation of a nation's morality to that of imperial subjugation: it is a shift in genre from the jeremiad to apocalypse.[2]

Baldwin's apocalyptic turn, his abandonment—further, condemnation—of the American experiment, disappointed critics. He forsook the idea, core to *Fire*, that the United States might deliver on the promissory note embedded in the country's founding documents. Instead, he turned to a genre that enabled an international framework within which individual moral agency loses its potentially redemptive force under the wheel of capitalism. One characteristically puzzled reviewer asked, how had "one of the most sensitive writers in the Western world . . . come to this?" (Ford 102).

[1] See Sacvan Bercovitch, *The American Jeremiad*; and David Howard-Pitney, *The African American Jeremiad.*

[2] In 1964, Baldwin still believed, though "we ourselves are far more dangerous for ourselves than Khrushchev or Castro" that nevertheless, "If we can hang on just a little longer, all of us, we may make it" ("What Price" 87; "White Problem" 97). Just two years later he wrote "A Report from Occupied Territory," which can be seen as a turning point, where the occupied territory is Harlem. With ironic derision, he writes, "The meek shall inherit the earth, it is said. This presents a very bleak image to those who live in occupied territory. The meek Southeast Asians, those who remain, shall have their free elections, and the meek American Negroes—those who survive—shall enter the Great Society" (738). Here Baldwin undercuts the pretensions of America's domestic and foreign policy and links the oppression of blacks in Harlem to the plight of America's opponents in the Vietnam War; his growing disillusionment with American ideology—America as a symbolic entity—is palpable. Baldwin garnishes the rhetoric in which he sarcastically distances himself from American myths with apocalyptic phrases—"those who remain," "those who survive"—which suggest that the link between blacks in America and the Vietnamese is the threat of cultural extinction. Already in 1966 Baldwin begins to shift his rhetoric from the jeremiad to the apocalypse. In an essay in 1967 he predicts that "the Western populations . . . will precipitate a chaos throughout the world" ("International" 248). In *Infrastructures of Apocalypse*, Jessica Hurley shows that Baldwin takes up the apocalyptic mode in 1968's *Tell Me How Long the Train's Been Gone*. The stage was set for Baldwin to unleash his full apocalyptic vision with *No Name in the Street.*

Near the end of *No Name*, Baldwin writes, "To study the economic structure of this country, to know which hands control the wealth, and to which end, seems an academic exercise—and yet it is necessary...for discipline, for knowledge, and for power" (462). The postwar boom created unprecedented wealth in the United States. African Americans migrated in vast numbers from the south to work manufacturing jobs in northern cities. Starting in 1965, these gains dissipated.[3] The consequences belong to a familiar story. Manufacturing jobs disappeared from the cities, "eroding [their] economic base," and "rapid suburbanization... left much of the central city impoverished" (Harvey 45). The erosion of the tax base and the decline of corporate profitability created fiscal and social crises. African Americans continued to migrate north through the end of the 1960s, increasing the population at a time when opportunities were decreasing (Wilson 111). Inner cities were populated largely by African Americans who faced "unemployment, underemployment, inferior education, inadequate housing, and police brutality" (Wilson 137). The postwar boom also created unprecedented class division within black America. The period saw "advances in jobs [and] civil rights" for some African Americans, even as, for others, "the quality of black urban life—poor housing, rat infestation, crime, high infant mortality rates, disease, poor public education—continued to deteriorate" (Marable 91). Class tensions, in the mid- to late 1960s, put pressure on the civil rights movement. What devastated it, though, was Lyndon Johnson's decision to fight the Vietnam War, the cost of which compelled him to sacrifice the War on Poverty, which was to be the government's attempt to address the economic wing of civil rights. Without economic justice, the legal gains of the civil rights movement were toothless for many—if not most—African Americans. Baldwin declared that civil rights had been "rendered moribund."

Baldwin came "to this," to apocalypse, through an appraisal of capitalism, which convinced him that the United States had an ineradicable

[3] As German and Japanese manufacturers caught up with the United States, global supply outpaced demand, creating a profitability crisis. Brenner writes, "Between 1965 and 1973, US manufacturers sustained a decline in the rate of return on their capital stock of over 40 per cent.... Well before the oil crisis, then, the advanced capitalist economies as a whole were facing a significant problem of profitability" (99). Baldwin was apt to turn, at this moment, from a national to an international framework for his thought.

flaw in its commitment to a system founded on racial inequality. Baldwin is not unique in this. Black writers and artists as varied as Toni Cade Bambara, Amiri Baraka, Audre Lorde, Sun Ra, Ishmael Reed, and Malcolm X participated in this aesthetic formation, an apocalyptic turn grounded in criticism of the racial inequality built into capitalism. This chapter tells a new story about the trajectory of Baldwin's oeuvre, about how he became part of this group of black writers well placed to feel the leading edge of the long downturn and to set the terms of black misgivings of the United States for decades to come.

Last Days of the American Empire

Malcolm X had, through the late 1950s and early 1960s, been prophesying that, just as slavery brought down ancient Egypt, Babylon, Greece, and Rome, and just as colonialism brought down modern European countries as world powers, so, too, would the United States's racism "bring white America to her hour of judgment, to her downfall" (Marable 270). In his time as a leading member of the Nation of Islam, Malcolm X preached the peculiar theology of its leader, Elijah Muhammad. Muhammad leaned on the Book of Revelation, which he claimed was written not 1,900 years ago by a man named John on the island of Patmos, but "6,600 years ago on the Island of Pelan" by the mad scientist Yacub, who poisoned the world by creating white people (125–6). According to Muhammad's reading of Revelation, its famous beast represents white people, whose behavior indicates that we are living in the end times. Muhammad published political pamphlets with titles like "The Day of America's Downfall" and "America is Falling, Her Doom Is Sealed." Malcolm X added political notes, insisting, for instance, on human rights, not civil rights, in an attempt to internationalize African American politics and foreground US imperialism.

Under Malcolm's influence, the Nation of Islam grew rapidly, especially in northern cities whose black residents preferred the message of self-defense and separatism to non-violence and integration into—as Malcolm and Baldwin would say—a burning house. In the years that followed Malcolm's assassination, with the Vietnam War, the abandonment of inner cities, and the growing sense that racial equality was hopeless, black writers had before them a script, left by Malcolm, to translate the hope of the jeremiad, the dream of one America, into visions of American cataclysm.

LeRoi Jones was listening. A key figure in the New York City poetry world in the 1950s and 1960s as a "poet, writer, playwright, critic, publisher, editor, and cultural organizer," Jones would make one of US poetry's most famous departures, upon Malcolm's assassination, leaving the loose network of the Beats, the New York School, and the Black Mountain School to move to Harlem, found the Black Arts Repertory Theatre/School (BARTS), change his name to Amiri Baraka, and become a motivating force within the Black Arts Movement (Smethurst 38). As early as 1964, Jones shared Malcolm's apocalypticism. That year Jones wrote "The Last Days of the American Empire (Including Some Instructions for Black People)," a polemical essay in which he addresses economic inequality, rejects, in homophobic terms, Baldwin's climactic call-to-arms from the end of *Fire*, and calls on African Americans to "erupt like Mt. Vesuvius to crush in hot lava these willful maniacs who call themselves white Americans" (235). He admonishes the black middle class for being complicit in the United States's "ceremony" of "blood violence and hatred" (222). The essay joins Malcolm in yoking black immiseration to US imperialism and economic exploitation, and to present, as the only possible future, the destruction of white America.[4]

Baraka made his debt to Malcolm X and the Nation of Islam explicit in his 1966 play, "A Black Mass," which dramatizes Muhammad's origin story of whiteness. In the play, Yacub creates the White Beast, or simply the Beast, which proceeds, in its evil, to destroy everything with which it comes in contact. The end of the play calls the audience to slay the Beast, and declares the jihad, or holy war, merging Christian and Islamic visions of the apocalypse. Baraka recorded the play in 1968 in collaboration with

[4] Six years later, in 1970, having changed his name to Amiri Baraka, and having taken up the cause of cultural nationalism, Baraka would write his epochal poem "It's Nation Time," which he recorded as a free jazz performance. In the poem, Baraka maintains his earlier call to destroy white America and end its economic exploitation, writing "strike close ford" and "close prudential burn the policies": destroy the factories and the insurance schemes that keep African Americans at the bottom (xx). Whereas in 1964, Jones focused on criticizing oppression and calling for white America's downfall, here Baraka's emphasis is on collective action toward building an alternative society: "the black man is the future of the world" (xx). The poem features the refrain "niggers come out," inviting his fellow blacks to "help us build a new world" (xx).

Sun Ra and the Myth Science Arkestra. Ra had been involved with the Black Arts Movement before, leading "one of the inaugural public events of BARTS in Harlem, a parade down 125th Street" (Smethurst 151). Like Malcolm X and Baraka, Ra turned to apocalypse to imaginatively resolve African American crises. As Anthony Reed notes, Ra "often posit[ed] the end of the world or the escape from the earth as an ambivalently utopian desire" (119).[5]

When Ishmael Reed was a young writer on the periphery of Baraka's circles in New York City in the mid-1960s, he would watch Sun Ra perform at small clubs (*Conversations* 272). During that time, Reed and Baraka both attended the Umbra Poets Workshop in the Lower East Side, a gathering spot for African American writers, and, despite their divergent politics and aesthetics, they would publish each other over the years. Reed moved to the Bay area in the late 1960s, where he wrote *Mumbo Jumbo*, published in 1971, a postmodern retelling of the 1920s and the Harlem Renaissance, in which black culture—arts, religion, dance—proliferates through the virus Jes Grew, and becomes a plague across the United States, threatening white America. Though whites manage to contain the virus, allowing them to maintain their "mundane 'system,'" dependent on the notion of "*homo economicus*"—the idea that humans are rational actors best suited for markets—the novel's protagonist, Papa LaBas, notes in the end that, in the 1970s, "the 20s were back again," yet stronger this time (218). LaBas cites Arna Bontemps's *Black*

[5] Consider John Coney's 1974 film *Space is the Place*, featuring Sun Ra. In it, Ra plays a game called "End of the World" with a figure named The Overseer. The contest takes place in the desert and is played with tarot cards "for the fate of the world" (Reed 123). "The Overseer plays a card emblazoned with a white Cadillac labeled 'Chariot' and Ra counters with a card featuring his Ark labeled 'Judgement'" (ibid.). In Reed's analysis, "The name 'The Overseer,' with its definite article, is wry commentary on the continuities of slavery and the gradual incorporation of blacks into liberal, civil society and public visibility: some may rise to positions of authority, which are jealously protected with flattery, trickery, coercion or violence as the situation requires" (134). Against the film's early-1970s context, we hear echoes of Baraka's criticisms of the black middle class who are complicit in an economic system that condemns most African Americans to poverty. As Reed puts it, The Overseer diverts "the fight for freedom into one of mere liberty, which within capitalist modernity is always at bottom the liberty to exploit your neighbor, and to be exploited" (ibid.). At the end of the film, Sun Ra's Ark escapes, and the Earth explodes, which calls us back to the beginning of the film, when members of the Arkestra sing, "It's after the end of the world." Baldwin, in *No Name in the Street*, observes that blacks in America are trapped, compelled either into complicity with capitalism, or, if they resist, to be crushed by it. With nowhere to turn, hopeless, Baldwin adopts apocalyptic rhetoric. Ra, through Coney's film, pursues this third way, an attempt at revising reality via apocalypse, an attempt to "imagine freedom beyond the bounds of extant ideology" (Reed 121).

Thunder, an account of Gabriel Prosser's 1800 slave revolt, which Bontemps takes as an occasion to foresee a black revolution. "Time," says LaBas, "is a pendulum" (218). The end of *Mumbo Jumbo* suggests that Jes Grew is back, is spreading, and this time *homo economicus* will be unable to stop the overthrow of white America by the forces of black culture.[6] Reed's allegory is plain. Black cultural life, at the outset of the 1970s, is apocalyptic, spelling the end of white people.

If Baraka, Ra, and Reed adopt apocalypse from the midst of the civil rights movement and its early aftermath as an aesthetics of refusal—a refusal to integrate, a refusal to accept America as the horizon of possibility for black politics and a black future—then Audre Lorde and Toni Cade Bambara step into and revise that refusal in the late 1970s and early 1980s. Both own their debts to Malcolm, both bring to black politics the feminist credo *the personal is political*, yet both criticize black politics for its neglect of patriarchy and feminism for its failure to address black women. Out of a rebuke to white feminists comes Lorde's famous apocalyptic slogan, "For the master's tools will never dismantle the master's house" (112). However untrue this may be as a literal statement—one can use the hammer that built a house to tear it down—it illustrates how Lorde understands as foundational for her vision of a new society grounded in difference and eros the total annihilation of capitalist patriarchy, toward "genuine change" (ibid.). She indicts the world under capitalism as unlivable, reproducing, as it does,

[6] Reed had been yet more explicit in a brief pamphlet from the previous year, *Cab Calloway Stands In for the Moon*, also titled, *D Hexorcism of Noxon D Awful*, written against "those who are devoted to Law and Order," a reference to Richard Nixon's rhetoric, deployed to shore up support for intensified policing of people of color (7, 10). In this tale, Papa LaBas infiltrates Noxon's dreams. (Noxon is an obvious parody of Nixon.) We learn that the United States, like Frankenstein's monster, originated as a mad scientist's experiment, which escaped, such that the US now is "crouched upon the midnight of the world ready to spring" (23). Noxon's private phone number is 666, which "*a secret society of aging white adepts who dwell in caves high in the Swiss Alps*" use to communicate with Noxon, their stooge (30, 32). These adepts are "*using the earth as a mere steppingstone to higher things: complete dominion of the Universe*" (30). Toward this dominion, the adepts are adorning Saturn's rings with department stores. Yet the planet OB is coming to crash into earth with its (the earth's) "dying race of Noxons" (37). Against the threat, which, at the end of the pamphlet, is "butting against the front door," Noxon's wife, Minnie D Moocher, puts "the needle to Stars and Stripes Forever" (ibid.). Next week, we learn, we'll read about "The Invasion of the Subway People" (ibid.). In other words, according to LaBas in this pamphlet, Nixon and the United States serve as subordinates to an international financial elite toward universal economic domination via consumerism, yet this system, which is shored up by American nationalism, faces apocalyptic threats both cosmically and from a revolt of "the Subway People," the black underclass.

the "horror" of defining "the good in terms of profit rather than in terms of human need," thus robbing us of the sustenance of eros (55). Yet, with and alongside Malcolm's call for an overturning of the structures of power, Lorde emphasizes the importance of not believing "that revolution is a one-time event, or something that happens around us rather than inside us" (141). Lorde makes immanent Malcolm's apocalypse, locating structural change within individual survival.

Bambara's 1980 novel, *The Salt Eaters*, takes as its premise the structural significance of individual survival in a white capitalist patriarchal world rushing toward apocalypse. The novel, set in the 1970s and early 1980s in the imagined southern US town of Claybourne among veterans of 1960s black politics, narrates the non-Western rituals that heal protagonist Velma Henry after her attempts at suicide. She sees now a repetition of Noah's apocalypse. She must dance toward "the Ark in the new tidal wave, racing in the direction of resurrection," while fleeing from "demons" who are "defiling the universe" (264). The earth overflows with dead bodies; the ice caps have melted and "tidal waves have inundated half the earth" (274). Pluto is in Scorpio, which signifies, "Annihilation and transformation…complete and total change" (282). Against this apocalyptic backdrop, Henry discovers that she needs "to believe in ordinary folks' capacity to change the self and transform society" (260). She and her fellow activists prepare for the new society on the power of "sheer holy boldness" (265).

This brief survey does not do justice to the careers of these figures or the movements with which they are associated, including the Black Arts Movement, Afrofuturism, and woman-of-color feminism. They are a diverse group with divergent politics and aesthetics. All the more striking, then, that they share a common apocalypticism.

From sites of political disappointment, out of despair and a sense of betrayal at the ongoing immiseration of black lives in the years after the accomplishments of the civil rights movement, these writers turned to apocalypse as a form that affords a vision of the demise of white capitalist patriarchy and the substitution of a just, if inchoate, society founded on difference. They adapted a script prepared by Malcolm X in which capitalism is a global system founded on black exclusion from wealth, which demands apocalypse. Baldwin's transformation, 1962 to 1972, from a writer of jeremiads to an apocalyptic visionary, a transformation that puzzled critics—how could Baldwin abandon a United States he vitally defended in *The Fire Next Time*? how could he become so embittered?—is, from this perspective, ordinary. Conditions had changed. Black political agency was in crisis. Apocalypse was, to many, the way out.

Sequel

Baldwin considered *No Name in the Street* his sequel to *The Fire Next Time* (Leeming 310). It was his first book-length essay in a decade, a self-consciously ambitious text from a leading African American writer that intervened in a crucial moment for black politics. Yet it has been neglected. In *The Critical Reception of James Baldwin*, Consuela Francis reports that it received, upon publication, "at best, mixed reviews" (112). Critics felt "that Baldwin trie[d] too hard in this collection to mimic the anger of the 'younger generation'" (112–13).

The notion that Baldwin's anger diminished his aesthetic sensibility became a common narrative to describe the trajectory of his career, contributing to the obscurity of his later work for more than two decades. In 2002, literary critic Morris Dickstein reproduced the familiar argument, writing that, "as his anger took hold…as success and acclaim freed him to vent his bitterness, his prose turned preachy" (184).[7] By constructing a narrative in which Baldwin's emotions corrode his work, critics missed how Baldwin's aesthetics developed in response to a changing world. Accusing Baldwin of allowing politics to contaminate his art, they establish a normative standard that does not prohibit political art, but circumscribes which politics produce acceptable kinds. As long as Baldwin was writing within the tradition of the jeremiad, his work was valuable, but when he departed from nationalism and exceptionalism,[8] criticizing the United States to its foundations, his art became too consumed by anger.

[7] Dickstein located where he thought Baldwin went wrong: "The best response to color is to be color-blind, to grant blacks a full measure of humanity. This was a simple message, but eventually Baldwin would find it almost impossible to sustain" (184).

[8] See n. 1.

The last fifteen years have seen a "renaissance" in Baldwin studies (Francis 126; Kaplan and Schwarz 2). Much of this attention has resisted the tired narrative of his decline, reevaluating and, in some cases, evaluating for the first time his less read works.[9] And yet despite the salutary redirection, few scholars offer a sustained analysis of *No Name in the Street.*

The edited collection *James Baldwin: America and Beyond* has been most attentive to *No Name.*[10] In their introduction, Cora Kaplan and Bill Schwarz note that, "By the time of *No Name in the Street,* [Baldwin's] emphasis on American exceptionalism had diminished . . . and he was more inclined to understand 'the American crisis' as a manifestation of what he came to identify as the 'global historical crisis' in an entire racial order" (17). Outlining an arc I have been tracing, they argue that from *Fire* to *No Name* Baldwin's "prophetic voice shifts from Jeremiah to Job" (23). (Baldwin borrows his title and his epigraph from a passage in the Book of Job.) Cheryl A. Wall takes up this shift in her essay from the collection. In a neat inversion of the old declension narrative, Wall argues that "Baldwin's [early career] rhetoric could resonate with that of numerous pro-U.S. Cold War intellectuals," because of his "strategic American exceptionalism" (36). But, she continues, "By the time he wrote *No Name in the Street,* Baldwin recognized the error" (36).

A Delicate and Dangerous Position

No Name in the Street contains two essays and a short epilogue. "Take Me to the Water," the first essay, revisits Baldwin's time in Paris from 1948 to 1957, a period that ends with his return to the United States to pay "his dues" and take part in the growing civil rights movement by traveling through the South (383). "To Be Baptized," the second essay,

[9] For an overview of the renaissance in Baldwin Studies, see Caplan and Schwarz's introduction to *James Baldwin: American and Beyond.* Important publications include Dwight A. McBride (ed.), *James Baldwin Now*; D. Quentin Miller (ed.), *Re-Viewing James Baldwin*; Lawrie Balfour, *The Evidence of Things Not Said*; Douglas Field, *Historical Guide to James Baldwin*; Magdalena J. Zaborowska, *James Baldwin's Turkish Decade*; and D. Quentin Miller, *A Criminal Power.* See also *The James Baldwin Review.*

[10] Along with Cheryl A. Wall's substantial treatment of *No Name in the Street* in "Stranger at Home," essays by Kevin Birmingham, Kevin Gaines, and Magdalena J. Zaborowska touch on *No Name,* or use passages from the text as a jumping-off point for inquiries elsewhere in Baldwin's oeuvre.

leaps to 1968, then jumps around the 1960s and early 1970s, narrating Baldwin's attempt to free a friend from prison, and remembering slain black leaders, especially Medgar Evers, Malcolm X, and Martin Luther King, Jr.

The temporal gap between the two essays, 1957 to 1968, elides the rise and fall of the civil rights movement, situating "To Be Baptized" at a moment of crisis for black politics. How to make sense of the limits of civil rights? What now? To answer, Baldwin goes transnational, beginning "Baptized," writing, "All of the Western nations have been caught in a lie, the lie of their pretended humanism" (404).[11] To clarify what he means by this "lie," this accusation that Western nations are not the good faith actors they claim to be, Baldwin quotes a character from Dostoevsky's *The Idiot* who reacts to the rise of railroads with cynicism, saying: "the wagons that bring bread to humanity, without any moral basis for conduct, may coldly exclude a considerable part of humanity from enjoying what it has brought; so it has been already" (ibid.). The lie? The false promise that liberalism—"the wagons," the uninhibited work of markets—will produce wealth for all, when in fact it produces wealth for a few and "misery" for most. By noting the system's lack of "any moral basis for conduct," Baldwin highlights the contradiction between liberalism's moral claims toward bettering all ("bring[ing] bread to humanity") and capitalism's amoral exigencies.

Baldwin lingers on the problem of exclusion: "it was on this exclusion that the rise of this power inexorably depended" (ibid.). Baldwin posits Dostoevsky's claim about the consequences of the railroads—exclusion in the name of inclusion—as necessary to capitalism from the start. Baldwin theorizes the implications of this originally inscribed exclusion:

> now the excluded—"so it has been already"—whose lands have been robbed of the minerals, for example, which go into the building of railways and telegraph wires and TV sets and jet airliners and guns and bombs and fleets, must attempt, at exorbitant cost, to buy their manufactured resources back—which is not even remotely possible, since

11 He credits Malcolm for making "increasingly articulate the ways in which this lie, given the history and power of the Western nations, [has] become a global problem, menacing the lives of millions" (ibid.).

> they must attempt this purchase with money borrowed from their exploiters. (Ibid.)

Baldwin's litany highlights that most of the stolen resources are used to support communication technology or war, profiting the elite few. The excluded are coopted into commodity exchange, required to buy the goods robbed from their land at an inflated price. To pay this price, the excluded must go into debt, borrowing from "their exploiters," establishing a fiduciary relationship of dominance and submission. Baldwin's analysis annuls his hope from a decade earlier that Americans might "achieve our country" with love (346). Love is no obstacle for capitalism.

What does this analysis mean for political action? Baldwin poses a double-bind. "If [the excluded] attempt to work out their salvation—their autonomy—on terms dictated by those who have excluded them, they are in a delicate and dangerous position, and if they refuse, they are in a desperate one: it is hard to know which case is worse" (404–5). Baldwin suggests that both reform (working within the "terms dictated" by those in power, i.e. the pursuit of civil rights, King) and revolution ("if they refuse," i.e. separatism, Black Power, Malcolm) are too risky ("delicate and dangerous" or "desperate"). Baldwin's adjectives are vague, but he is clear that the excluded have little freedom to practice their agency and achieve autonomy. Both reform and revolution fail to bring freedom to the excluded within the context of global capitalism.

What, then? Baldwin writes, "for power to truly feel itself menaced, it must somehow sense itself in the presence of another power—or, more accurately, an energy—which it has not known how to define and therefore does not really know how to control" (406). He elaborates what this cryptic "energy" that power can neither define nor control might be, and how to acquire it. We must attend to "the people who are the most spectacular recipients of the benefits of this prosperity [that costs millions their lives]" (ibid.). These, the wealthy and the powerful,

> cannot, or dare not, assess or imagine the price paid by their victims, or subjects, for this way of life, and so they cannot afford to know why their victims are revolting. They are forced, then, to the conclusion that the victims—the barbarians—are revolting against all established civilized values—which is both true and not true—and, in order to

> preserve these values, however stifling and joyless these values have caused their lives to be, the bulk of the people desperately seek out representatives who are prepared to make up in cruelty what both they and the people lack in conviction. (Ibid.)

Baldwin's first move is psychological: he calculates that, for the well-off, it would cost too much—("price paid," "afford")—and threaten the benefit of one's comfort to recognize the suffering on which that comfort depends. It's difficult to enjoy one's iPhone while imagining the Foxconn suicides. The rest of the passage explains the consequences of this disavowal. Because the well-off refuse to understand the suffering that motivates people to riot, they respond by distancing themselves from "the barbarians" and electing politicians who vow to crack down on the black underclass, such as Richard Nixon, who campaigned, in 1968, on the promise of "law and order."

This disavowal and cruelty "is a formula for a nation's or a kingdom's decline" (ibid.). The disavowal prevents the powerful from being able to "define" the energy manifested in riots. The election of politicians like Nixon only intensifies this indefinable and uncontrollable energy. In the end, "the victor," by which Baldwin means the United States, will "become the prisoner of the people he thought to cow, chain, or murder into submission" (407). Baldwin envisions this uprising as less a matter of human agency than the result of an inevitable, impersonal process— "a formula." Thus, he advocates endurance: "the excluded begin to realize, having endured everything, that they *can* endure everything" (ibid.). In the meantime, the excluded must begin "to forge a new morality, to create the principles on which a new world will be built" (ibid.).

Baldwin turned to apocalypse to solve a problem of political agency. It seemed that reform and revolution had failed African Americans. Civil rights were moribund. He had long felt that the dream of building a separate black state, carved out of the United States, was fantastical. Worse, he now saw that Elijah Muhammad's idea of separatism entailed capitalism, which Baldwin theorized could not be disentangled from racism. If capitalism was the problem, nothing short of its undoing would do. Seeing this as a task unsuited to human agency, Baldwin eschewed the jeremiad and called up apocalypse: wait, endure, plan for the radically new world that is inexorably coming.

The Ultimate Justice of Things

Baldwin patiently dismantles the pretensions of liberalism that sustain a US political order that showed itself dependent on black immiseration, a dependence Baldwin finds confirmed by the US government's treatment of the Black Panthers. Baldwin observes that the government needed to "smash" the Panthers—through, for example, the FBI's COINTELPRO efforts at sabotage—because they made visible, with free breakfasts and practices of self-defense against the police, "the truth of the American black situation" (462–3). Imagining an honest attempt on the part of the United States to solve the problem presented by the Panthers, Baldwin writes,

> any real commitment to black freedom in this country would have the effect of reordering all our priorities, and altering all our commitments, so that, for horrendous example, we would be supporting black freedom fighters in South Africa and Angola, and would not be allied with Portugal, would be closer to Cuba than we are to Spain, would be supporting the Arab nations instead of Israel, and would never have felt compelled to follow the French into Southeast Asia. (463)

The United States would have to pursue justice against its economic priorities. But "such a course would forever wipe the smile from the face of that friend we all rejoice to have at Chase Manhattan" (ibid.). Baldwin anticipates financialization: the United States must keep investment banks happy by using its military power to maintain stable conditions for finance capitalism. He writes, "The course we *are* following is bound to [wipe the smile from the face of our friend at Chase], and with dreadful repercussions" (463). He compares African Americans to "those outnumbered Christians, running through the catacombs: and digging the grave, as Malcolm put it, of the mighty Roman empire" (ibid.). If the United States is the Roman empire, sowing the seeds of its own collapse, black Americans are the early Christians, oppressed, imprisoned, but coming together to imagine a new world that will rise ascendant from the ashes of the old. One of those early Christians, John of Patmos, penned a vision of that collapse and ascension. So too Baldwin.

Baldwin's apocalypse synthesizes Malcolm's with the black Christian tradition. More than Amiri Baraka or Sun Ra, Audre Lorde or Toni Cade Bambara, Baldwin looks to the scriptures for his apocalyptic paradigms. We learn in *The Fire Next Time*, after all, that, "on the blindest, most visceral level," he has never left the excitement of the church, and "never will" (306).[12]

Slaves mixed Christianity with cultural elements transmitted across the Middle Passage to develop the vernacular genre of the spiritual.[13] W. E. B. Du Bois closes *The Souls of Black Folk* with a chapter on spirituals. He writes, "Through all the Sorrow Songs there breathes a hope—a faith in the ultimate justice of things" (213). The spirituals became a unique African American expression of the desire for freedom. They draw, especially, on two biblical narratives: the exodus, in which Moses guides the Israelites out of slavery and into the Promised Land, and the Book of Revelation's destruction of an unjust empire and the installation of the New Jerusalem.

Baldwin takes quotes from spirituals for his epigraphs to "Take Me to the Water." The first speaks in the voice of Samson, from Judges 16, singing, "If I had-a-my way / I'd tear this building down" (353). Samson, an early Jewish leader, called on God to give him the strength to destroy a building, killing himself and his oppressors in the process. As a spiritual, it expresses the desire to destroy the edifice that upholds slavery. As Baldwin's epigraph, it expresses his desire to destroy white America, even at the expense of his own life. The second epigraph—"Just a little while to stay here / Just a little while to stay"—conveys the singer's anticipation that her arrival in heaven is imminent. Baldwin frames *No Name* with a note of reassurance: we *will* demolish America, we *will* find freedom yet, even if we lose America, and I sacrifice myself, in the process.

"No name in the street" is a quote from the Book of Job. Baldwin uses the passage from which it comes as an epigraph for the book as a whole. One of Job's interlocutors, Bildad, describes the fate of the wicked:

[12] Literary critic Maxine Lavon Montgomery argues that studies of the African American apocalyptic tradition must "begin with a consideration of the forms of cultural expression indigenous" to African Americans (2).

[13] Melville Herskovitz provide one of the earliest accounts that argues for the transmission of elements of African culture across the Middle Passage through the spirituals. His work is taken up by Lawrence W. Levine in *Black Culture and Black Consciousness* and Amiri Baraka in *Blues People*, among many others.

> His remembrance shall perish from the earth
> and He shall have no name in the street.
> He shall be driven from light into darkness,
> and chased out of the world.
>
> (18:17–18)

This passage prophesies the annihilation of any memory of the wicked. As a title, *No Name in the Street* issues a coded warning to white Americans. The threat of the fire next time—the apocalypse that would come without the embrace of an interracial politics of love—fell on deaf ears. The time for pleading with white America has passed. They are wicked, they have failed to address their wickedness, they shall be cast from earth, leaving behind, for the post-apocalyptic world, no legacy, no memory, no name.

The Last Witness

Baldwin may have been lending his prominent voice to the growing disillusion with the American project, but he was also trying to stay relevant with a new generation of black activists. *The Fire Next Time* made him a leading spokesman on behalf of integration. As noted above, LeRoi Jones (Amiri Baraka) offered a rebuke as early as 1964: "America will not change because a few blacks and whites can kiss each other" (235). In 1968, Eldridge Cleaver accused Baldwin of "the most grueling, agonizing, total hatred of the blacks, particularly of himself, and the most shameful, fanatical, fawning, sycophantic love of the whites" (99). Despite the fact that Baldwin "didn't like what [Cleaver] had to say about me," he confesses in *No Name* that he admired his book. He even internalized Cleaver's criticism, mocking himself as "the Great Black Hope of the Great White Father" (410). As black politics became defined by economic injustice, hegemonic masculinity, and disillusion with the civil rights movement, where did Baldwin—who, despite his poor Harlem upbringing, was now a famous, well-off, queer, cosmopolitan black man—fit in?

Baldwin felt he needed to authorize himself anew as a prophet for his people. What good were his words if he weren't respected as a vessel? He needed to describe his journey, show that he, too, walked the same roads.

He needed to find a way to traverse class lines. *No Name* conveys its apocalyptic vision through spiritual autobiography. Baldwin revisits his childhood, recounts his years in France, reminds his readers how he came to the United States in the late 1950s to pay his dues, and reports on his reactions to the deaths of black leaders.

He stakes his claim for authority, above all, by positioning himself as a successor to Martin Luther King. *No Name* begins with Baldwin's attempt to give the suit he wore to King's funeral to a friend, and ends with his description of the funeral. Though Baldwin shows the highest regard for King, his engagement with the slain leader is neither hagiographic nor uncritical, asserting, as he does, that King's strategy of "petitioning" the government for political gain had lost its force (440). Portraying himself as an associate of King, Baldwin makes his case as a candidate to fill the void King's death has left: an elder with the wisdom, experience, and critical acuity to lead African Americans into the wrath to come.

Baldwin considered the suit he wore to King's funeral "too heavy a garment" (360). He "could not put it on, or look at it, without thinking of Martin, and Martin's end" (ibid.). A childhood friend, with whom he had not been in touch, having read in the paper that Baldwin could no longer wear the suit, contacted him to ask if he could have it. Baldwin returns to the Bronx to give it to him. To get there, Baldwin must cross the distance that has grown between them: socioeconomic distance, which Baldwin expresses as the distance across New York City. "Naturally, the car which picked me up that particularly guilty evening was a Cadillac limousine about seventy-three blocks long, and, naturally, the chauffeur was white. Neither did he want to drive a black man through Harlem to the Bronx" (361). Baldwin, who grew up poor in Harlem and went to high school in the Bronx, is returning home ostentatiously, as a wealthy man. He imagines himself "eyed bitterly... by a totally hostile population. I held the suit over my arm, and was tempted to wave it: *I'm only taking a suit to a friend!*" (ibid.). We learn more from this passage about Baldwin, projecting what those in Harlem and the Bronx think of a black man in a limo, than we do about what they actually think. Baldwin's return confronts him with his class difference, and he feels guilty.[14] With

[14] Cheryl A. Wall observes that "the adjective 'guilty' recurs five times in one paragraph," and always with regard to Baldwin himself (43).

regards to himself and his friend, Baldwin thinks, "the guilt of the survivor is a real guilt" (359). Baldwin recognizes that he has "'made it'" and could "sign a check anywhere in the world," which, to him, signifies "that [he] had betrayed the people who had produced [him]" (359).

Baldwin's encounter with his friend grows increasingly uncomfortable. Baldwin feels he has special access to the truth of the black situation. He writes, "what I could not understand was how nothing seemed to have touched" his friend, namely, that, "we are living through what our church described as 'these last and evil days,' through wars and rumors of wars" (ibid.). Though they grew up together in the church, Baldwin alone interprets these apocalyptic passages from the Bible as applicable to the present. When Baldwin decries the Vietnam War, his old friend responds by saying, "'let me stand up and tell you what I think we're trying to do there'" (364). Baldwin explodes: "'*We*?' I cried, 'what motherfucking *we*? You stand up, motherfucker, and I'll kick you in the ass!'" (ibid.).

A decade earlier, Baldwin had been the boldest black voice to proclaim an interracial *we*, an American *we*. Now he cannot abide the use of his old tactic "sans critique," he cannot stand being grammatically coerced into "common cause" with white America in Vietnam (Wall 44).[15] The fury he feels at a pronoun misused is a symptom of his reinvention as an apocalyptic visionary. African Americans are no longer—as in *Fire*—central to the American imaginary, but excluded from it. Attempts to imagine blacks as part of the American *we* make them complicit with a system that depends on their suffering.

This scene in his friend's home stages Baldwin's dilemma. What good is his vision if he cannot communicate it to those who need to hear it? He must show that he has been down the line, that he is not, in his words, "an aging, lonely, sexually dubious, politically outrageous, unspeakably erratic freak" (363). *No Name* follows him to France during the Algerian

[15] Baldwin tells his old friend, "black people certainly had no business there, aiding the slave master to enslave yet more millions of dark people, and also identifying themselves with the white American crimes: we, the blacks, are going to need allies, for the Americans, odd as it may sound at the moment, will presently have none" (364). Here, Baldwin shows himself working through the voice that he establishes for himself throughout *No Name*, linking the U.S. to the world, U.S. blacks to the global poor, identifying ("we") with blacks, and prophesying a racial apocalypse. For years, Baldwin had used "we" strategically in his writing; it "played a critical role in Baldwin's strategic American exceptionalism. It enabled him to claim a citizenship that had not been fully granted" (Wall 44). But now Baldwin has given up his former strategy and speaks as a black writer to a black audience.

uprising, to the American South during the early years of the civil rights movement, and to the deaths of Evers, Malcolm, and King. These are the dues he has paid.

Baldwin revises earlier accounts of his time in France to fit his apocalyptic turn. Writing from Paris while he lived there, in the mid-1950s, Baldwin described how the encounter between the "American Negro" and the "French African" led the American to reflect upon his distinction *as* an American: "They face each other, the Negro and the African, over a gulf of three hundred years" of black history in the Americas (89). He believed that white America would accept black history, which would "bring Americans," white and black, "at last their own identity" (90). In 1972, Baldwin admits, "Not only was I operating within the American frame of reference, I was also a member of the American colony, and we were, in general, slow to pick up on what was going on around us" (375). Nevertheless, he declares, in retrospect, in a reversal of his conclusion from the earlier essay, that "the Algerian and I were both, alike, victims of this history [of European colonialism], and I was still a part of Africa, even though I had been carried out of it nearly four hundred years before" (377). The old gulf of "three hundred years" has been bridged by Baldwin's recognition of the shared history of European colonialism.

He builds on this recognition by comparing French and US wars in southeast Asia, arguing that both led to increased brutality at home. He writes, "The French were still hopelessly slugging it out in Indo-China when I first arrived in France, and I was living in Paris when Dien Bien Phu fell" (367). The Battle of Dien Bien Phu was the final turning point that led to the end of the French occupation of Indo-China, which itself instigated uprisings against French colonial rule elsewhere, marking, broadly, the end of French imperialism. Baldwin turns from the distant Battle of Dien Bien Phu to domestic life in Paris.

> The Algerian rug-sellers and peanut vendors on the streets of Paris then had obviously not the remotest connection with this most crucial of the French reverses; and yet the attitude of the police, which had always been menacing, began to be snider and vindictive. This puzzled me at first, but it shouldn't have. This is the way people react to the loss of empire—for the loss of an empire also implies a radical revision of

> the individual identity—and I was to see this over and over again, not only in France. (Ibid.)

Baldwin argues that empires respond to their diminution by intensifying their domination at home through sanctioned police violence. Baldwin continues this thought—that we would see this pattern "over and over again, not only in France"—later in *No Name* by turning his gaze to the United States, arguing that the US, in response to its losses in Vietnam, responds to imperial decline the same way France did: with police brutality. African Americans feel US economic decline through the business end of police batons. Baldwin's tactic is to imagine the United States through the history of empire and the black situation through the history of imperial subjugation. This allows him to recognize that if the French empire, like all empires, could come to end, so could that of the United States.

In 1957, Baldwin realized that he "could no longer sit around in Paris discussing the Algerian and the black American problem. Everybody else was paying their dues and it was time I went home and paid mine" (383). He closes "Take Me to the Water" with a long section on his journey across the American South, which he figures as a descent into hell. This serves to further his self-authorization in two ways: it demonstrates his long, personal involvement in black politics; and it calls, formally, on the apocalyptic trope in which the author-visionary takes an "otherworldly journey," often to hell (Collins [2015] 7). "I felt," Baldwin writes about his arrival in the South, "as though I had wandered into hell" (386). He goes to "Birmingham," to "Montgomery," to "Tuskegee," presenting the names as badges (387). He travels to "Little Rock" in the midst of school integration (389). He suffers sexual assault at the hands of a white sheriff (390–1). Quoting Dante, he writes, "I would not have believed that death had undone so many" (389). By figuring his experiences in the South as a katabasis, Baldwin dramatizes the lengths he has gone, following the path of many previous apocalyptic visionaries, to understand, and thus be able to speak for, the black masses.

Near the end of *No Name*, Baldwin matches his earlier New York class-crossing drive with a similar drive across Los Angeles. Now, after proving his authority, he can rewrite it without the embarrassing outburst. As before, he is staying in a wealthy part of town, "the Beverly Hills Hotel" (428). He makes a point of emphasizing that, while "people have their environments... the Beverly Hills Hotel was not mine" (ibid.). So he goes to Watts. "The drive from Beverly Hills to Watts and back again is a long and loaded drive—I sometimes felt as though my body were being stretched across those miles" (429). But he no longer imagines himself viewed by a "hostile population." Instead, he feels "stretched" toward the black underclass. His "guilt" has been replaced with "helplessness" (ibid.). He writes, "everything that might have charmed me merely reminded me of how many were excluded, how many were suffering and groaning and dying" (430). His wealth highlights his complicity in the exclusions of capitalism. Though he refrains from claiming a total identification with the black underclass, Baldwin, in Los Angeles, confidently asserts himself, in contrast to the parallel scene in New York, as a steadfast voice on the underclass's behalf. His journey, his revised narrative, has, he hopes, authorized him as a complicated visionary for 1972.

The Silence That Undid Me

"I went to Atlanta alone," Baldwin writes about King's funeral (448). Pushing through crowds, he makes it into the church. "The atmosphere was black, with a tension indescribable—as though something, perhaps the heavens, perhaps the earth, might crack. Everyone sat very still" (ibid.). His description recalls a tense moment from the Book of Revelation, after the first six seals have been opened and have caused destruction and death on earth: "And when he had opened the seventh seal, there was silence in heaven" (Rev. 8:1). Baldwin describes "the long, dark sister, whose name I do not remember," who sang for the service, and whose "song rang out as it might have over dark fields, long ago; she was singing of a covenant a people had made, long ago, with life, and with that larger life which ends in revelation and which moves in love" (449). Baldwin bridges slavery ("dark fields, long ago") with apocalyptic freedom in the present (a "covenant... with life... which ends with revelation"). Then it is over and Baldwin finds himself outside.

> I had not been aware of the people when I had been pressing past them to get into the church. But, now, as we came out, and I looked up the road, I saw them. They were all along the road on either side, they were on all the roofs, on either side. Every inch of ground, as far as the eye could see, was black with black people, and they stood in silence. It was the silence that undid me. (450)

He had entered the church alone, as an individual, but leaves awed—undone—by the collective black silence in response to death and destruction on earth. *No Name* is Baldwin's attempt to bear witness from that silence. "With Evers, Malcolm, and King gone," Baldwin believed, "I'm the last witness . . . that's my responsibility. I write it all down" (Leeming 310). In writing, he returns to the silence that undid him to find the center of his new political vision: the silence of endurance.

King's funeral closes the frame that opened with the story of the suit. *No Name* then arrives at Baldwin's current moment. He details how landlords, storekeepers, and insurance companies "bleed the ghetto," how the police are deployed "not for the protection of the ghetto but for the protection of American investments there," how the "administration, increasingly, can rule only by fear: the fears of the people who elected them, and the fear that the administration can inspire. In spite of the tear gas, mace, clubs, helicopters, bugged installations, spies, *provocateurs*, tanks, machine guns, prisons, and detention centers, this is a shaky foundation" (453–4, 457). He is precise about how capitalism dispossesses African Americans. Capitalism means keeping the black underclass in ghettos where the police work not for them but for shop owners and insurance companies, and, if the population dares to resist this subjugation, the police and the state respond with Baldwin's litany of techniques, from SWAT team violence to COINTELPRO subversion to what will become mass incarceration. This, to Baldwin, is a world with "a shaky foundation," trembling before apocalypse. Against these circumstances, he takes solace in history, from which:

> the rulers of empires assuredly learn the least. This unhappy failing will prove to be especially aggravated in the case of the American rulers . . . who do not know what the passion of a people can withstand

> or what it can accomplish, or how fatal is the moment, for the kingdom, when the passion is driven underground. (Ibid.)

Baldwin closes this section with his clearest—if still enigmatic—vision for a black future:

> The government cannot afford to trust a single black man in this country, nor can they penetrate any black's disguise, or apprehend how devious and tenacious black patience can be, and any black man they appear to trust is useless to them, for he will never be trusted by the blacks. It is true that our weapons do not appear to be very formidable, but, then, they never have. Then, as now, our greatest weapon is silence. As black poet Robert E. Hayden puts it in his poem to Harriet Tubman, 'Runagate, Runagate': *Mean mean mean to be free.* (457–8)

Baldwin uses the words "disguise," "devious," "patience," and, earlier, "underground" to describe black tactics; they help us understand what Baldwin means by naming "silence" the "greatest weapon." This silence is a turning away from whites, a masking, a dissimulation, and a willingness to wait for the end to come. Baldwin's phrase "then, as now," and his allusion to Harriet Tubman remind us that silence has long been a central tactic for black survival in America, amid slavery to avoid the lash, or to find joy in life beyond the eyes of whites, or to plot revolution or escape, beyond slavery through Jim Crow to the present. This kind of silence—silence toward one's oppressors—has long characterized black vernacular, with "its in-group and, at times, secretive, defensive, and aggressive character: it is not, generally speaking, produced for circulation beyond the black group itself" (O'Meally 3).

Baldwin structured *No Name* around the absent figure of silence. In his form of address, his use of pronouns, and the spirituals he cites, Baldwin practices the silence toward whites that he advocates. In envisioning *the wrath to come*, Baldwin turns his back on white America. "It was the silence that undid me"; "our greatest weapon is silence." Baldwin takes the silence he felt at King's funeral, the power he felt in its black collectivity, and absorbs it into his literary form. The endurance of silence is a transformative political agency to which Baldwin gains access through apocalypse. The tragedy of *No Name in the Street*, and of Baldwin's career, is that this endurance, this silence, has not outlasted white supremacy or the capitalism onto which it is inextricably grafted.[16]

Baldwin published *No Name* in 1972. That year, Richard Nixon, in a radio address, said that what many called an "urban crisis" he liked to think of as an "urban opportunity" (Nixon). He went on to trumpet how his administration had "spent more than two-and-a-half times as much on fighting crimes this year as four years ago, and eleven times as much on fighting drug abuse" (ibid.). Nixon's law and order has been devastating for African Americans. Conditions for the black underclass are worse today than in 1973.[17] Mass incarceration solved the problem Baldwin saw: "that this country does not know what to do with its black population now that the blacks are no longer a source of wealth" (432). Again today, we are seeing how white Americans, in response to black activism and economic anxiety, elect "representatives who are prepared to make up in cruelty what both they and the people lack in conviction." They are doing it in the name of making America great again.

[16] The black apocalypticism that spanned from Malcolm X to Toni Cade Bambara would, by the 1990s, find a home in hip hop. See "When Disaster Strikes" by James Edward Ford III.

[17] The statistics to support this are ubiquitous. Helpful graphs can be found at this link to a *Washington Post* article from 2013: http://www.washingtonpost.com/blogs/wonkblog/wp/2013/08/28/these-seven-charts-show-the-black-white-economic-gap-hasnt-budged-in-50-years/.

2
White Rage, White Rapture

In December 2015, while reporting on the Iowa caucuses, I attended a training for supporters of presidential candidate Donald Trump. It was held in the community room of a local bank in a small town on a cold night. Thirty of us sat in folding chairs under fluorescent lights. Attendees were mostly older, white, and eager to be there.

Each of us in turn stood up to testify—to talk about the road that had brought us to Trump. People complained about radical Islamic seed cells across America and about how "the illegals" get free health care. A man near me, by way of explaining his support, said, "I get pretty well educated by this ministry that comes on TV every Sunday morning." Unlike the pastor at his church, this show addressed the threat of Islam. What show, I wondered. Moments later, I watched him bond with another Trump supporter who watched it, too. It's called *Jack Van Impe Presents*.

Jack Van Impe Presents masquerades as a news show. Jack and his wife, Rexella, sit behind a desk and discuss the week's "headlines." These headlines tend to be about Islam, such as reports on ISIS beheadings, opinion pieces on Saudi Arabia and sharia law, and investigations of preachers who claim that Allah and Jesus are the same God. Rexella, blond and frail, editorializes with phrases of grandmotherly astonishment: "oh my word" and "whoa boy." She then turns to Jack for interpretation. Jack—whose website claims that his nickname is "The Walking Bible"—recites a string of verses that prove the headlines are signs of the rapture, Armageddon, and the second coming of Christ (np). In an episode from early 2016, Van Impe implored, "We need a strong president, a man who will stand for convictions, a man who will say, 'You Muslims can't do this and kill our people!'" He expressed astonishment that the United States has a Muslim congressman and condemned President Obama for "letting it happen." Then he prayed, "I'm a sinner. Lord, I want you, the world's in such a mess. Soon Armageddon will be

American Literature and the Long Downturn: Neoliberal Apocalypse. Dan Sinykin, Oxford University Press (2020).
DOI: 10.1093/oso/9780198852704.001.0001

here. Soon bombs will be flying. But even sooner, we're going to be taken away in the rapture" (Sinykin).[1]

Since the 1970s, this arcane apocalyptic reading of the Bible has become commonplace; undergirding its popularity is a message to white Americans that validates and imagines an end to their felt loss of economic, social, and political power. It is called dispensationalism. Billy Graham held to it. Media mogul Pat Robertson preaches it. *Left Behind*, a book series that narrates the events of the final dispensation, from the rapture to the second coming, has sold more than sixty million copies, making it one of the all-time best-selling novel series. Tim LaHaye, a co-author of *Left Behind*, helped found the Moral Majority, transforming evangelicals into a political force, uniting them with business conservatives to elect Ronald Reagan. The rapture—the notion that believers will be snatched from earth and taken to heaven before the apocalypse—has served largely white Americans as an outlet for their frustration with the civil rights movement, second wave feminism, economic anxiety, and rapid globalization.

In the wake of the civil rights movement, African Americans felt betrayed, disappointed, and hopeless because of economic injustice, police brutality, and FBI subversion, all of which, as I argued in the previous chapter, James Baldwin identified as belonging to capitalism in a moment of imperial decline. White Americans saw the same world differently. Riots and economic crisis were threats to white power. Richard Nixon galvanized these Americans, calling them his "silent majority." Facing the limited scope of governmental allocation that would lead to stagnant wages and increasing inequality, Nixon encouraged his silent majority to see the racial other as a threat to white well-being in this economically constrained America. Against black militancy, he would restore "law and order," a coded way to say white supremacy.

But police brutality and mass incarceration alone were not enough to calm anxieties about white obsolescence. It felt too late for whites, for capitalism, for America. Until candidate Donald Trump arrived, apocalypse sated the thirst for an undiminished white world.

[1] Nasia Anam argues that contemporary anxieties about mass migration—especially the fear that "the Western world is projected to meet its demise at the hands of colonizing Muslim migrants"—have inspired a trend of "apocalyptic migrant fiction" (655–6).

Whiteness Studies

In 1953, before even *Brown v. Board of Education*—the standard marker for the start of the civil rights movement—James Baldwin announced in *Harper's*: "This world is white no longer, and it will never be white again" ("Stranger" 129). His ambitious thought proved wishful thinking. Yet it remains the tightest formulation of the egalitarian wish that motivated the retrenchment of whiteness after the civil rights movement, Black Power, and a politics of scarcity. Whites fought to keep the world white. Almost thirty years later, Baldwin, in *The Nation*, revised his earlier declaration, with the apocalyptic tone that characterized his later work: "we have survived, children, the very last white country the world will ever see" ("Notes" 807). Across his career, Baldwin sought to know the white mind. At the heart of this pursuit was his conviction that "one cannot deny the humanity of another without diminishing one's own" ("Fifth" 179). He charted the contours of this diminishment. His work, and mine in this chapter, belongs to a tradition of studying whiteness. This tradition has shown that efforts to shore up whiteness against its perceived threats have a long history in the United States.

Toni Morrison, in her fiction but especially in *Playing in the Dark*, her brief book of literary criticism, assumed Baldwin's mantle, analyzing the white mind through its fantasies about African Americans. After puzzling over the portrayal of African Americans in canonical American fiction and the paucity of critical attention to that portrayal, she realizes that, "the subject of the dream is the dreamer" (17). White writers' portrayal of black people tells us little about black people and a lot about the white mind. She finds "an extraordinary meditation on the self; a powerful exploration of the fears and desires that reside in the writerly consciousness. It is an astonishing revelation of longing, of terror, of perplexity, of shame, of magnanimity" (ibid.). Her thesis is that "the process of organizing American coherence through a distancing Africanism became the operative mode of a new cultural hegemony" (8). White writers have maintained supremacy through the invention of blackness, an invention that allows them to align being American with being white.

Being American and being white serve as compensation for whites who lack class power. David Roediger follows W. E. B. DuBois in showing how whiteness emerged in tandem with the working class in the nineteenth-century United States (6). He argues that the "status and privileges conferred by [whiteness] could be used to make up for alienating and exploitative class relationships" and that, "whiteness was a way in which white workers responded to a fear of dependency on wage labor and to the necessities of capitalist work discipline" (13). He insists that, though whiteness gained traction as an empowerment tool in response to class, race must not be reduced to what some argue is the greater reality of class. Racism had long been naturalized as a justification for slavery. White supremacists are not racist *because* of their economic status. Racism lay at hand as a ready salve, through the promulgation of whiteness, for the indignities of class. The appeal of whiteness as a mode of recuperating power is an old story. It was renewed for the long downturn.[2]

What Lives Inside You

In "The White Album," Joan Didion writes that the Manson Family's night of murder marked, as word spread the next day, an abrupt end of the Sixties. "The paranoia was fulfilled" (47). This timeworn tale, which Didion helped codify with "Slouching towards Bethlehem," tells us that the idealism of the Sixties descended into nihilism and violence. Manson—along with the Altamont Speedway Free Festival and the violence of the Weather Underground—punctuates this end.

[2] One way whites used race to recuperate power in this period was through the ethnic revival, an appeal to particular identities rather than whiteness. Matthew Frye Jacobson has described how the Civil Rights Act and the Voting Rights Act were "electrifying" for "white ethnics whose inchoate sense of social grievance required only the right vocabulary to come alive" (20). In Jacobson's telling, "the Civil Rights movement had heightened whites' consciousness of their skin privilege, rendering it not only visible but uncomfortable" (2). In response to this discomfort, and after "the example of Black Nationalism and the emergence of multiculturalism," whites *en masse* took up their "Italianness, Jewishness, Greekness, and Irishness" as "badges of pride, not shame" (2). This shift was itself a way to "bolster" whiteness, while relocating its symbolic site from "Plymouth Rock" to "Ellis Island" (7). Like Roediger, Jacobson acknowledges that "ethnic pride might provide some solace in a time of general malaise" (314). In the end, he notes, "the diversity-loving heritage project merged with the idioms of white primacy" (388). From well into the second decade of the twenty-first century, the retrenchment of whiteness through claims of ethnicity looks less forceful than the retrenchment of whiteness qua whiteness. Writing from the Trump era, I locate a genealogy of white supremacy concerned not with ethnicity (Irish, Italian, Greek) so much as with *whiteness* as identity.

"It was, and is, too pat: 'the Sixties blew up,'" writes Todd Gitlin (400). But he seduces himself into that narrative, admitting, "The habit of thinking in decades is hard to break" (ibid.). For him, March 6, 1970, when members of the Weather Underground accidentally blew up their own house, was the end of the Sixties. "As word spread about what was being manufactured in the townhouse, there was the toll of an ending, the subliminal sense that what blew up was not just three people but the movement's innocence and its larger logic" (402). Manson, for Gitlin, was an exemplary figure of this logic: "the way revolutionaries can shade into nihilism" (ibid.). He writes, "For the mass-media, the acidhead Charles Manson was readymade as the monster lurking in the heart of every longhair" (404). Hippie as murderer-in-waiting.

Manson ended the Sixties. But, a pivotal figure, he also inaugurated the apocalyptic logic of the long downturn. We hear it when Gitlin, riffing off Didion, who was riffing off W. B. Yeats, calls Manson "the rough beast slouching to Beverly Hills to be born for the next millennium" (ibid.). Like a railroad pointsman, Manson switched the United States from one track (counterculture) to another (white apocalypticism). He was born in 1934, raised as a poor Appalachian boy, and came of age in the boom years amid a culture of prosperity. He wanted to be a rock star. But as the 1960s progressed, as Vietnam deepened in quagmire, as civil rights turned to riots, as Martin Luther King looked to class and was killed, Manson found his voice. He supplemented the Book of Revelation with Malcolm X and Dale Carnegie. He took his revenge on an America that promised a Dream it would not deliver by giving America the nightmare he felt it deserved.

At his trial, Manson defended himself by declaring, "I'm only what lives inside you, each and every one of you" (40). He was the monstrous conscience of capitalism and imperialism. He indicted Americans for sustaining their wealth at the expense of the poor. He prophesied that they could not escape the suffering they imposed on others. He described surviving off capitalism's detritus. "I have ate out of your garbage cans to stay out of jail," he said. "I have wored your second-hand clothes" (42). He criticized the government for funding war instead of addressing poverty. Nixon "should have been on the side of the road picking up his children. But he wasn't. He was in the White House sending them off to war" (45). The consequence, he said, would be apocalyptic. "When it comes down around your ears and none of you know what you are doing, you better believe I will be on top of my thought" (46).

He sounded, that is, like the black apocalypticists I surveyed in the previous chapter, who saw, "spinning above the thoughtless American head, the shape of the wrath to come." Like them, he saw the United States as an empire that would collapse under the weight of those it excluded. He observed the Nation of Islam during his last stint in prison before becoming a cult leader, and his rhetoric, like Elijah Muhammad's, would feature a racially motivated rewriting of the Book of Revelation. Manson believed that whites were genetically superior to blacks and, in time, envisioned his white cult as the true biblical remnant that would rise to power after the end, when he himself would be recognized as Jesus (Guinn 74).

Your Tomb That You Built

Prisons, warehouses for those stripped of the rights of citizenry and excluded from the nation, were generative sites for black and white apocalypses alike in the long downturn.[3] Apocalypse as a form afforded prisoners a way to understand America not as it presented itself, not as an inclusive nation, but as an empire that regenerated itself on their exclusion.[4] Manson had spent most of his life in prison—"your tomb that you built," he called it at his trial—when he arrived in Haight-Ashbury in April 1967, in time for the Summer of Love. He joined the influx of young people from around the country, though, at 32, he was older than most. Haight-Ashbury in 1967 in one crucial way resembled the Harlem that Malcolm X found when he left prison fifteen years earlier, in 1952: "Virtually everywhere Charlie looked in the Haight there were street preachers pontificating to ... misfit listeners desperately seeking someone special to tell them what to do, how to live, what to think" (Guinn 95).

[3] Lee Bernstein writes about the importance of prison to the Nation of Islam in "Prison Writers," *New Thoughts on the Black Arts Movement*, 314.

[4] For a study of how prisons have shaped American literature, see Caleb Smith, *The Prison and the American Imagination*.

Manson became another street preacher in the Haight. He borrowed the idea of free love from the hippies, the idea of free food from the Diggers (94). As a child living with his strict Christian grandmother in Appalachia, Manson had absorbed the Bible, "including colorful sections from the apocalyptic Book of Revelation that described a bottomless pit" that "were cited so often that Charlie had ample opportunity to learn them by heart" (49). He blended Bible lessons with his variation on Elijah Muhammad's rewriting of the Book of Revelation. For Muhammad, the Revelation spoke to the corruption of whites and the need for a black separatist apocalypse. Manson shared the corruption, the separatism, and the apocalypse, but made himself Muhammad, incarnation of the divine. Whether it was this odd collagist theology or the manipulative techniques he learned from Dale Carnegie's *How to Make Friends and Influence People*, which he studied in prison, Manson soon gained committed followers, mostly young vulnerable women and girls, who came to call themselves the Family (60).

The Family moved to southern California, living in several places, including the home of Dennis Wilson of the Beach Boys, before settling into Spahn Ranch in the Simi Hills west of Los Angeles. Out there, Manson "preached and supervised acid sessions, and at night amused himself by soaking in a hot tub while Leslie [Van Houten] read to him from the Bible, always the Book of Revelation" (192). He wrote pop songs, aspiring to be a rock star. He worshiped the Beatles, treating their lyrics as sacred text. Revelation, he noted, "predicted that locusts would come, and locusts were, of course, beetles—the Beatles" (195). At other times, he told the Family that the Beatles were four angels from Revelation, and he was the fifth (195–6). The release of the White Album in late 1968 was a turning point. Manson interpreted the lyrics of "Blackbird" to prophesy an imminent black uprising. "Blackbird singing in the dead of night / . . . / you were only waiting for this moment to arise." The uprising would amount to an apocalypse, to which he gave the name "Helter Skelter." He said the song predicted the cataclysm: "Look out, helter skelter / She's coming down fast."

Manson used current events and numerology from Revelation to build his vision of Helter Skelter. He pointed to riots, black militancy, and the rhetoric of Black Power as evidence of the uprising in which "blacks were going to kill most . . . whites and enslave their surviving oppressors" (196). At the beginning of Helter Skelter, the Family would enter a bottomless pit to wait out the violence. There, they would reproduce until their numbers reached 144,000, as "specified in Revelation 14:3" (ibid.). Above ground, "blacks would discover that they lacked the intelligence and organizational skills to run the world" (ibid.). The Family would emerge from the pit and be hailed as superior, with Manson recognized as Jesus.

Manson's rhetoric escalated as it became increasingly clear that he would not make it as a rock star. His friendship with Dennis Wilson never garnered him a record contract. Wilson's friend Terry Melcher, a producer at Columbia Records, offered Manson his best shot. It was only after Melcher rejected him that the Family resorted to murder. The most famous murders, the ones on Cielo Drive, took place at a house that Melcher had recently vacated. Manson had recently come by, looking for Melcher. But to the Family, Manson said that the murders were necessary to initiate Helter Skelter. They hoped to make it look like it was committed by Black Panthers—by, for instance, writing "PIGGIES" on the wall in the victims' blood (201). The crime was meant to aggravate racial tensions and incite a race war. Did Manson plot the murders to take revenge on Melcher for failing to get him a record contract? Or did he do it for the reason he gave the Family, to accelerate apocalypse?

It would be foolish not to see these narratives as intertwined, the murders overdetermined. He was a poor white Appalachian aspirant to an American Dream made ubiquitous by the boom years. When he felt the inheritance promised him by his skin color slip away, he entered wholly into the apocalyptic logic he'd been preaching, in which he was the Messiah for inferior African Americans. The loss of his fantasy of what he could be—a rock star—triggered the set of affects Morrison found characteristic to whiteness: longing, terror, perplexity, shame, magnanimity. It is a mistake to think Manson was exceptional, a sociopath whose aberrant behavior can be discounted. We should heed the words he spoke in self-defense at his trial, his sense of himself as a symptom. "I'm only what lives inside you, each and every one of you." The feeling that a fantasy of whiteness was slipping away would soon gain traction. His apocalyptic white supremacy would echo down the decades.

Attack!

Many have committed murder, since Manson, in the name of inciting race war. On June 17, 2015, Dylann Roof, with that hope, killed nine African Americans in a church in Charleston, South Carolina. On April 19, 1995, Timothy McVeigh bombed the Murrah Federal Building in Oklahoma City, killing one hundred and sixty-eight. He carried photocopies from a novel that provided his blueprint: William Luther Pierce's *The Turner Diaries.*

Pierce was a physicist turned into an ideologue by anger at the civil rights movement. He befriended George Lincoln Rockwell, founder of the American Nazi Party, and quit his job to devote himself to writing and activism (Berger, "The Turner Diaries," 8–9). "After falling out with Rockwell's successors over the prolific display of Nazi branding, which Pierce felt was counterproductive to recruitment, [he] founded his own group, the National Alliance, in 1974. At the beginning of 1975, in an effort to boost circulation of the National Alliance's racist newspaper *Attack!*, Pierce launched the first chapter of a serialised 'future history' novel entitled *The Turner Diaries*" (9). He published *The Turner Diaries* as a book under the pseudonym Andrew McDonald in 1978.

The Turner Diaries tells how an underground white militia overthrew the US government and slaughtered the world's non-white population. A "textbook millenarian narrative," it predicts "an imminent apocalyptic change in the world with cosmic war as violent precursor to a utopian era of peace" (39). In its own words, it tells the story of "the men and women whose struggle and sacrifice saved our race in its time of greatest peril" (1). It takes the form of a diary written by Earl Turner, a martyr who gives his life in a crucial moment of the race war. The United States is infected by a "Jewish-liberal-democratic-equalitarian plague" (42). Jews control the government and use African Americans, depicted as mindless thugs, as muscle. Fearing further abrogation of white rights after the "Gun Raids," in which the government stripped citizens of their firearms, Turner writes, "we are already slaves. We have allowed a diabolically clever, alien minority to put chains on our souls and our minds" (33). The degradation has come to a point that apocalypse is the only (final) solution. "There is no way a society based on Aryan values and an Aryan outlook can evolve peacefully from a society which has succumbed to Jewish spiritual corruption" (111).

Turner joins a group called the Organization and, later, its central cabal, the Order, in an effort to take down the government, murder all non-white people, and inaugurate an Aryan world. Eventually, the Organization orchestrates "one of the biggest mass migrations in history," Turner's euphemism for the forced evacuation of "Blacks and mestizos" from southern California (153). Afterward, "it was heartwarming to see pretty, White children playing quietly where previously hordes of screaming, young Blacks had swarmed" (159). To ensure obedience, the Organization hangs tens of thousands of whites who "betrayed" their race through intermarriage or other forms of complicity (160–1). This is all preparation for "the new order which will serve our race for the next thousand years," on the model of the Book of Revelation's millennial kingdom (175). The Organization drops nuclear bombs on New York City and Israel, destroying "two of world Jewry's nerve centers" and transforms "some 16 million square miles of the earth's surface from the Ural Mountains to the Pacific and from the Arctic Ocean to the Indian Ocean" into "the Great Eastern Waste" through "chemical, biological, and radiological means" (191, 210). The epilogue reports, "the dream of a White world finally became a certainty" (210).

The book's publisher claims that, before he began to carry it in 1996, it had sold more than 185,000 copies, and "not more than a dozen or two of these" through bookstores (vii–viii). J. M. Berger writes that, though he could not verify this number, the book "was, at least, already well-known to the authorities" (29). Berger quotes an FBI terror expert who told *The New York Times* in 1995 that *The Turner Diaries* could be found "everywhere you turn" (ibid.). It inspired a white nationalist revolutionary group called the Order. The Order murdered radio host Alan Berg and penned the Fourteen Words—"we must secure the existence of our people and a future for white children"—a common slogan among white nationalists. Berger claims, "*The Turner Diaries* is the best-known racist novel written in the English language and arguably the most influential work of white nationalist propaganda since the fall of Nazi Germany" (6).

William Luther Pierce was born in 1933. He was almost 12 when World War II ended. The holocaust discredited eugenics and other scientific bases for racial difference. The civil rights movement validated, legally and socially, the notion that all races are equal. Jews became white. Threats to white supremacy for a racist anti-Semite were everywhere visible.

Arguably, the civil rights movement could happen because the postwar boom made the United States seem capacious enough for everyone's flourishing. The government could extend labor and voting rights to African Americans because there was room for them in the economy. This is not to say that recalcitrant whites did not resist violently against African American gains. Of course they did. But when the economy was good, the civil rights movement could gather enough force to change the government. In the late 1960s, the end of the boom made race feel like a zero-sum game. For whites like Pierce, for whom race had always felt like a zero-sum game, to the indignities of racial equality were added economic woe.

It is not quite right to say that, for Pierce, economic woe *was added* to racial equality. As depicted in his novel, both belong to the "natural decay of America" (111). By 1975, when Pierce published *Turner*'s first serialized segment, the United States was dealing with inflation and unemployment, deindustrialization and brownouts. These are the conditions of his novel's world. The "grumbling" of the "masses" "has increased steadily over the past six or seven years as living conditions have deteriorated" (55). Turner's Organization cell takes up residence in an abandoned welding and machining building, signaling the gutting of US manufacturing (21). Economic decline has taken its toll on the electric grid, such that "power blackouts and brownouts . . . have become a weekly, if not daily, phenomenon in recent years" (25). Later, Turner adds, the "power failures are only one crack among thousands in this crumbling edifice we are trying so desperately to pull down" (55).

The downturn provides the Organization the opportunity it needs. Recognizing that most whites will remain unconvinced by racist arguments, the Organization goes for their wallets. "As long as the government is able to keep the economy somehow gasping and wheezing along, the people can be conditioned to accept any outrage. Despite the continuing inflation and the gradually declining standard of living, most Americans are still able to keep their bellies full today" (6). If money is what moves people—"what is really precious to the average American is not his freedom or his honor or the future of his race, but his paycheck"—the Organization will reach them there (101). Turner explains the strategy. The Organization attacks "carefully selected economic targets: power stations, fuel depots, transportation facilities, food sources, key industrial plants" to further hack at "the already creaky American economic structure" (102). And again: "what we are doing with our program of strategic sabotage is hastening along the somewhat natural decay of America. We are chipping away at the termite-eaten timbers of the economy, so that the whole structure will collapse a few years sooner—and more catastrophically—than without our efforts" (111).

William Luther Pierce was terrified by what he saw happening in 1975 to the United States. Against racial equality and economic decline, he wrote an apocalypse. As a form, apocalypse divorces humans from agency, delivering them to a larger inexorable force. Here that force is decadence, "natural" decay. It was the same for Malcolm X and James Baldwin. For Baldwin, this was a way to resolve the failures of political agency. Human action could not end capitalism, but that was okay, because capitalism would collapse under its own weight. Baldwin counsels endurance.

But *The Turner Diaries* is a terrorist handbook. It counsels action. Pierce's apocalypticism introduces a conflict between agency and fatalism. What point is there in acting if the United States is going to collapse on its own? Pierce negotiates this conflict with the metaphor "termite-eaten timbers." He advocates accelerationism. The United States will collapse on its own. The downturn has made that much obvious. Racists can hurry it up by targeting an economy in decline.

Pompeii Has Returned!

Timothy McVeigh bombed the Murrah Federal Building two years to the day after the FBI's final assault on the Branch Davidian compound in Waco, Texas, in which seventy-six Davidians were killed, including their leader, David Koresh. The siege on Waco, which lasted fifty-one days, began because the Bureau of Alcohol, Tobacco, Firearms, and Explosives suspected the Davidians of weapons violations. McVeigh traveled to Waco during the siege, moved by his anger at the idea of the federal government taking guns from citizens. He sold bumper stickers to that effect. Though he was not a Branch Davidian, and the Branch Davidians are not white nationalists, their affinities hint at the larger cultural formation that encompasses them both.

The Branch Davidians are a religious group that splintered from the Seventh-day Adventist Church. They believe we are living in the end times as foretold in the Book of Revelation. Koresh claimed he was the lamb from Revelation 5:2. Most scholars interpret the lamb as Jesus, but Koresh understood it as preparing the way for the Second Coming.

An obscure far-right religion called Christian Identity unites the theology of the Davidians with the racism of Charles Manson and William Luther Pierce. Manson claimed no affiliations to any religion. And Pierce evacuated *The Turner Diaries* of ideological affiliations and theological commitments in an effort to attract as many adherents as possible. But their beliefs resemble those propagated by Christian Identity writers who "foresee a period of mounting violence in which the destruction of the white race will be narrowly averted, their racial adversaries either killed or subordinated, and a Jesus-led 'Aryan' regime installed for earthly rule from Jerusalem" (Barkun, "Racist Apocalypse," 132). Christian Identity is motivated by "resentments against the civil rights movements, civil rights legislation and court decisions, and affirmative action programs"—resentments that "have thus been channeled into religious myths" out of fear of a "white genocide" (126).

Manson, Pierce, and their white nationalist peers represent only part of a much larger set of figures who defended whiteness by giving apocalyptic form to the long downturn. As early as 1965, Billy Graham, possibly the best-known religious figure in the United States at the time, responded to youth culture, riots, third world revolution, and what he saw as lawlessness in US cities—the last three of which, at least, are code for people of color—by writing an apocalyptic manifesto, *World Aflame* (221). Ten years later, in 1976, Francis Schaeffer, a theologian who influenced key figures in the Christian Right such as James Dobson, Jerry Falwell, Tim LaHaye, and Pat Robertson, published *How Should We Then Live?* (Maltby 18). Schaeffer argued that secular humanism—in which man is the measure of all things, rather than God—was leading Western civilization to its collapse. "Pompeii has returned!" he declared. "The marks of ancient Rome scar us: degeneracy, decadence, depravity, a love of violence for violence's sake" (226). Schaeffer believed that the postwar boom had instilled the values of "personal peace and prosperity," a culture of affluence that threatened Christianity. He felt that affluence led to spiritual emptiness, which youth sought to fill with degenerate behaviors, and made people susceptible to despair during what he saw as an imminent "economic breakdown," which he compared to the Weimar Republic (246). Like Weimar, like Rome, America's decadence would bring its collapse.

In 1965, when Graham published *World Aflame*, the end times theology he preached was still marginal. By 1980, tens of millions of Americans would hold these beliefs and would become powerful enough to elect Ronald Reagan, and to inform the worldview from which he governed.

The Pieces Are Scattered in Small Bits

The influence of dispensationalism cannot be overstated. One scholar estimates that there are one hundred million evangelicals in the United States, of whom "approximately 40%" hold to dispensationalism (Maltby 20–2). They believe God divided history into seven dispensations, or epochs, of which we are in the sixth. The seventh begins with the rapture, when believers will be taken to heaven in the twinkling of an eye, then proceeds according to an end times narrative drawn from different passages of the Bible, especially the Book of Daniel and the Book of Revelation. Hal Lindsey, who popularized dispensationalism, writes, "these predicted movements of history are interrelated in their general time of beginning and ending. This is why the prophecies can be pieced together to make a coherent picture, even though the pieces are scattered in small bits" (Lindsey 43).

Dispensationalism is new. Historians have identified several key moments in its rise. John Darby, an Anglo-Irish Bible teacher, developed dispensationalism in the 1830s. He influenced the Plymouth Brethren, an evangelical movement that splintered from Anglicanism, which, in turn, influenced popular American preacher Dwight Moody, who incorporated dispensationalism into his sermons. One of Moody's students was Cyrus Scofield, who developed a version of the King James Bible annotated with footnotes that promoted dispensationalism. Oxford

University Press published the Scofield Reference Bible in 1909 and it circulated across the United States in the interwar years. One of Scofield's followers founded the Dallas Theological Seminary in 1924, which has been a central site for the dissemination of dispensationalism. Hal Lindsey studied at Dallas before writing *The Late Great Planet Earth*, which claims on its cover to have sold more than fifteen million copies, and which *The New York Times* called the best-selling nonfiction book of the 1970s. In 1995, Jerry B. Jenkins and Tim LaHaye, writing in a mode of dispensationalism pioneered by Lindsey, published the first volume of the *Left Behind* series, which would eventually sell more than sixty million copies, becoming one of the best-selling series of all time.

Dispensationalists have saturated American life. Historian Paul Maltby observes how they have accomplished this saturation via "strategic presence on town councils and school boards, via hundreds of TV and radio stations controlled by fundamentalist media moguls, [and] via vast, well-financed publishing houses such as Tyndale, publishers of the Left Behind novels" (30). Key figures in the politicization of American evangelicals, like Jerry Falwell and Tim LaHaye (Moral Majority) and Pat Robertson (Christian Coalition), were dispensationalists.

Dispensationalism gave voice to white Americans anxious about losing power. Paul Boyer argues that this anxiety gathers around "two motifs": "fears of underclass turmoil and violence, and fears of an emerging economic and technocratic order that will destroy individual freedom" (463). People of color and neoliberalism drove millions of whites to fantasize about the rapture.

The Late Great Planet Earth, responsible for the exponential growth of dispensationalism in the 1970s, manipulates these fears. Hal Lindsey presents his book as "a direct account" of what the Bible tells us about the future. He claims to "step aside" to "let the prophets speak" (7–8). He shows how current events correspond to biblical signs of the end times.

Important to Lindsey is the establishment of the Israeli state and, later, in 1967, its conquest and occupation of Jerusalem. He predicts that "within forty years or so of 1948" the rapture will occur. "Many scholars who have studied Bible prophecy all their lives believe that this is so," he adds (54). Palestinian resistance further confirms prophecy. He writes, "The Arabs are joining in a concerted effort to liberate Palestine under Egyptian leadership. The black African nations are beginning to move from sympathy…to an open alliance in their 'liberation' cause" (80). He turns his attention to Asia in a chapter titled, "The Yellow Peril." Though "for centuries Asia has had a tradition of backwardness," the rise of China suggests that "the dragon is awake" (83–4). He describes the Chinese army as an "Asian horde" that threatens the West (82). Domestically, Lindsey worries about decadence and anarchy. He worries about crime at home and revolutionary movements abroad (101). He is concerned that "established standards of morality" have been "thrown aside for a hedonistic brand."[5]

Lindsey pays close attention to the possibility of a European Common Market—the idea of a free trade economic community in Europe that preceded the European Union. He predicts that the European Common Market signals the decline of the United States as a global power: "the United States will cease being the leader of the West and will probably become in some way a part of the new European sphere of power" (95). This shift of the center of power will coincide with technological developments, permitting authoritarian control via our economic behavior. To participate in the economy, "everyone will be given a tattoo or mark on either his forehead or forehand, only if he swears allegiance to the [Antichrist] as being God. Symbolically, the mark will be 666" (112–13). In practice, the Antichrist will track our behavior through the unification and electrification of money: "in the near future…we will have just one number for all our business, money, and credit transactions. Leading members of the business community are now planning that all money matters will be handled electronically" (113). He adds, "the cleverness of this economic vise is ghastly to contemplate" (ibid.).

After World War II, a group of evangelical leaders "transformed fundamentalism from a dispersed, decentralized movement into one carefully directed by a powerful and culturally influential white male elite" (Sutton 295). But after just a short couple of decades, this power and influence appeared to be waning, threatened by the agitation of

[5] With the AIDS crisis in the 1980s, dispensationalists intensified their attacks on hedonism, with virulent attention to gay men, whose deaths they claimed were deserved, and seeing homosexuality and AIDS as signs of the apocalypse. Gay writers and artists, including Keith Haring and Tony Kushner, made use of apocalypse for their own ends, expressing the terror of the compounding losses. Dagmawi Woubshet writes about how, "in the hands of Haring, the figure of the apocalypse is freed of its literalism and moreover exposes the very people who exploited the book of Revelation for homophobic ends" (101).

people of color, and by economic turbulence. Leading evangelists like Billy Graham and Francis Schaeffer preached a narrative of American decadence. Lindsey cannily capitalized on the moment, taking the dispensationalism he learned at the Dallas Theological Seminary and the cultural cues he'd observed as a missionary for the Campus Crusade for Christ to write a book of pop prophecy that recognized its audience's fears and gave them hope for vindication through war and rapture.

Enslave the American Economy, Enslave the World

Hal Lindsey opened doors for Christian publishing: "major media companies were taking notice of [Christian] houses and moving in to acquire them. ABC acquired Word Publishing in 1974, while Rupert Murdoch's Harper bought Zondervan" (Gutjahr 213). Other writers turned out popular books in Lindsey's mold, including Paul Billheimer's *Destined for the Throne* and David Wilkerson's *Set the Trumpet to Thy Mouth*. In addition to these pamphleteers, novelists had been fictionalizing dispensationalism, according to Amy Johnson Frykholm, since 1905, but only achieved blockbuster success in 1995 with Pat Robertson's *The End of the Age* and the first volume of the *Left Behind* series (29).

At the peak of its success in 1995, *The End of the Age* hit number one on several bestseller lists (Boyer 461). Robertson's novel's sales were helped by the fame of its author. As the founder of the Christian Broadcasting Network and star of its most popular show, *The 700 Club*, Robertson wielded great influence in evangelical circles. Outside those circles, he is famous for inflammatory contributions to the culture wars. At the time of writing, an extensive Wikipedia page is dedicated to "Pat Robertson controversies," with twenty-nine sections. In 1992, he wrote that feminism is "a socialist, anti-family political movement that encourages women to leave their husbands, kill their children, practice witchcraft, destroy capitalism, and become lesbians" (np). He believes members of mainline Protestant denominations serve the Antichrist. He has called liberal professors "racists, murderers, sexual deviants, and supporters of Al-Qaeda." He has mocked the appearance of East Asians. It is surprising, then, that *The End of the Age* appears to embrace multiculturalism.

In the novel, an asteroid crashes into the Pacific Ocean, ushering in the final dispensation: the ascendance of the Antichrist, his defeat, and the final arrival of the New Jerusalem as an eternal paradise. Robertson makes a point of including a diverse cast. Manuel Quintana—born in the United States to undocumented immigrants from Mexico, raised in a "blue-collar family"—is a communications engineer who joins the Christian resistance (13). Dave Busby, an African American and ex-star basketball player, is another key member of the resistance. The Treasury Secretary is James Wong, an Asian American who studied economics at Stanford (106). The stereotypes are the first sign of disingenuousness.

Robertson pits good identities (Mexican American, African American, Asian American) against sinister ones (Arab American, queer). Percy DuVal, "the head of the office of White House personnel... had used every trick in the book to fill the highest government positions with those who shared his lifestyle and philosophy" (163–4). Robertson depicts the US government as corrupted by queers like DuVal, who "allowed himself to be enticed into group sex with a number of very young Ethiopian boys," a scene that was caught on videotape, leaving DuVal open to blackmail by the Antichrist, and putting the White House at risk (164). The occupant of the White House is Mark Beaulieu who started as a dissipated aristocrat. Though white, his French surname arouses suspicion. Beaulieu feels guilty over his unearned wealth, leading him "to loath the free-enterprise system that spawned his wealth, as well as capitalism, the United States, Christianity, and the whole of Western civilization in general" (167). While serving in the Peace Corps in India, he is possessed by Shiva and "controlled and directed by powerful demonic forces" (170). As President, he ushers in a new era of US globalism, calling US citizens "citizens of the world," and initiating "a new order of unity and cooperation in the world" through "a new coalition—a world Union for Peace" (259–60). The Union for Peace is a thinly veiled version of the United Nations, widely disliked among evangelicals, who feel that it "could potentially serve as a tool for the devil to use to assert his power over the world's nations" (Sutton 300).

Robertson reserves the most vitriol for the power behind Beaulieu: Tauriq Haddad, the Antichrist. Robertson writes, "his eyes were deep, dark brown, and they seemed to burn like hot coals. They were a paradox: attractive, yet strangely repellent; malevolent, yet kindly," invoking Orientalist tropes about the sinister mystique of Arabs (114). It's Haddad who directs Beaulieu to the Presidency, and then makes himself, first, chairman of the Federal Reserve, and then, "in effect, the surrogate president, chief of staff, and vice president" (293).

As the placement of the Antichrist as head of the Fed suggests, Robertson channels his fears about threats to white Christian identity through economic anxieties. James Wong is plagued with "doubts about the future of the American economy," as he watches the "burgeoning financial power of Asia" (118, 106). Meanwhile, "all of the major banks" are "clamoring for a system to transfer money without checks," working instead, "computer to computer" (121). Members of the Christian resistance worry about the move to digital currency. One Christian predicts to another, "the world government of the Antichrist will start the financial ball rolling by issuing each person credit on a chip" (224). Haddad takes advantage of the bankers to advance his "long-range plan to introduce a global financial system based solely on numbered computer accounts" and to institute a "single, unified currency" (279, 284). In case the implications are not clear, James Wong reckons, "it would be only a matter of time before [Haddad] enslaved the American economy and used it to enslave the world" (279).

Before Haddad can enslave the world, white men save it. The protagonists are all straight white Protestant men. Busby and Quintana fade. Wong dies. Carl Throneberry, who has a degree in astronomy from Cal Tech, is "extraordinarily gifted. Besides his ability to write, he [is] good-looking and charming" (5). Al Augustus, the Secretary of Defense who defects to the resistance, attended Yale and Harvard. And John Edwards, or Pastor Jack, who leads the resistance from his secret hideout, El Refugio, looks "like a cowhand with faded jeans, rough hide cowboy boots, a blue workshirt, and denim jacket" (134). Together, these men defeat Haddad.

Robertson's multiculturalism—aimed at an identity-based outreach—reveals itself: "good" minorities will die or remain subservient to white men. Robertson latches fear of foreign influence onto Arabs. He paves the way for Trump's hostility, in rhetoric only, to pieces of neoliberalism, associating global finance, banking, and monetary policy with the Antichrist.

The End Is Near, You Will Be Saved

A much bigger blockbuster brought Robertson's vision to millions more readers. *Left Behind* was published the same year as *The End of the Age*.[6] The *Left Behind* series stretches the story of the seventh dispensation across sixteen novels. It tells the story of those *left behind* by the rapture who suffer the terrors of the tribulation. The Antichrist rises to power with the help of a secret cabal of global finance capitalists who control the world economy (85). In the climactic scene of the first volume, upon acceding to power, the Antichrist dramatically murders the finance capitalists on whose shoulders he climbed.[7] A small group of Christians who convert after the rapture form a militia to battle this hostile world. The series promises white men who will guide the faithful to paradise. Morally imperfect but virile leaders emerge with names like Rayford Steele and Buck Williams. Like all dispensationalism, the series has deciphered a pattern in the Bible. It appeals to the sense of being among a besieged people, surrounded by chaos and decadence.

The long downturn felt frightening to white evangelicals in the United States for reasons now well-rehearsed in this chapter. Amy Johnson Frykholm, who conducted ethnographic research on the readers of *Left Behind*, finds that "the rapture emerged in American Protestant culture at a moment when conservative Protestants felt a decline of cultural power" (18). The rapture "promised an escape," it "divided the saved from the unsaved," and it "became a way for these Christians to reject a

[6] In addition to its own extraordinary success, the "franchise catalyzed a boom in prophecy fiction.... As many rapture novels were published in the decade since the mid-1990s as were published in the century to that date" (Chapman 5).

[7] Chapman argues that the series "participates in a shift away from earlier rapture fictions in which the domain of finance and the market was highly suspect, and toward a pragmatic and utilitarian concept of money as a neutral medium that can be harnessed for beneficent or maleficent purposes" (98). Chapman rightly recognizes how the series attempts to negotiate ambivalent feelings toward neoliberalism. *Left Behind* wants a certain kind of wealth to signal virtue—the wealth of an airplane pilot or a journalist. It also wants to celebrate consumer culture. In these ways, "the texts become complicit in a neoliberal discourse that conflates personal choice and volition with the ability to participate in a free market economy that interpellates individuals as consumers. In doing so, the novels participate in an ideological discourse that seeks to naturalize the mechanisms of the market" (Chapman 100). But the characterization of the financiers illustrates, again, the evangelical anxiety about finance capital and globalization. Far from offering an endorsement of the economics of the long downturn, the *Left Behind* series aims to adopt neoliberal innovations on the older Protestant work ethic while rejecting the financialization and globalization that—because they enable at least limited economic growth, however unfairly distributed—are concomitant.

disorienting new social terrain" (19).[8] The civil rights movement threatened white supremacy, second wave feminism and post-Stonewall sexual politics threatened male privilege and heteronormativity, the post-WWII international order, emblematized by the United Nations, threatened US sovereignty, as did financialization.[9] Inflation and unemployment in the 1970s and the subsequent, and ongoing, wage stagnation, fueled rising wealth inequality, from which many poor and working class white evangelicals suffered. All this felt inexorable, like it was happening at a scale that far exceeded the understanding of the single human, and a single human's actions in response felt meaningless to stop the change. Apocalypse ameliorates this sense of lost power, lost agency. Texts like *The Late Great Planet Earth*, *The End of the Age*, and *Left Behind* narrate worlds in which these white wounds are at the center.

But these texts do more than soothe white wounds with imaginary stories. By making white evangelical Christians into the victims of the long downturn, these texts establish, for their large readerships, a consensus worldview that justifies political agency on behalf of white supremacy. Pat Robertson's novel followed his unsuccessful presidential bid. Tim LaHaye wrote *Left Behind* in the middle of a long career fighting to make evangelicals a political force. In the guise of escapist fiction, these novels perform insidious political work.[10]

[8] Like *The End of the Age*, the *Left Behind* series gestures to multiculturalism by including diverse characters. But, as Jennie Chapman, in her astute book-length study of the series, argues, *Left Behind* maintains "a subtext of regret that the time when evangelicalism 'belonged' to white Americans has passed. In *Left Behind*, this undercurrent of regret is disclosed in its white protagonists' anxiety about their own authority and leadership, and their subtle and not-so-subtle efforts to withhold these privileges from nonwhite characters" (93). Thus, despite appearances of embracing multiculturalism, the series promotes "a tacit schema in which whiteness is understood as normative and nonwhiteness as aberrant or deviant, thus legitimizing and naturalizing white authority" (Chapman 81). (Many scholars, including Matthew Frye Jacobson, have argued that the discourses and practices of multiculturalism play this role in the contemporary United States, offering a front for the perpetuation of systemic white supremacy.) Jonathan Freedman addresses the series' apparent philosemitism to argue that "the basic narrative structures and figurative associations that have marked antisemitic discourse... remain strikingly in place. Indeed, they are effectively reanimated, retrofitted for a seemingly tolerant, multicultural age" (143).

[9] Quinn Slobodian argues that Geneva School neoliberals, including Friedrich Hayek, "were stalwart critics of national sovereignty, believing that after empire, nations must remain embedded in an institutional order that safeguarded capital and protected its right to move throughout the world" (9).

[10] Heather Hicks shows how, in apocalyptic texts including but extending well beyond those written by dispensationalists, "the Whore of Babylon continues to serve as a punitive archetype that demonizes women and lays the risk of human annihilation at their feet" (*Smoke Follows Beauty* 624).

The worldly power of white apocalypticism is striking in contrast to the political impotence of the black apocalypticism I discussed in the previous chapter. Both come from disappointment and despair at the same phenomena. Yet Baldwin must ultimately retreat from the world. Because his people lack power, they must endure, they must plot toward a future world, in apparent silence to the white majority. Cruelly, conservative politicians leverage white apocalypticism to gain the support of white evangelicals, millions of whom have suffered from the long downturn, only to persist with the policies that motivate evangelical apocalypticism in the first place.

It becomes clear, to return to where I began, how Trump seduced evangelicals into his fold. Trump and white apocalypticism alike portray the white majority as "a marginalized minority, as 'outsiders' to the evil majority" (Frykholm 15). Evangelicals have managed to construct their movement "as both broadly popular and paradoxically exiled at the same time," inverting identity politics on behalf of white Christians (ibid.). Trump tapped into this narrative and the anxieties that drive it. He too depicts the world as chaotic and decadent and promises to restore order. His people are besieged by inexorable forces. On the campaign trail, he announced that his presidency would restore borders, and bring jobs, and clarify who the Americans are. Salvation awaits his presence. Threatening invaders will be repulsed by a big, beautiful wall. America will be great again. All these years, Jack Van Impe has been preaching a certain emotional truth. It took Trump to make it revelation.

3

Evening in America

James Baldwin's observation that "American investments cannot be considered safe wherever the population cannot be considered tractable" could serve as a précis for Cormac McCarthy's *Blood Meridian* (*No Name* 405). Published in 1985, McCarthy's novel's apocalyptic vision marks the turn from the economic crisis of the 1970s and early 1980s to the flourishing of finance capital. This turn to finance aimed to solve the long downturn's structural limits to growth by forgoing the manufacture of commodities in favor of making money from money, with the long-term effect of "having deepened rather than solved the contradictions that underlay the preceding" crisis (Arrighi 300). US investment banks began lending extensively to developing countries, placing them in debt, and, when the countries defaulted on their debt, as Mexico did in 1982, the banks, with the help of the United States, the World Bank, and the International Monetary Fund, leveraged their power to impose structural adjustments, opening debtor countries to free trade and making their populations tractable to US power. Mexicans, for example, lost the ability to earn a living growing corn, unable to compete with subsidized big agriculture in the United States, a major impetus behind the revolutionary Zapatista uprising in Chiapas, Mexico, in 1994, timed to coincide with the start of the North American Free Trade Agreement (NAFTA).

McCarthy's novel traces US scalp hunters in northern Mexico in 1849, in the aftermath of the US-Mexican War, as they work to clear the land of intractable Indians—i.e. to slaughter them for cash—so that the United States can pivot from settler colonialism to economic imperialism, instituting the longue durée of US investment abroad that would lead, eventually, to financialization in the late 1970s. The scalp hunters prove as bad for capital as the Indians they decimate, debauching cities, taking Mexican scalps that might pass as Indian, and destroying the industrial means of production. McCarthy depicts a constitutive violence

American Literature and the Long Downturn: Neoliberal Apocalypse. Dan Sinykin, Oxford University Press (2020). © Daniel Sinykin.
DOI: 10.1093/oso/9780198852704.001.0001

that imperial capitalism has unleashed, but cannot control, presciently registering impending crises of the long downturn, like the Zapatista uprising, the 2008 financial crisis, and the repercussions of climate change. What remains, for McCarthy, beyond capitalism is the excess that fells it, a drive to violence.

Apocalypse shapes narrative, history, and experience according to a logic of linear time and imminent cataclysm. With *Blood Meridian*, McCarthy invites readers to see American history as plotted apocalyptically, proceeding toward the cataclysm that will occur when the violence the United States has deployed to secure its dominance turns back on the empire and levels it to ruins. This is, perhaps, why Harold Bloom in his introduction to the Modern Library edition of the novel, writes, "*Blood Meridian* seems to me the authentic American apocalyptic novel" (v).

The Way of the World

McCarthy's strange title—*Blood Meridian, or, The Evening Redness in the West*—hints at the apocalyptic vision awaiting its reader. "Meridian" means both a line of longitude and, common in the mid-nineteenth century when the novel takes place though now obsolete, the time when the sun reaches its peak, or noon. Figuratively, "meridian" means the "point or period of highest development or perfection, after which decline sets in; culmination, full splendour" (*OED*, "meridian," 4.b.). *Blood Meridian*, then, suggests a perfectly violent time and place: in this case the southwestern United States and northern Mexico in 1849 and 1850. Yet, if *Blood Meridian* invokes a zenith, *The Evening Redness in the West* sounds like an elegiac end.

At about its midpoint, the novel expands on the significance of its title. A gang of scalp hunters under contract with the state of Chihuahua is camped for the night "in the ruins of an older culture," the Anasazi, who built impressive cities and then mysteriously disappeared (139; Lange 128). Judge Holden, the gang's most loquacious member and an amateur anthropologist, tells a parable to his fellow scalpers in reference to the lost tribe, at the end of which he generalizes to the whole of humanity. "The way of the world," says Holden, "is to bloom and to flower and die but in the affairs of men there is no waning and the noon of his expression signals the onset of night. His spirit is exhausted at the peak of its achievement. His meridian is at once his darkening and the evening of his day" (146–7). Holden takes the example of the Anasazi as a single case of the general truth that, compared to the cycles of the natural world, human civilizations suddenly end upon reaching their meridian. Here we can recognize how it resonates with the novel's title and the story it tells. In an earlier draft of this passage, McCarthy notes, "(meridian = evening / as in title)" ("Early"). The note highlights what is strange: McCarthy uses a metaphor from the natural world—the movement of a day—but denaturalizes it by excising the afternoon, by making noon become immediately night. The fusion of *Blood Meridian* and *The Evening Redness in the West*, Holden's "at once," marks temporal collapse at multiple levels: of the quotidian distance between noon and evening; of the chronological distance between the mid-nineteenth century and the years of the novel's genealogy and publication, 1975–85; and of the distance between mid-nineteenth-century US scalp hunting in the southwest borderlands and the contemporary imperial capitalism this practice worked to institute.

The title opens peculiar questions. In what sense did the United States peak in the years the novel spans, between 1833 and 1878? What sense does it make to suggest the nation's decline when, in 1985, when the novel was published, it seemed to many as strong as ever? *Blood Meridian* follows its protagonist, "the kid," from birth to death, as he moves west, joins first a band of filibusters who intend to invade Mexico, then a gang of scalp hunters paid with hopes of exterminating the Apaches, before finally, after many years, meeting his end in an encounter with Holden. The novel centers on the intersection of the United States, Mexico, and Indians from both sides of a border they did not recognize, in the years 1849 and 1850. After the US-Mexican War, the United States faced pressing questions regarding its empire: would it continue settling new lands by force, as the filibusters hoped, or would it turn its focus to the economic penetration of foreign lands?

My study of new historical sources leads me to identify *Blood Meridian*'s scalp hunters as agents for the US consul Bennet Riddells, whom McCarthy calls Riddle: McCarthy has hidden his meticulous historicism in this quizzical pun. With attention to the history of the southwest (or, for Mexico, northern) borderlands and the novel's genealogy in travelogs and historical romance, I show how the scalp hunters serve as ignorant actors in the institution of US imperial capitalism. (Most accounts of the history of US empire date the origin of its economic imperialism to the early twentieth century, after the wars of 1898; *Blood Meridian* suggests 1849, more than forty years before Frederick Jackson Turner declared the closing of the frontier and the turn to Asian markets.) McCarthy aspires to grander claims than this particular historical intervention. He configures his scalp hunters as a violent force inscribed in the origin of the nation's imperial capitalism, an original violence collapsed into, and threatening, the novel's contemporary historical moment. The 1970s and early 1980s witnessed a crisis for capitalism, a circumstance that the persistent emphasis on the Cold War sometimes obscures. *Blood Meridian* emerges from this crisis to prophesy the unraveling of capitalism's order and the return of violence, to denounce Ronald Reagan's "Morning in America" and to see, instead, the onset of an American—including, for all its attention beyond the border, Mexican—night.

Illusions of Progress

My account of *Blood Meridian*'s scalp hunters moves beyond the recognition that Manifest Destiny entailed repressed violence to show how the novel transforms our understanding of the US progress narrative. The scholarship on *Blood Meridian* can be divided heuristically into that which takes the novel's relationship to history as central and that which finds this relationship secondary, even irrelevant.[1] In the latter camp are essays by Denis Donoghue and Harold Bloom, who, in the late

[1] Vereen Bell published the first academic study of *Blood Meridian* in his *The Achievement of Cormac McCarthy*. This wide-ranging chapter introduces several themes that scholars have continued to address, including the novel's relation to Turner's "frontier thesis" and the Enlightenment; how the novel exposes us to normally repressed evil; several of the figures to whom Judge Holden has been compared (Ahab, Kurtz, Satan, God, Nietzsche); and the centrality of the natural world in the novel. In 1992, Leo Daugherty analyzed the novel's debt to Gnosticism. John Sepich published his excellent genealogical work, *Notes on* Blood Meridian, in 1993. That same year saw the first academic conference on McCarthy and the origins of an author society. In 2009, Stephen Frye published a helpful, even-handed account of *Blood Meridian* in *Understanding Cormac McCarthy*, perhaps the best introduction to the criticism. See Leo Daugherty, "Gravers False and True," 159–74.

1990s, near the end of the culture wars, found in *Blood Meridian* an aesthetic triumph that disregarded the pious moralisms of the day.[2] Bloom praised McCarthy extravagantly: "no other living American novelist, not even Pynchon, has given us a book as strong and memorable as *Blood Meridian*" (v). Dana Phillips's early and influential article contends that the novel envisions a world in which humans exist on the same ontological plane with rocks and all else. More recently, Amy Hungerford has read McCarthy's novel in light of US literature's response to what she calls postmodern belief, or "belief without meaning" (49).

The historicist argument usually contends that the novel's violence critiques US imperialism. In taking up the transnational turn in American studies and attending to the geography of the US-Mexico borderlands, Mark Eaton concludes that *Blood Meridian* is "McCarthy's attempt to contest in his work the official story of Manifest Destiny"; that the novel records the "forgotten atrocities committed in the name of nationhood"; and that "[r]emembering the dead becomes . . . a way of coming to terms with how the West was won" (157, 158, 164).[3] Yet Eaton's attention to geography is not careful enough, for the bulk of the novel concerns the scalp hunters doing their killing in Mexico, for Mexican pay, not in the name of nationhood or the conquering of the West.[4]

Blood Meridian is a deeply researched account of the moment when the United States turned from conquering new land to developing economic enterprises abroad. Given its recent military victory, the United States deemed Mexico available for its imperial investments, but the presence of antagonistic Indians prohibited these plans. The scalp hunters enter here to facilitate this transition by slaughtering the Indians, thereby opening northern Mexico to US mining corporations and business enterprises. The novel sees the scalp hunters as symbolizing,

[2] See Donoghue, "Teaching Blood Meridian," *The Practice of Reading*, 258–78.

[3] See also Neil Campbell, "Liberty beyond Its Proper Bounds," 217–26; Robert L. Jarrett, *Cormac McCarthy*; and Sara Spurgeon, "The Sacred Hunter and the Eucharist of the Wilderness," 75–102. For an account of how the novel uses Yuma mythology, see Stacey Peebles, "Yuman Belief Systems," 231–44

[4] Timothy Parrish straddles both historicist and ahistoricist modes. He emphasizes McCarthy's engagement with history only to argue that "the events that the novel draws on are incidental to its actual narrative" (85). What matters to Parrish is how a "will to violence" undergirds history; history is only an epiphenomenon of, or excuse for, violence (83). The generality of his assertion reduces McCarthy's nuanced historical engagements to a metaphysical formula, a reduction I try to counter in this article. See Parrish, *From the Civil War to the Apocalypse*.

further, a violence that unravels ideas of progress central to the American imaginary.

As if to suggest the novel's rejection of progress, McCarthy considered the following as an epigraph: "There is a deep truth in what the school of Schopenhauer insists on—the illusoriness of the notion of moral progress. The more brutal forms of evil that go are replaced by others more subtle and more poisonous" ("Holograph").[5] Ultimately, he opted for more discretion, and indeed he takes pains to demonstrate the triumph of violence against specific forms of mid-nineteenth-century ideologies of progress, including the tent preacher (Reverend Green), a figure of millennialist fervor, a form of Christianity in which the moral improvement of man will result in a state of perfection that will institute the millennium and initiate Christ's return; the filibuster (Captain White) who exerts his own initiative to annex foreign lands by force in the name of the US empire and, here, as elsewhere, the moral superiority of Anglo-Saxons; and the sentimentalist woman (Sarah Borginnis) who believes in moral improvement as a force for social progress. Each becomes an object of mockery, which suggests the persistence of bloodshed with one of the three epigraphs that McCarthy did include, one which notes a newspaper article telling of a "300,000-year-old fossil skull" that "shows evidence of having been scalped" (xix). Yet the unchosen epigraph indicates that violence changes its form over time. *Blood Meridian* ends with the breakup of the scalping gang, the death of the kid, and the closing of the West. The implication is that the "more brutal forms of evil" give way to "more subtle and more poisonous" forms of imperial economic violence.

Against Enclosure

"What do you think of the treaty?" Captain White asks the kid, referring to the 1848 Treaty of Guadalupe Hidalgo, which ended the war between the United States and Mexico and annexed to the United States all or parts of what became eight states (33). Historian Brian DeLay writes that,

[5] McCarthy mistakenly attributes this to Henry James, but the passage comes from an address his brother William gave, "The Dilemma of Determinism."

though divisive at the time, "the war with Mexico helped make the United States a world power," yielding "the immense and varied resources of the conquered territory" (*War* 263). For Mexico, by contrast, the war was a disappointment not entirely unexpected. Only a few decades earlier, in 1821, Mexico had emerged from an exhausting eleven-year war for independence from Spain in political and financial turmoil.[6] The national situation did not improve in subsequent years. "Between May 1833 and August 1855 the presidency changed hands thirty-six times. . . . [T]he three chaotic years preceding war with the U.S. [have been] characterized," writes David Weber, "as 'the most turbulent period of Mexican history'" (32). Instability in Mexico City resulted in the neglect of its immense northern frontier, which had been enjoying a tenuous if imperfect peace with Apaches, Comanches, Kiowas, and Navajos (DeLay *War* 155). New Spain had built across the north a series of presidios, "military institutions" that served also as centers of commerce and diplomacy with independent Indians, perhaps their more important function (3050). Under the Mexican state these presidios deteriorated, which, coupled with the decision by Chihuahua and Sonora, in the northwest, to end in 1831 a longstanding ration program to Apaches, made the region vulnerable to renewed marauding. For their own complex reasons, the Apaches and Comanches, scarcely friends and each internally heterogeneous, began raiding northern Mexico extensively in the early 1830s.

Several decades of devastating warfare across the region followed. DeLay, whose recent book is the best synthesis of the sources on this warfare, calls it "the War of a Thousand Deserts," because of the "creation of man-made deserts where once there had been thriving Mexican settlements" (162). Numerous contemporaneous accounts attest to the devastation, the crumbling presidios, the desecrated churches, and the abandoned villages that comprise the setting for *Blood Meridian*. By 1849, when the historical Glanton gang joined the war as mercenaries, partly funded by US money that had traveled to Mexico City by the Treaty of Guadalupe Hidalgo, which was then sent by the Mexican Congress to northern states to pay for the war against independent

[6] See DeLay's prologue to *War of a Thousand Deserts*, 16–29.

Indians, the scalp hunters were stepping into the later stages of a prolonged series of conflicts (5994).

Blood Meridian is cobbled together from dozens, perhaps hundreds of sources from this period.[7] McCarthy spent years researching and revising his manuscript for historical accuracy. He even asked himself at one point whether he should "footnote the novel?" ("Photocopy"). A brief account of several of the novel's most important sources suggests how it appropriates mid-nineteenth-century genres, which yields surprising insights about its relationship to older forms. Especially of note are the many details originating in travelogs by people passing through northern Mexico in the 1840s, like British explorer George Ruxton or John Woodhouse Audubon, son of the famous ornithologist and himself a gifted naturalist.

These narratives attune us to the vast sections of *Blood Meridian* devoted to landscape writing, many more pages, in fact, than McCarthy gives either to depictions of violence or to Holden's speeches. Many passages detail the war-torn countryside as an apocalyptic wasteland, yet others poetically catalog flora and fauna. For instance,

> the scalpers passed through a highland meadow carpeted with wildflowers, acres of golden groundsel and zinnia and deep purple gentian and wild vines of blue morninglory and a vast plain of varied small blooms reaching onward like gingham print to the farthest serried rimlands blue with haze and the adamantine ranges rising out of nothing like the backs of seabeasts in a devonian dawn. (187)

We hear in this passage the transformation of a traveling naturalist's catalog into the lyrical memorialization of a pastoral landscape, imagined in association with an even earlier ("seabeasts," "devonian") time. Yet, as Audubon and others like him knew, the presence of these travelers marked the beginning of this pastorale's end, an end inscribed in the travelogs by their cataloging of not only flora and fauna, but of natural resources, too. Ruxton's "impression is, that the mines of Mapimi,"

[7] McCarthy wrote that "he had, indeed, read hundreds of books to make his *Blood Meridian*" (Sepich i). Sepich's *Notes on 'Blood Meridian'* is indispensable to scholars searching for McCarthy's sources. The acquisition of his papers by Texas State University's Wittliff Collections in 2007 introduced another excellent resource for McCarthy scholarship.

through which the scalp hunters of *Blood Meridian* pass, "if properly worked, would be the most productive in the country" (2470). Again and again, these travelogs highlight the extravagant wealth waiting in northern Mexico upon the extermination of the Indian threat.

Consider the travelog of John Russell Bartlett, which McCarthy drew from for his novel. The US government sent Bartlett to survey the new border between the United States and Mexico, created by the Treaty of Guadalupe Hidalgo. Bartlett emphasizes the possibilities of exploiting the natural resources of, especially, Chihuahua and Sonora, the states where most of *Blood Meridian* takes place. He writes, "the mineral wealth of Chihuahua is not surpassed, if equaled, in variety and extent by any State in the world" (13058). He encourages the United States to follow through with plans to develop a railroad through northern Mexico, portions of which seem "almost graded by nature for a railway" (14914). Likewise, one of Bartlett's contemporaries writes, "the construction of a railroad should afford the means of actually redeeming the country to possession, which Spain never accomplished, and Mexico can never accomplish" (Wilson 4431). One motive for the Gadsden Purchase in 1854 of these northern regions of Sonora and Chihuahua was to build this railroad, though it would be delayed until 1877. McCarthy's sources chart how the United States laid plans to profit off its neighbor's land, paradisiacal landscapes that these passing travelers read as both timeless in their beauty and ripe as possessions to be redeemed by cleansing them of Indians and developing their resources. These sources, in other words, bequeath to *Blood Meridian* a history of western expansion as a story of enclosure, the process by which capitalists capitalize on that which lay outside of capitalism. In place of "golden groundsel and zinnia and deep purple gentian," the "highland meadow" and "vast plain" will soon feed cattle and grow monocrops.

Samuel Chamberlain's *My Confession: Recollections of a Rogue* (1996) is the most significant primary source for *Blood Meridian*. Like the novel, this autobiographical romance describes a violent teenager who heads west, first to St Louis, then to New Orleans, Texas, and northern Mexico, before ending up with the Glanton gang and finally in a peculiar feud with the formidable Judge Holden. More revealing than the plot itself is how *My Confession* transmits to *Blood Meridian* a foundation in the genre of the historical romance. Early in his memoir—which like many such accounts deviates from the historical record and at times looks little different from a novel—Chamberlain tells of his youthful reading of the Bible and "the usual books of a Sabbath School Library," especially, "Scott's immortal works. What a glorious new world opened before me! How I devoured their pages and oh how I longed to emulate its horrors" (27). Walter Scott was easily the most popular writer in the antebellum United States, with "some five hundred thousand volumes" in print (Horsman 161). Chamberlain proceeds to emulate Scott's horrors, turning northern Mexico into the setting for a historical romance. The Comanches, he observes, "certainly made a most gallant appearance, and reminded me of the description in *The Talisman* of the reception the Saracens gave to him of the Lion Heart," referring to Scott's 1825 novel (71).

Blood Meridian inherits the historical romance's underlying logic. For Winfried Fluck, the historical romance derives its meaning through the description of a "historical process" rather than "merely" the illustration of "moral laws." Historical romances interpret past events "on the basis of a historical law." For Scott, historical law worked through "a sequence of stages from savagery, barbarism, and a pastoral agricultural state to modern commercial society," a development he regards ambivalently (Fluck 121). McCarthy is less enthusiastic about this progression. The setting of a terribly violent war becomes the occasion for a historical romance whose central figures—the scalp hunters—in an ironic revision of the mid-nineteenth-century romance, evince the perpetuity of violence as agents who unintentionally usher in a new age of technological modernity and the ideology of progress.

I turn now to *Blood Meridian* to specify the history it engages. The kid first arrives in Mexico with Captain White's band of filibusters; after Comanches destroy the band, he joins Glanton's scalp hunters. Filibustering and scalp hunting represent two different forms of armed intervention in mid-nineteenth-century imperialism, with the novel's narrator adopting different tones toward each: during the filibustering episode, a mocking irony directed at grandiose ambitions; an earnest seriousness for the grim business of the scalpers.

While recruiting the kid, Captain White invokes the classic rationalization of imperialism: "We are to be instruments of liberation in a dark and troubled land" (34). Beginning around 1848, enterprising individuals recruited private militias from within the United States to invade

Mexico and Central American countries to claim these lands for these filibusters' greed and glory. Filibusters united the belief in Anglo-Saxon superiority and Mexican weakness with liberatory pretension as an opportunistic play for land. In the novel, Captain White delivers a lengthy speech that reflects the conditions of northern Mexico as seen through a filibuster's eyes while offering an oblique history lesson for both the kid and the reader.

After lamenting the kid's ignorance of the Treaty of Guadalupe Hidalgo, White explains that the soldiers who fought in the war "were sold out," a common opinion among many Americans, especially Democrats, who believed the nation should have annexed more of Mexico (33). (Many Whigs believed the United States should have taken none of Mexico.) The treaty, and the acquisition of the Oregon territory shortly before, forced to the foreground a dilemma at the heart of what "America" means. "The American experience," argues Edward Said, "was from the beginning founded upon the idea of an *imperium*—a dominion state or sovereignty that would expand in population and territory, and increase in strength and power" (9). After reaching the Pacific, where could the United States grow? Reginald Horsman states the problem cogently. "After the Mexican War," he writes, "it was clear that if American expansion was to continue into populous areas it either had to be through colonial rule or economic penetration," but regardless of which, "Americans were determined to participate fully in shaping the economic future of not only the American continent but of the world" (247). Filibusters stood at the front of those who opted to extend US imperialism through settler colonialism, that is, the project of settling foreign land as a step toward annexation.

"We fought for it," says Captain White about Mexico. "Lost friends and brothers down there. And then by God if we didnt [sic] give it back" (33). Yet White does not accept the current boundaries as the end of the story. Despite the "mollycoddles in Washington," he says, "I dont [sic] think there's any question that ultimately Sonora will become a United States territory. Guaymas a US port" (34). White's belief is ubiquitous in the travelogs and primary accounts from the borderlands of that time. Robert A. Wilson writes, "Once in ten years [the United States] requires a portion of the wild land nominally belonging to Mexico, and once in ten years she must take it" (1400). Contrary to what White believes about

US politicians, the expansionist desire even gripped his "mollycoddles in Washington." Before settling on a purchase of the land in Chihuahua and Sonora just south of the Gila River, US ambassador James Gadsden tried to purchase most of Sonora, Chihuahua, Coahuila, Nuevo León, and Tamaulipas and the entirety of Baja California (Argüello "Interesa" 137). A few years later, President James Buchanan tried again to buy Sonora and Chihuahua, and when he failed he suggested in his State of the Union address that the United States occupy those states (1). We have become accustomed to recognizing the border as it currently exists, but *Blood Meridian* testifies to its radical instability in 1849.

White makes clear that his vision of himself as a liberator depends on his ideas about this "mongrel race": "We are dealing with a people manifestly incapable of governing themselves. And do you know what happens with people who cannot govern themselves? . . . Others come in to govern for them" (34). White represents those many Americans who viewed the turbulence of the Mexican government as a sign of racial and religious inferiority rather than the legacy of Spanish colonialism or internal class divisions. Plainly linking his racism to his settler colonialist project, he argues that "unless we act, Mexico—and I mean the whole of the country—will one day fly a European flag. Monroe Doctrine or no" (35). In White's construction, filibustering is the liberation of an inferior people from themselves and the otherwise inevitable encroachment of "toadeaters," not an aggressive act against a sovereign nation (34).

He expresses in his speech the opportunistic goal toward which his racist ideology is directed. He describes the abandoned locale that the reader will shortly encounter. He promises the kid that "There will be a section of land for every man in my company. . . . Some of the finest [grassland] in the world. A land rich in minerals, in gold and silver I would say beyond the wildest speculation" (34). Here White echoes the discourse of natural resources laid to waste by independent Indians that we have seen in the travelogs that McCarthy consulted. DeLay explains that "Americans saw [in northern Mexico] perversion and opportunity: perversion because Mexican settlers seemed to be reversing the arc of history by falling back before Indians, and opportunity because, characteristically, Americans thought they could do better" (*War* 202). Beneath the racist cant are dreams of incredible wealth. But the captain's imperial plan requires minimizing the Indian threat. When he mentions Indians, he does so to shame the Mexicans: "a heathen horde rides over the land looting and killing with total impunity. Not a hand raised against them. What kind of people are these?" (33).

White's speech provides the historical context for what comes next, if slanted through mid-nineteenth-century racist ideology. Readers gain a picture of the War of a Thousand Deserts from an Anglo-American's perspective in the aftermath of the US-Mexican War. The speech also indicates that the dilemma of US imperial expansion will animate McCarthy's depictions of armed US citizens in northern Mexico. Finally, what follows the speech deflates the pretensions of an ideology of racial superiority that conceives of Anglo-Saxons as agents of progress. The filibusters assume wholly that "America" is robust, eternal, and pure. *Blood Meridian* will prove White's filibusters to be fragile, finite, and impure.

The novel reveals its judgment of the filibusters and transitions toward the scalp hunters in its most grotesquely violent scene. The filibusters set out across the border into difficult, barren country. Before long, men of the company are dying, their animals failing (46–7). McCarthy ironically describes them as "elect, shabby and white with dust like a company of armed and mounted millers wandering in dementia" (48). White's confidence in Americans as chosen makes him, and his company, look mad. Soon the Comanches, whom White dismissed, appear in an astonishing and itself racist scene to annihilate the filibusters, called here "the unhorsed Saxons," as if to ridicule their racist ideology. The Comanches attack "like a horde from a hell more horrible yet than the brimstone land of christian reckoning, screeching and yammering and clothed in smoke," a scene of apocalyptic cataclysm (53). Indeed, we have a remnant, a resurrection. "With darkness one soul rose wondrously from among the new slain dead and stole away in the moonlight—the kid" (55). He survives to make a punch line of the filibusters and their pretensions. After encountering Captain White's head in a jar, the kid says, "Somebody ought to of pickled it a long time ago. By rights they ought to pickle mine. For ever takin up with such a fool" (70). He also survives to participate in a very different, indirect, and unusual form of US imperialism: scalp hunting.

As much as *Blood Meridian* mocks filibusters, it takes scalp hunters seriously. Compared to the pontificating but hapless Captain White, terse Captain Glanton, who leads the scalp hunters, is capable and cruel. We first see him test Colt revolvers by shooting a cat, a goat, and a chicken (82). Shortly thereafter he executes an old woman for her scalp (98). Yet later, he is described as "equal to whatever might follow for he was complete at every hour," words that might apply to the hero in a Louis L'Amour pulp Western (243). Like such heroes, Glanton occupies an ephemeral role in a moment of national transition marking the end of the code by which the hero lives; in Glanton's case, he inadvertently helps usher in the new age. *Blood Meridian*'s narrator suffuses the scalp hunters with ambivalence, at once apocalyptically horrible, committing cataclysmic violence, and crowned with nostalgia for a life before modernization, before capitalism, a life closer to nature, when no gap existed between a man's actions and his code and when he was "complete at every hour."

The scalp hunters serve as mercenaries in a much larger story. Both the Judge and the narrative voice characterize them as instruments of destiny, working for a higher agency of which they are ignorant. Holden, our satanic misinterpreter, reveals this agency as deified war; literary critics have named the agency nature, Schopenhauerian will, or the whims of the author.[8] Nonetheless, McCarthy provides a bevy of details to make evident that the scalp hunters are instruments of government interests as well as the moneyed power brokers with particular agendas for northern Mexico. For US and Mexican businessmen to capitalize on the wealth of resources in the region, they need it made safe for capital through the extermination of the independent (really, any) Indians. Yet in doing so, the scalp hunters, ironically, exceed their economic role and prove as bad for business as the Indians they were supposed to kill.

The United States, Mexico, and independent Indians each had distinct agendas for northern Mexican land in the mid-nineteenth century. We have seen how US filibusters attempt to settle land, but they represented a less than common plan for US imperialism. As Horsman observes, "A minority argued that [ongoing colonization] meant that Americans would have to settle other regions, act as a ruling elite, and create a colonial empire or sister republics, but the majority thought that a

[8] See Dana Phillips, "History and the Ugly Facts," 433–60; Dwight Eddins, "'Everything a Hunter and Everything Hunted,'" 25–33; and Amy Hungerford, *Postmodern Belief*, 91–2, respectively.

vigorous commercial penetration of the globe would create immense wealth" (274). Daniel Walker Howe puts it more bluntly: "Chihuahua would 'buy American' at gunpoint" (760). In fact, "[e]conomic investment by U.S. citizens in Mexico increased after 1848, especially on the frontier" (Stout xiii). The United States realized that, with the development of new technologies and the expansion of global markets, it could extend its empire more easily through capitalism than settler colonialism. Mexican historian Ana Rosa Suárez Argüello argues that, given the role US businessmen played during this period in growing their capital through the Mexican economy and, she notes, with the help of local Mexican businessmen, "*es casi imposible explicar por qué ha sido ignorado*" 'it is almost impossible to explain why [the role of US businessmen] has been ignored' (*Batalla* 12). In northern Mexico, as we have seen, aspiring imperial businessmen had a problem: the region was at war. The war was usually depicted as the aggression of the Indians; the United States could at least do business with the Mexicans.

Mexican businessmen and the northern Mexican state governments also wanted to eliminate the Indian threat so as to develop capital. During the 1830s, politicians from three northern Mexican states argued that "their states could be enormously productive if only Indian raiders could be kept in check" (DeLay *War* 3105). Years later, "the Border Commission sent out by Mexico in 1873 declared that one of the greatest damages resulting from these raids had been the suspension of every kind of industry and the lack of confidence in beginning afresh arising from the insecurity of the fruit of their labors" (Rippy 389). When northern states financed scalp bounties that drew Anglo Americans across the border, they highlighted a class tension. While wealthy businessmen needed to eliminate the Indians, villagers were not pleased to see the same people who had recently pillaged their land return. Indeed, "To patriotic Chihuahuans, these well-armed, well-mounted intruders riding over their land so soon after the Mexican War were camouflaged Yankee imperialists" (Smith "Scalp Hunt" 119). *Blood Meridian* raises this tension to its peak when Glanton and his gang begin to slaughter entire Mexican villages for their scalps.

Meanwhile, the different raiding Indians—the Apaches, Comanches, Kiowas, and Navajos—had their own complex agendas for northern Mexico, not least of which were also economic, though nevertheless hostile to capitalism. These raiders relied on economic markets through which they could turn "captives, mules, and horses into almost anything they wanted" (DeLay *War* 1941). Yet, as the scene in *Blood Meridian* in which the Comanches massacre the filibusters evokes, the independent Indians could be roused to raid for noneconomic purposes: "Comanches and Kiowas united their broader communities in the [raiding] enterprise in part by submerging economics in a discourse about honor, pity, and, especially, revenge" (DeLay "Independent" 48). From the perspective of capitalists, these Indians needed to be expelled or, more often, annihilated to allow economic development.

Given the financial and organizational difficulties confronting the Mexican state, "Northwesterners . . . looked to the market to do what government could not or would not do": they hired scalp hunters (DeLay *War* 3320). The market for scalps rose and fell during the War of a Thousand Deserts, but it received a boon from the money that came from the United States via the Treaty of Guadalupe Hidalgo: "soon scores of mercenary outfits were doing across the north what [famous scalp hunter] James Kirker and others had done" (DeLay *War* 5994). Significantly for Blood Meridian, "On May 25th, 1849, Chihuahua adopted the *Ley Quinto* (Fifth Law), under which the state paid for scalps as late as 1886" (Smith "Scalp Hunt" 17). It is about this time that the kid falls in with Glanton.

McCarthy makes a point of reflecting the historical role of the scalp hunters in the larger story of conflicting business interests. The Glanton gang receives funding from both the Chihuahuan state under governor Angel Trías and US consul Bennet Riddells, known in the novel only as Riddle. Just before they join the gang, the kid's companion, Louis Toadvine, says, "His name is Glanton. . . . He's got a contract with Trias. They're to pay him a hundred dollars a head for scalps and a thousand for Gómez's head" (79). The gang then rides to the edge of Chihuahua, "where the governor gave them his blessing and drank their health and their fortune in a simple ceremonial" (80). Soon after, during the scene in which Glanton tests the Colt revolvers on animals, he tries to haggle over the cost, to which the merchant replies, "Mr Riddle thinks that it's a fair price" (83). When Glanton counters, "Mr Riddle aint payin it," the merchant corrects him, "He's putting up the money" (83). As Ralph A. Smith notes, "Benjamin Riddel [sic], U.S. consul in Chihuahua, old friend of Yankee scalp hunters and proprietor of the American hotel... had staked [Glanton] to $2,500" ("Glanton" 9). From the beginning of the scalp-hunting portion of *Blood Meridian*, McCarthy presents the details that demonstrate whom the Glanton gang ostensibly works for: the state of Chihuahua, which pays for the scalps, and the US consul tasked to support business interests and who supplies the start-up funds for new Colt revolvers. This money enlists the scalpers in the War of a Thousand Deserts and the project to exterminate Indians and thus open the land for capitalist investment.

Once they set out, the scalp hunters are well received by the Mexican elite. Riding through "the wretched town" of Corralitos, "Glanton and the judge with the Brown brothers" eat dinner with "General Zuloaga" and spend the night at his hacienda (88–9). Zuluoga would later become president of Mexico and an opponent of Benito Juarez's populist reforms. McCarthy would have known, through Bartlett, that Riddle, as US consul, had worked with the elite in Corralitos to defend its mines against the "persecutions" of the Indians (12871). From Corralitos, the gang rides to the desolated mines of Santa Rita del Cobre, "abandoned these dozen years past when the Apaches cut off the wagontrains from Chihuahua and laid the works under siege" (113). The novel lingers over the defunct mine's waylaid capital, "the slag and rubble and the dark shape of shaft mouths and . . . the smeltinghouse where piles of ore stood about and weathered wagons and orecarts bonewhite in the dawn and the dark iron shapes of abandoned machinery" (114). The mine had been owned by American Robert McKnight and Frenchman Stephen Cuicier (Smith "Scalp Hunters" 7). The famous scalp hunter, James Kirker, who had once worked for the mine, avenged his former employers, launching a "surprise attack" on a nearby Apache village. McCarthy rewrites this battle as Glanton's. The gang leaves Santa Rita and proceeds to massacre Apaches in a surprise, morning attack (155–6). If the scalp hunters' initial funding tells us whom they work for, their journey, moving between wealthy haciendas, sites of desolated capital, and massacres of Indians, indicates how they follow their appointed destiny: as mercenaries slaughtering Indians on behalf of a transnational elite who strive to mine the land, pursuing enclosure.

Although I have interpreted *Blood Meridian*'s scalp hunters as ignorant agents performing what in Marxist terms is called "primitive accumulation," *Blood Meridian* is no Marxist parable: after they receive their payment for the Apache scalps, the gang outstrips their economic imperative, madly wreaking havoc across the region, as if the realization of their role in a market economy unleashes a force opposed to capitalism, attempting to expose it as absurd because, from the outset, it has tried to harness a violent irrational force that denies enclosure. *Blood Meridian* charts how this force, in its excess, destroys the capitalism it was meant to institute.

When the Glanton gang returns to Chihuahua with scalps from the Apache massacre, the city throws "a hero's welcome" and the gang's patrons—Trías and Riddle—host a dinner "in their honor" (165, 167). Afterward, they take their pay and begin an extended debauch of the city, quickly nullifying any benefits of their slaughter in the minds of the townspeople: "Mr Riddle, who was acting consul in the city, descended to remonstrate with the revelers and was warned away. . . . Charcoal scrawls appeared on the limewashed walls. Mejor los indios [We prefer the Indians]" (171). After the debauch, they leave the city to procure more scalps, but something has changed. Before they only slaughtered en masse those, the Apaches, for whom they had a contract. This time out the scalp hunters begin by killing every member of a peaceful band of Tiguas (174). Members of the gang wonder at the change. After conferring with the kid, Toadvine objects, "Them sons of bitches aint botherin nobody" (173). But on they ride. Soon after, the gang finds itself in a bar fight in which they kill thirty-six Mexican citizens. In the smoking room, Glanton commands, "Hair, boys. . . . The string aint run on this trade yet" (180). Given the presumed difficulty of distinguishing among Mexican, Apache, and other Indian scalps, Glanton intends to cash in on them all.

Once they take Mexican scalps, it seems they cannot turn back. They proceed to massacre a series of Mexican villages. They return to Chihuahua "filthy and reeking with the blood of the citizenry for whose protection they had contracted" (185). The authorities pay the gang but within a week post a reward for Glanton's own head (185). The gang, as Bloom observes, having "broken away from any semblance of order," leaves the city, "infatuate and half fond toward the red demise of that day, toward the evening lands and the distant pandemonium of the sun" (xi, 185). As the scalp hunters approach the titular evening redness in the west, they also move toward a sun that represents an elemental chaos rather than standing as a symbol of order. They have become half-mad ("half fond"), a turning point from which the narrative only delves deeper into the chaos of violence.

The Glanton gang begins as a mechanism of primitive accumulation but transforms into an irrational, apocalyptic force that performs a *reductio ad absurdum* on the capitalism—specifically US imperial capitalism—it was supposed to implement. Glanton soon goes completely mad, ties a Mexican flag to the tail of a donkey, and whips the animal into a fury so that it drags the flag through the mud (193). Chased out of town, the gang disrupts "a conducta of one hundred and twenty-two mules bearing flasks of quicksilver for the mines," leaving most of the mules dead at the bottom of a cliff and the mercury dashed (194). Whatever help they had offered to the mining industry, they have now negated. These "Americans" are described as "dark and smoking and apocalyptic," and Glanton is represented as one of St John's horsemen of the apocalypse: "like some storied hero [riding] toward what beast of war or plague or famine with what set to his relentless jaw" (190, 272). Thus are we invited to read its ending as an apotheosis of endings, an apocalypse.

The scalp hunters reject Riddle, slaughter peaceful Tiguas and Mexican citizens, and destroy the necessary tools of mining. US economic expansion was to be the form of "the more potent flame which the Anglo-Saxon seems just now disposed to shed over benighted Mexico" (Ruxton 93). The scalp hunters seem to transform at the party thrown in their honor by their patrons and upon the distribution of their pay, as if the consummation of their participation in the markets of capitalism itself unleashes the latent force in "that communal soul," "a thing that had not been before" (*Blood Meridian* 152). Earlier, McCarthy notes that the gang members display no regard for exchange, the basis for market capitalism: "The Americans might have traded . . . but they carried no tantamount goods and the disposition to exchange was foreign to them" (121). Once they have money, they refuse to use it by the rules of the market, repeatedly paying in absurd excess (200, 266–7). They exceed the logic of capitalism, an excess that has implications for how we think about the economic text of this novel, for the violence figured by the scalp hunters institutes capitalism's order, lies at the origin of capitalism's sense-making, and haunts the world it has created with the threat of a return to chaos.

McCarthy brings his story of enclosure to an end by flashing forward to 1878, to the West Texas plains and the near-extinction of the American bison. In the final chapter, the kid (who has become "the man") comes to Fort Griffin, a bison-hunting outpost, where he meets a veteran of the hunts who describes "the hides pegged out over actual square miles of ground and the teams of skinners spelling one another around the clock and the shooting and shooting weeks and months till the bore shot slick and the stock shot loose" (316–17). He recalls for the man "the meat rotting on the ground and the air whining with flies" (317). The diminution of the bison herds from thirty million to a few hundred destroyed the means of life for plains Indians and served as method by which the US government could "force Indians to submit to the reservation system" and, finally, enclose the West within barbed wire (Isenberg 3).

The bison hunts complete the Glanton gang's work. McCarthy describes these bison in the chapter heading as "the millennial herds," punning on the millions killed and the apocalyptic significance of their destruction and the subsequent enclosure (316). In his notes on Fort Griffin, McCarthy lists a series of dates and facts about the bison trade, closing with a lyrical line that provides insight into his process of transforming the historical record into the apocalyptic stuff of his novel: "The rabble in off the plains coagulate and seething within the raw board structures erected for their containment (enclosure)" ("Photocopy").[9] These rabble are the bison hunters. With his parenthetical note, McCarthy signals how he sees the hunters repeating the allegorical movement of the Glanton gang. Coagulate and seething, the hunters embody a violent force barely contained by human-built walls; again the forces of enclosure threaten to destroy that which they institute. (In the next chapter, I discuss how Leslie Marmon Silko imagines the return of the bison as a sign of apocalyptic rebirth, overturning the enclosures of neoliberalism.)

Blood Meridian's cryptic epilogue features a man "progressing over the plain by means of holes which he is making in the ground" (337). He "chucks" an implement "with two handles" into the holes, "striking fire

[9] The final version of this line, as published in the novel, becomes: "A dimly seething rabble had coagulated within. As if the raw board structure erected for their containment occupied some ultimate sink into which they had gravitated from off the surrounding flatlands" (324).

out of the rock which God has put there" (ibid.). With his posthole digger, this man brings infrastructure (barbed wire fences) and culture (Promethean fire) to the plains. It is a parable about the myth of progress and civilization, about the entwinement of cultural forms in their material foundations. But *Blood Meridian*, exemplary in its apocalypticism, shrouds the parable in the shadow of death, as the novel prophesies the violent destruction of civilization itself.

Apocalyptic Finance

In Holden's gloss of the novel's title, the two options, meridian or evening, are linked by the uncanny excision of the afternoon, especially to be perceived in his claim that "in the affairs of men there is no waning and the noon of his expression signals the onset of night." This removal also suggests, as a cryptic prophecy, the temporal collapse between the novel's setting and its publication date. How, then, should we read the novel's implications for 1985?

McCarthy started the novel at least as early as 1975; it reached near-final form by 1982. The years of its genealogy ripened the conditions for predicting US decline: the superpower had recently lost a war to a small southeast Asian country; a president had resigned in disgrace; and, most importantly here, throughout the period the nation fell ever deeper from the heights of the post–WWII golden age of capitalism into the long downturn.[10] To name the problem again in its broadest terms, capitalism needed to expand and regain profitability, but, by 1973, it had reached a point where growth was limited.[11] In the short term, policymakers allowed inflation to mask the crisis of capital scarcity (Krippner 63–4). Decline, however, would soon open onto transformation.

In *Capitalizing on Crisis*, Greta Krippner explains how the United States solved its various crises of the late 1960s through early 1980s by stumbling into the spiraling expansion of credit that spurred financialization, a byproduct of deregulation, the emergence of transnational

[10] See Robert Brenner, *The Economics of Global Turbulence*; and Daniel T. Rodgers, *Age of Fracture*.

[11] For an extended account of the end of the post-WWII boom and the subsequent challenges for global capital growth, see Brenner (1–11).

capital flows, and the turn to the market to solve political problems. These same mechanisms created what David Harvey calls a neo-imperial "accumulation by dispossession" (160). This dispossession is effected by economic agreements, not scalp hunters. "In 1984 the World Bank, for the first time in its history, granted a loan to a country in return for structural neoliberal reforms," Harvey asserts (100). That country was Mexico, and the reforms generated a transformation, beginning a decade of mass dispossession, migration to cities, the rapid rise of crime and violence, and the emergence of the drug cartels that are laying waste to northern Mexico, the land of *Blood Meridian*, conditions McCarthy went on to explore in *No Country for Old Men* (2005) and *The Counselor* (2013). As a Mexican man tells the scalp hunters in a forlorn cantina, "This Mexico. This is a thirsty country. The blood of a thousand Christs. Nothing" (102).

The temporal collapse inscribed in *Blood Meridian*'s alternative title marks the nearness of 1849 to 1985 as well as how each peak contains its own instantaneous undoing: progress entails its mockery; capitalism entails destruction; US financial wealth entails Mexican dispossession. The novel's narrative arc implies that this destruction cannot be contained, that it exceeds its imperial purposes and turns back on the empire.

In the meantime, financialization and the sudden widespread availability of previously unheard-of amounts of credit created the impression of a resurgent US economy and the conditions, beginning in the mid-1980s, for a new trend of finance-inflected US literature.[12] In *Bright Lights, Big City* (1984), Jay McInerney could have a character say, "'The new writing will be about technology, the global economy, the electronic ebb and flow of wealth'" (65). The family at the center of Don DeLillo's *White Noise* (1985) and its narrator repeat international brand names seen on TV. Protagonist Jack Gladney shops as therapy, purchasing "existential credit," internalizing the expanded debt economy to

[12] The numbers are striking. Consumer credit began to spike in the mid-1980s (Glick and Lansing). This new credit staved off a "serious repression or depression" by fueling consumption (Brenner xxiii). At the same time, the new credit assisted the decline of manufacturing in the United States and the rise of finance, initiating the economic conditions that persist today (Krippner 52–7). See Reuven Glick and Kevin J. Lansing, "U.S. Household Deleveraging and Future Consumption Growth." FRSBF Economic Letter May 15, 2009.

boost his self-esteem (84). For Andrew Hoberek, the novel "functioned to obscure the actual decline of the postwar boom with anecdotes of well-off boomers who were, also, champion consumers" (126). The reason these boomers could appear well off was because finance capital created the credit that buoyed the economy.

What sense does it make to suggest the nation's collapse when, in 1985, the year that the novel is published, the economy seemed to many as strong as ever? Did financialization moot McCarthy's doomsaying? *Blood Meridian*'s response to the global economic crisis of its time, its tale of the origins and ends of US imperial capitalism, its insistence on an imminent American dusk, was less misguided than appears at first. Krippner concludes her investigation into the US economy since 1970 with the observation that "the policy regime associated with financialization *suspended* rather than eliminated scarcity"—a truth we learned with painful certainty in 2008 (139). Indeed, as Krippner notes, "we now know that financial exuberance rested on exceedingly fragile economic, as well as normative, foundations" (149). Fragility, in the end, lies at the heart of *Blood Meridian*, especially the fragility of economic and normative foundations, of human bodies, of nation-states. The novel posits a metaphysics of violence to imagine the cataclysm entailed in imperial finance's rage for order. This is what *Blood Meridian* tells us about 1985: the apparent US economic resurgence through financialization and the regained faith through Reagan in US progress rested on chaos, a violence always ready to consume us.

4
Human Capital

With the money awarded her in 1981 as an inaugural recipient of a MacArthur Fellowship, Leslie Marmon Silko set to work on *Almanac of the Dead* (1991), a novel about the end of European colonialism in the Americas. It would take her a decade to complete. During that time, she collected countless clippings from newspapers and periodicals. She focused on US interventions in Latin America, the US mafia, the international drug trade, and global economics. She heavily underlined, for example, William J. Quirk's "The Big Bank Bailout," published in *The New Republic* on February 21, 1983. The article discusses the shift in the United States from manufacturing to finance. Silko underlined the following: "30 to 50 million jobs were lost during the 1970s as a result of plant relocations, closings, and contractions. The US, at an extraordinarily fast rate, underwent 'deindustrialization,' a process that will be fatal to the future strength of the country." Quirk describes how US banks began lending to foreign countries to increase profits, leading to a situation in which Mexico came to owe, "in interest alone, $250 million *a week*." He discusses how this debt led to the IMF's imposing on debtor countries "higher taxes, less spending, lower subsidies for industry, and currency devaluation.... In a word, austerity." He adds, "a Mexican peasant may think things are pretty austere already."

That was just the beginning. The decade that Silko spent writing *Almanac* witnessed the rapid neoliberalization of the Mexican economy. "Between 1982 and 1991," observes Nora Lustig, "the Mexican economy underwent a profound change... external trade was liberalized, markets were deregulated, and ownership restrictions removed" (v). Since the Mexican Revolution in the early twentieth century, Mexico had been known for its institutionalized populism and economic protectionism.

American Literature and the Long Downturn: Neoliberal Apocalypse. Dan Sinykin, Oxford University Press (2020). © Daniel Sinykin.
DOI: 10.1093/oso/9780198852704.001.0001

Yet, beginning with its debt crisis of 1982,[1] neoliberalism progressed at such speed that by 1991 Mexico had become "an open economy in which . . . the tendency is for the market to replace regulations, private ownership to replace public ownership, and competition, including that from foreign goods and investors, to replace protection" (Lustig 1). These changes benefited Mexico's elite, but hurt most Mexicans. As Lustig notes, "in the 1980s, real income fell, poverty rose, and social indicators deteriorated. Some of this damage, such as the contraction in investment in physical and human capital, may produce lasting effects" (10).

Two of the groups affected most deleteriously by Mexico's economic policies provide key figures in Silko's novel: peasants from the state of Chiapas, and Yaqui Indians in the northwest and in diaspora. In Chiapas, already one of Mexico's poorest and most indigenous states, poverty more than doubled between 1984 and 1989 (204). Meanwhile, the Yaquis became "worse off than any other social group in the northwest," writes Evelyn Hu-Dehart. "[W]hile Yaquis own considerable land, they are at the mercy of outside financiers. In short, the loss of their economic autonomy lies at the root of their current dependency" (217). Drawing from this devastation, Silko makes several of her leading characters Yaquis. Lecha, Zeta, and Calabazas have left the violence and economic colonization of their Sonora homeland to live in Tucson, Arizona. The indigenous revolution in the novel originates in Chiapas, led by Chiapans, notably Angelita La Escapía, a colonel in the "Army of Justice and Redistribution."

Almanac of the Dead takes the news of the 1980s as signs of the apocalypse. The novel describes dozens of characters struggling to survive amid the austerity imposed by neoliberalism in the US-Mexico borderlands. These characters participate in various ways in the destruction of US and Mexican governance—which the novel also portrays as destroying itself, according to the prophetic dictates of an enigmatic almanac—and they contribute variously to the uprising of the dispossessed who prove poised to take over in the wake of the collapse. For now, they live within scripts provided by neoliberalism, above all the

[1] The Mexican debt crisis of 1982 was instigated by rapacious loans from transnational commercial banks, which were "making enormous profits on their cross-border lending to the developing countries and by excessive spending predicated on future oil income" (Sachs 8; Lustig xx).

concept of "human capital," which defines people by the knowledge, skills, health, and values that comprise their market value and capacity to earn. Following the logic of neoliberalism spelled out by theorist Michel Feher, these characters are entrepreneurs who capitalize on the fever for privatization, monetizing policing, human organs, torture, and suicide. For Silko, anticipating Wendy Brown's claim that neoliberalism heralds the end of democracy, these depravities, culled and extrapolated from her folders full of news clippings, reveal the West at its furthest limit, at which point it must collapse into itself.

Neoliberalism came to hold sway in the 1980s because it served as an effective response for state and business actors struggling to deal with the ongoing difficulties produced by the long downturn. The different aspects of this history have been described by Brown, Angus Burgin, David Harvey, Greta Krippner, Daniel T. Rogers, Quinn Slobodian, and others. Economists at the University of Chicago and the transnational Mont Pèlerin Society began developing neoliberal thought after World War II, arguing that only economic liberty afforded political liberty. In subsequent years, economics proceeded to subsume politics, social science, and the humanities. In the 1950s and 1960s, Gary Becker developed a theory of "human capital" that conceives of the various skills, tendencies, and dispositions of a human being as economic attributes. (Hence Nora Lustig, quoted above, writing for the Brookings Institution, expresses concern about the fallout of Mexico's new economic policies not for humans but for human capital.) Becker read phenomena as varied as criminal justice, family life, personal taste, and addiction as principally economic, work for which he was awarded a Nobel Prize. Reading Becker and others, Michel Feher argues that the shift from liberalism to neoliberalism entails a shift in the categories that shape experience: the entrepreneur replaces the laborer, self-esteem replaces satisfaction, and credit replaces profit.[2] Randy Martin argues that "risk will replace labor as something taken rather than given, as a venture rather than an appropriation of one's effort" (35). We see the implementation of these shifts with the decades-long decimation of unions and the rise of the gig economy, exemplified by companies like Uber and Airbnb.

[2] Michel Feher, "On Credit, Self-esteem, and Sharing."

In the United States, post-boom limits to economic growth challenged the state's ability to allocate funds to the satisfaction of lobbyists and interest groups, leading the state to abdicate responsibility, turning over policy decisions to the market. Krippner writes, "with the deterioration of economic performance beginning in the 1970s, policymakers sought to depoliticize economic policy by returning to the market aspects of policy implementation formerly attributed to the state" (108). This compelled Americans to "*take upon* [*themselves*] the costs and risks externalized by the State and corporations" (Lazzarato 51). Against the promises made by neoliberal theorists that such externalization would bring widespread prosperity, "to become human capital or an entrepreneur of the self means assuming the costs as well as the risks of a flexible and financialized economy, costs and risks which are not only—far from it—those of innovation, but also and especially those of precariousness, poverty, unemployment, a failing health care system, housing shortages, etc." (ibid.).

Enter *Almanac of the Dead.* It opens with a scene of precarious entrepreneurship. Diasporic Yaquis, a banished Pueblo, a felon, a former sex worker, and a self-loathing queer gather in the kitchen of a heavily guarded compound on the outskirts of Tucson, where "pistols, shotguns, and cartridges [are] scattered on the kitchen counters, and needles and pills all over the table" (20). Zeta runs a smuggling business that ships drugs and arms across the border. Her nephew Ferro and his associate Paulie clean and order the guns. Lecha, now injecting Demerol, has just returned to Tucson after having traveled the country as a television talk show psychic; though ostensibly she has come to decipher the family's treasured almanac, she will continue to work as a freelance psychic with a strict pay-scale, adding her worknotes to the almanac itself (174–7). The scene's two other characters, Sterling and Seese, have both recently arrived at the ranch as outcasts from their previous communities (the reservation and a cocaine cartel, respectively). They take jobs working for Zeta and Lecha (19–30). By beginning with this cast of outsiders who suffer from the policies she scrupulously tracked during the years of the novel's genealogy, Silko indicates that *Almanac* will explore the human cost of neoliberalism.[3]

It was the specter of a precipitous end built into capitalism that undergirded my analysis in the previous chapter. Cormac McCarthy

[3] For an account of Silko's imagined alternative to human capital, see Breu, *Insistence*, 159.

imagined chaos from within and violence from without bringing an imminent end to capitalism's order. He wrote in the context of US policies of financial deregulation, part of the project to turn policy decisions over to the market, which destabilized the economy. As Greta Krippner writes of the deregulation of credit in the 1970s and 1980s, "the market was not a very effective source of restraint, and transferring control to the market ultimately served to loosen rather than restrict credit [as was the intended effect], propelling financialization to its most intense phase before bringing it to what appears to be a precipitous end" (Krippner 137). In this chapter, I show how Silko rewrote the narrative of neoliberalism—the uplifting story of human capital, entrepreneurship of the self, feeding the poor by unlocking their access to capital through privatization—as a story of apocalypse.

Wire Racks at the Grocery Store

Silko had specific ambitions for *Almanac of the Dead*. Her earlier work was high modernist in style, densely lyrical, exploring the interiority of trauma. Accordingly, she had achieved the kind of prestige that leads to a MacArthur Grant, but not impressive sales. In 1983, she told *The Arizona Republic* that she was aiming for new audiences with her next novel. "I've had positive critical attention," she said. "Now I want to make the wire racks at the grocery store checkout stands." She wanted to move stock with the proficiency of Tom Clancy, John Grisham, and Danielle Steel. Stylistically, *Almanac of the Dead* mimics mass-market fiction. The prose is plainspoken, the plot sensational. It features mobsters, sex workers, and drug traffickers. Yet Silko couldn't keep herself from Freud and Marx and extensive allusions to Maya codices and other indigenous texts and practices in a mode less Dan Brown than James Joyce, which might help explain why *Almanac* failed to reach the large audience she hoped for.[4] (Critics and scholars, for their part, ranged from dismissive to laudatory.)[5]

[4] Silko also refused to play the scripted part of the multicultural writer. See Breu, *Insistence*, 160.

[5] The novel was panned as over-the-top and sensationalist in the mainstream press (Dickstein 184). Sven Birkerts, writing for *The New Republic*, critiqued Silko's "premise of

It is normal for an author to aspire for sales, but Silko also had less conventional ambitions for *Almanac*. From the beginning, she modeled her novel on the few extant Maya codices—or, as she sometimes calls them, almanacs—that were not destroyed by Spanish colonists. She hoped that the novel "would fit together much as the old Maya almanacs had fit together" (*Yellow* 1619). We can gather from comments made in interviews and from the role the indigenous almanac plays in the novel that she meant she wanted the novel to serve anti-colonial indigenous politics and that she imagined the novel as visionary, prophetic. She writes that its "characters would foretell the future" (*Yellow* 1618). In particular, she claims that the novel's almanac "correctly predicted the Zapatista uprising" (*Yellow* 1782). Briefly alluded to in the previous chapter, the Zapatista uprising developed out of the immiseration of Mexican peasantry under neoliberalism in the 1980s and early 1990s. Notably, Mexican farmers could no longer compete with highly subsidized US agriculture, strangling the market for Mexican corn, which was especially important culturally in the highly indigenous southern states of Oaxaca and Chiapas. On New Year's Eve, 1993, the eve of the implementation of the North American Free Trade Agreement (NAFTA), which would exacerbate this situation, Zapatistas in Chiapas staged an armed insurrection and claimed several small regions as autonomous from the state. Reportedly, in the summer of 1993, a few months before the uprising, *Almanac*—with its depiction of an anti-colonial armed insurrection originating in Chiapas—circulated among the Zapatistas.[6]

Silko's distinct ambitions—for massive sales and political influence; to write a bestseller and a book modeled on pre-columbian codices—while by no means necessarily in conflict, create tensions that the novel itself, dramatizing these tensions through the fate of its eponymous almanac, is uncomfortable with. Is there a conflict between profiting from a text and

revolutionary insurrection" as "tethered to airy nothing. It is, frankly, naive to the point of silliness" (1). *Entertainment Weekly* called it "the windiest kind of bombast served up in the name of 'multiculturalism,'" (np). Academics working in Native American Studies, on the other hand, have lauded it, calling it "a supreme Native novel of innovation" and "one of the most important books of this century" (Teuton 117; Womack 233).

[6] See Collier and Lowery Quaratiello, 1.

presenting it as a work of prophecy? If a work is prophetic, is the future it foretells determined—in which case, what is the point of political action? Further, what does it mean to model a mass-market commodity on pre-columbian codices when these forms differ radically? These questions, central to the novel, have a history in Native American literature. Elizabeth Cook-Lynn, who holds a strong nationalist position on American Indian lit, arguing for its separation from the forces of colonialism, laments that "much of what is called American Indian fiction and scholarship is validated as such by non-Indian publishers, editors, critics, and scholars" (96). Cook-Lynn criticizes Indian writers like Silko who publish with houses complicit with global capitalism, advocating instead for community-based indigenous publishing. Yet the notion of the author is saturated by the history of capitalism.[7] Louis Owens recognizes that "through the inscription of an authorial signature, the Indian writer places him- or herself in immediate tension with [the] communal, authorless, and identity-conferring source [of traditional Indian discourses]" (11).

Almanac illustrates how the tensions described by Cook-Lynn and Owens were intensified by rapid privatization under neoliberalism. When everything becomes economic, what good does it do to write political fiction, which is immediately branded in terms of entertainment? Can our words and stories, in the form of fiction, still circulate with political force, or ought we relinquish the power of the meaning of words and stories and look to them instead for their ritualistic use? Should we privilege practices over meaning in the battle against capitalism? *Almanac of the Dead* takes on these questions but fails to resolve them. Instead, it turns itself over to the magical thinking of apocalypse.

Laughter, the Best Medicine

Silko is not always unclear on the relationship between politics and form in *Almanac*. The fate of several major characters depends on how they take to neoliberalism: if they embrace it, they are punished; if they resist, they are rewarded.

[7] See Foucault, "What is an Author?"

The novel begins and ends with Sterling, a Laguna Pueblo man who comes to Tucson to work on Lecha and Zeta's compound after he is banished from his reservation. His is an inverted bildungsroman, a journey toward his disarticulation from a society contaminated by neoliberalism. He is good-natured and pragmatic, but bumbling. Toward the end of the novel, he remembers how his earlier self, "had always worked hard on self-improvement. He had never paid much attention to the old-time ways because he thought the old beliefs were dying out" (762). His tribe banishes him after he fails to prevent Hollywood filmmakers, who he was tasked to chaperone, from filming a sacred stone snake, leading it to disappear. When we meet Sterling, he reads popular magazines such as *True Detective*, *Police Gazette*, and *Reader's Digest* for their pop-psychological advice, rather than consulting tribal knowledge (26, 23). He lives by the phrase "Laughter, the Best Medicine"; he tries not to think about his difficult history because the magazines recommend considering the past "'irreparable' and 'better forgotten'"; in the end, to Sterling, the magazines "all seemed to be in agreement: to cure depression one must let bygones be bygones" (23, 24, 36).

Almanac's closing sequence features Sterling as he returns home to the reservation. After living with revolutionaries on the brink of a new world, Sterling's reading habits have changed. "The magazines referred to a world that Sterling had left forever, a world that was gone, that safe old world that had never really existed except on the pages of *Reader's Digest* in articles on reducing blood cholesterol, corny jokes, and patriotic anecdotes" (757). Now, Sterling tries "to remember more of the stories the old people used to tell" (759). Tucson has "changed" him (762). He feels "haunted": "Sterling saw them over and over in dreams, ghost armies of Lakota warriors, ghost armies of the Americas leading armies of living warriors, armies of indigenous people to retake the land" (ibid.). Most important for Sterling is the reappearance of the stone snake on the reservation. The almanac, held at the Tucson compound, contains the "*Spirit Snake's Message*," which culminates with the prophecy: "What I have to tell you now is that / this world is about to end" (135). The novel's final line has Sterling with the snake, which "was looking south, in the direction from which . . . the people would come" (763).

The implications of Sterling's story arc are not subtle. The "safe old world" had kept him on a track of "self-improvement," but—in the neoliberal mode of human capital, self-esteem, and self-appreciation—the self being improved was an empty shell propelled by self-help pablum that prevented him from reckoning with the tribal "old-time ways." Sterling's journey to Tucson, his newfound interest in "the stories the old people used to tell," disarticulates him from neoliberalism, earns him his peace with the spirit snake, and allows him to return home.[8]

But *Almanac* teems with schemers who never arrive at such reckonings and thus face the consequences meted out by a world with a keen sense of justice. The neoliberalization of Mexico involved "converting water, education, and other resources and processes held in common and supplied collectively into commodities controlled by private enterprises and sold at 'market prices'" (Greenberg 247). The changes were vast. "From 1983 on, public enterprises were privatized, closed, merged, or transferred from federal to state or regional entities. From the more than 1,000 public enterprises at the end of 1982, there were only 269 in mid-1991" (Lustig 105). Silko's schemers scheme in this context. They are delirious with the fever for privatization on both sides of the US-Mexico border.

Trigg is a wheelchair-bound entrepreneur based in Tucson who owns and operates plasma donor centers, and is looking to expand. He thinks "the health care industry" is "a sleeping giant" (382). He plans to profit from addiction. "There were millions and millions to be made from treatments for people addicted to alcohol and other drugs" (ibid.). In the meantime, he discovers "a whole new market beyond plasma and whole blood. Trigg wanted to use the plasma donor centers to obtain donor organs and other valuable human tissue" (389). He enters the organ and tissue business in two ways. He buys "a great deal [of corpses] in Mexico where recent unrest and civil strife had killed hundreds a week. Mexican hearts were lean and strong" (404). He also—as has been frequently discussed in the criticism[9]—murders the homeless by performing oral sex on them while taking plasma until they die. Then he harvests and sells their body parts: a darkly literal take on human capital

[8] As Jessica Hurley notes, the stone snake is associated with uranium tailings. Hurley argues that the snake inscribes the colonial history of nuclear infrastructures into Silko's novel and that central to Sterling's arc is his recognition that US colonialism is not of the past but an ongoing practice inflicted on Indians. See Hurley, "Impossible Futures."

[9] See Brigham; Jarman; and Olmsted.

(443–5). He ends up getting his comeuppance: his "skull smashed" and his body "neatly arranged in an organ-freezer compartment" in the basement of his company's headquarters (750).

Menardo sells insurance from his base in the capital of Chiapas, Tuxtla Gutiérrez. Like most Mexicans, he is mestizo, with Spanish and indigenous heritage. As a child, he loved listening to his indigenous grandfather tell stories, "right up until the sixth grade when one of the teaching Brothers [at his Catholic school] had given [students] a long lecture about pagan people and pagan stories" (258). Menardo internalizes colonialism's racism, disavowing his indigenous heritage and inventing a story to explain the appearance of his characteristically indigenous nose. Silko links Menardo's vanity and his internalized racism to his business success, slipping from his explanation of his nose to the assertion that, "Menardo had risen quickly in the insurance business because he knew exactly what people wanted to hear" (260). Menardo owns Universal Insurance, which, true to its name, grows to insure against more and more risks, toward insuring against every eventuality. "What Menardo offered were special policies that insured against all losses, no matter the cause, including acts of God, mutinies, war, and revolution" (261). To fulfill its promises, Universal Insurance becomes "the first insurance company to employ a private security force to protect clients from political unrest" (ibid.). From there, the company grows to build "its own private air force" (292). Finally, Universal Insurance displaces one of the functions most central to the state: policing. Silko ventriloquizes commercial rhetoric, writing, "Whenever revolution, mutiny, uprising, or guerilla war might strike, Universal Insurance *would be there* to offer complete protection to clients. No need to depend on poorly equipped government forces" (ibid.).

As Universal Insurance becomes universal, Menardo applies the idea of total protection against risk to his own body. He obsesses over wearing a bulletproof vest at all times. Feeling the need to prove to himself that the vest will keep him safe, he asks his servant, an indigenous man named Tacho, to shoot him in the chest with a pistol. Tacho does, the vest fails, and Menardo dies. Menardo's death is allegorical: the event happens in a section titled "How Capitalists Die" (509). Just after the shooting, Tacho remembers indigenous teachings about "the eventual disappearance of the white man," adding that, "a great many fools like

Menardo would die pretending they were white men" (511). Menardo crystallizes, on his body and in his character, a narrative in which the attempt to extend the monetization of risk to its totalizing end—an attempt associated with whiteness and colonization, against indigeneity—leads to apocalypse: for one man, for a civilization.

Of Course, the Book Will Be Mine

Not all characters in the novel can be so easily contained by morality tales. Consider Lecha, who, as a psychic responsible for the eponymous almanac, is an avatar for Silko. Through Lecha, Silko grapples with the tension between making money and serving her people with her writing. What does she owe anyone? What are her political obligations?

Lecha is a TV psychic. She discovers that she "had been born for television talk shows" (147). As far as she's concerned, she "had never felt she owed anyone the truth, unless it was truth about their own lives, and then they had to pay her to tell them" (142). When a producer meets with her to arrange her first appearance, she opens with, "Business first... I want to know how much this TV show will pay me" (145). She has a strong sense of her own worth—and how to appreciate it. She recognizes that her "high Indian cheekbones and light brown skin give her an exotic quality that television... desperately needs" (141). On camera, she hams it up. "It was all an act," Silko writes, "the way Lecha would lower her voice and say she regretted what she was about to say, then reveal the location of the victim" (146). Years go by like this. Canny schemer that she is, she exemplifies Michel Feher's notion that, under neoliberalism, "life may be thought of as a strategy aimed at self-appreciation" of one's human capital (28).

But when the novel begins she has left the gigging life behind and moved to the compound in Tucson. Good neoliberal that she is, she attends to herself as a portfolio of investments and speculates that the vogue for racial others on TV is about to wane. "Lecha takes pride in knowing when to fold her cards. She is no gambler. She only goes for the sure things. The TV talk show circuit had been one of those sure things. But nothing lasts forever; she laughs to herself. The fascination the United States had had for the 'other'—the blacks, Asians, Mexicans, and Indians—ran in cycles" (142). Though she denies being a "gambler," Lecha's poker metaphor—*knowing when to fold her cards*—reveals that that's exactly what she is, if one who plays it safe.

Lecha returns to Tucson to work with the old almanac. She hires Seese to type the almanac's "notebooks" into "the word processor" (21). Lecha inherited the almanac from Yoeme, her Yaqui grandmother, who also bestowed Lecha with her prophetic gifts. Whereas Sterling came to embrace his indigeneity and Menardo to disavow his, Lecha lingers with hers, at turns putting it to work for white audiences and allowing it to remind her of the homeland she left behind. Her move to the compound suggests she feels the need to do right by Yoeme, to put her gifts to use for political rather than financial gain.

But her work on the almanac is self-serving. She tells Seese not to worry about the "old notebooks" because they "are all in broken Spanish or corrupt Latin that no one can understand without months of research in old grammars" (174). She says she "wants her personal notebooks transcribed and typed because [they are] necessary to understanding the old notebooks Yoeme left behind" (ibid.). Silko reports that "Lecha had already done translation work, and her notebooks contained narratives in English" (ibid.). Yet Lecha's notebooks, which Silko shows us, do not contain translations of the almanac—they contain notes for her freelance work, including passages like: "The computer posits models of possible routes taken by the abductor and victim" and "The abductor drives the victim west and then north into the desert foothills" (175). This is to say, Lecha is at least deceiving Seese, if not herself. On the pretense of caring for the almanac, she is adding her business papers to it. Her return to Tucson proves less a turn toward her indigeneity than a continuation of her neoliberal habits, a fact reinforced by a comment Lecha makes to her sister Zeta. Zeta says, "'You are going to copy [Yoeme's] book," to which Lecha replies, "her eyes dreamy and distant, 'You could say "her book," but of course, the book will be mine'" (177).

The notion of anyone possessing the almanac as her own is contrary to its origins as a pre-columbian text. As an avatar for Silko, Lecha's capitalizing on the almanac foregrounds Silko's complicated authorship as a writer modeling her mass-market novel to profit from Maya codices. It is far from clear whether we're meant to applaud or censure Lecha for her treatment of the almanac. What is clear is that she is one of the good guys. She helps with the revolution from the Tucson compound and eventually moves to the revolution's "secret headquarters" in North Dakota (754). She, with the help of the almanac, offers a definitive vision of the end of European colonialism in the Americas (756). In this novel where often characters get their just deserts, what do we make of "bad" behavior from a "good" character? Do we conclude that Lecha's profiting from the almanac—and Silko's from her *Almanac*—are necessary complicities on the road to revolution? But then why does Lecha feel the need to deceive Seese and maybe even herself? A closer look at the almanac will help us see the novel's own uncertainty on this point.

Up and Away Like Flocks of Small Birds

Lecha remembers the remarkable tale Yoeme had told her about the origin of the almanac. It suggests that the almanac matters not for its meaning or what it says, but for how it's used.

In the early days of European colonization of the Americas, an indigenous people, facing extinction, decided to send four children north with a book that described "who they were and where they had come from" (246). The children's elders told them the book held "all the days of their people. These days and years were all alive, and all these days would return again" (247). The book could also revive the tribe itself. "The people knew if even part of their almanac survived, they as a people would return someday" (246). The children pass through apocalyptic terrain: they "saw few birds or rodents and no large animals because the aliens had slaughtered all these creatures to feed themselves and their soldiers and their slaves.... [A]s the children continued on, they began to find entire villages that had been abandoned" (247–8). Eventually, the children come to a village with water where they rest, falling into the company of "a hunchbacked woman" with hostile designs (248).

Suffering from hunger, the children stop to eat with the woman, who cooks them a pot of stew. Secretly, the eldest girl slips a page of the book they are tasked to save—made, as it is, of "horse stomach"—into the "simmering vegetable stew": "The thin, brittle page gradually began to change. Brownish ink rose in clouds. Outlines of the letters smeared and then they floated up and away like flocks of small birds" (249). Thanks to the addition of the page, the stew is unusually sustaining, allowing the children to recover their strength. As it turns out, the woman had had plans to cannibalize the children, which are thwarted by the consumption of the book.[10] As Yoeme says, "if the eldest had not sacrificed a page from the book, that crippled woman would have murdered them all right then, while the children were weak from hunger" (253). Instead, the book survives and becomes, years later, central to the revolution that begins to unfold across the pages of the novel.

From the beginning of its tumultuous history, the almanac creates problems for determining how to read it. On the one hand, we learn that the almanac's power consists in its containing stories about "who [the people] were and where they had come from," stories that have the power to resurrect the people. On the other, the children "had been told the pages held many forces within them, countless physical and spiritual properties to guide the people and make them strong" (252). These *physical* properties *within* the pages that give the almanac its strength have nothing to do with reading at all. In fact, the almanac's key quality in Yoeme's story is not what it says—the eldest girl "could no more read the writing than she could understand the language of the hunchbacked woman"—but that, when eaten, it provides unexpected sustenance (249). After the eldest girl drops the page in the stew, the letters, identified in terms of their materiality as ink, fly away and it is the material qualities—the fact that the page is made of horse stomach and is surprisingly nutritious—that save the young refugees.

The sources of the almanac's power, its stories and its physical and spiritual properties, invite two modes by which critics might read *Almanac*. Most have chosen the former, reading the almanac and the novel as depositories of stories whose dissemination is a revolutionary political act. These readings highlight a few passages from the almanac that can be read programmatically, in which the spread of stories

[10] The novel historicizes the old woman's cannibalism as an effect of colonialism, known in the novel as the period of Death-Eye Dog. Everyone living within colonialism, according to *Almanac*, whether colonizer or colonized, is subject to the danger of personal corruption. The anecdote of the almanac ends: "As long as all our days belong to Death-Eye Dog, we will continue to see such things [as the old woman's plotting cannibalism]. That woman had been left behind by the others. The reign of Death-Eye Dog is marked by people like her. She did not start out that way. In the days that belong to Death-Eye Dog, the possibility of becoming like her trails each one of us" (253).

works as a mystical force that will induce the apocalypse. Here is one of the key passages:

> One day a story will arrive in your town. There will always be disagreement over direction—whether the story came from the southwest or southeast. The story may arrive with a stranger, a traveler thrown out of his home country months ago. Or the story may be brought by an old friend, perhaps the parrot trader. But after you hear the story, you and the others prepare by the new moon to rise up against the slave masters (578).

This story promises to instigate an uprising through the subversive transformation of consciousness. Yoeme confirms that "power resides within certain stories; this power ensures the story to be retold, and with each retelling a slight but permanent shift [takes] place" (581).

Critics adopt this notion of storytelling to read *Almanac* as exposing political truths and to theorize political strategies.[11] Rebecca Tillett, for instance, argues that the novel's "foregrounding of the lengthy history of colonialism in the Americas exposes the violent, repressive, and exploitative means by which empires, including the contemporary empires of global capital and corporate enterprise, are established and maintained" (331). Ann Brigham brings concepts from geography to the novel to consider how "constructions of geographic scale contribute to both the survival and overthrow of colonialist capitalism" (306). Several essays use *Almanac* as a model of political organizing in the face of the rise of the transnational capitalism of the 1980s. Channette Romero asserts that *Almanac* "attempts to overcome the limitations of the American Indian Movement" through "the promotion of cross-cultural connections" (623, 624). Eva Cherniavsky and Laura Shackleford both see the novel as developing a resistance movement that transcends identity politics. Cherniavsky writes that, "the novel's insurgent peoples evade" identity politics "to open up a front as broad and mobile as the flows of global

[11] Jessica Hurley, in "Impossible Futures," is a notable exception. She argues that Silko resists realist storytelling that depends on the logic of verisimilitude and plausibility, deploying apocalypse "to reveal the contingent nature of the present and to allow for other possibilities in both the present and the future" (778–9). Rather than turning to the novel's almanac as a model, Hurley looks to the novel's apocalyptic form and its tactics drawn from speculative fiction.

capital itself"; Shackleford claims, "subjecting global capitalist networks to its own networking logic, the novel attempts to reverse the former's suppression of historical time... developing an analogous model of transnational, material modes of resistance" (121, ¶13). Each of these essays turns to the novel for political analysis and, in their tone, risks triumphalism, a sense that by identifying a political vision in the novel, substantial political work has been done.[12] In these readings, the almanac's "proliferating storytelling," which transforms the world within the novel, serves as the model for the novel's own storytelling, which, thus, ought to transform the world beyond the novel (Donnelly 249).[13]

But this scholarly consensus depends on selective reading and wishful thinking. Only a few passages from the almanac are readable as such. Most are fragments that make little or no sense. Critics have neglected modes of reading offered by these fragments, which resist interpretation, or approaches guided by the parable of the children in which language floats *up and away like flocks of small birds*. At the far end of the mode that attends to storytelling, critics strive to create the conditions in which "even the marginalia and additions to [*Almanac*'s almanac] make sense" (Reinecke 77). But the parable about the departure of language from a book, leaving it useful as a material object, invites not reading at all, but rather *using* books. Here critics ought to consider the uses to which the almanac—and, thus, *Almanac*—might be put. The conflict between these modes stages a debate that has been contentious within literary studies since 2009:[14] is the task of literary critics critical, to rescue the conditions

[12] These essays participate in a "world-literary mode [that] impl[ies] that literature reaches a substantial audience of uninitiated readers who need to learn what writers want to teach them" (Brouillette *UNESCO*, 3). Heather Houser offers a more tempered reading of *Almanac*'s political work, arguing that it helps readers "become aware of how emotion puts pressure on the activist leanings of fiction" (217).

[13] Scholars often base their readings of Silko's novel on their analysis of the almanac. Catherine Rainwater writes, "We watch as the world seems to conform to Silko's story, just as the story reflects the shape of things intimated by Yoeme's notebooks" (141). Yvonne Reinecke asserts that "the novel functions much like the notebooks of the almanac contained within the narrative itself. Repeatedly, the novel highlights the resurgence and emancipation of the colonized and the repressed" (71). T. V. Reed makes the identity between the almanac and the novel most explicit, writing, "*Almanac of the Dead* is the almanac the characters in the novel seek to restore" (34). Channette Romero notes "the important political and spiritual work both the almanac and *Almanac of the Dead* are hoping to accomplish by engaging the audience/reader in a similar storytelling process" (631).

[14] Stephen Best and Sharon Marcus propelled "reading" to the forefront of keywords in literary studies with their special issue of *Representations* in 2009 called *The Way We Read Now*, in which they introduced the much-discussed term "surface reading." Rita Felski has been an

for the legibility of a text? or ought critics forgo critique and pursue instead what lies at the surface of a text, the various ways readers use texts?

They Are Not Intended to Make Sense

A closer look at the almanac reveals a politics of illegibility, a politics of use. To give a better sense of the enigmatic text, let me offer a long excerpt:

> "Death Dog traveled to the land of the dead where the God of death gave him the bone the human race was created with.
>
> Scorpion uses his tail as a noose to lasso deer. Scorpion is a good hunter. He has a net bag in which he carries his fire-driller and fire-sticks.
>
> The sign of the human hand = 2. The hand that holds the hilt of the dagger is plunged into the lower body of the deer.
>
> Those cursed with the anguish, and the despairers, all were born during the five 'nameless' days.
>
> On the five nameless days, people stay in bed and fast and confess sins.
>
> Black Zip whistles a warning. He is the deer god.
>
> In the year Ten Sky, the principal ruler is Venus.
>
> Big Star is a drunkard, a deformed dog with the head of a jaguar and the hind end of a dog with a purple dick. He staggers like Rabbit, who is also a drunkard. Nasty, arrogant liar! Troublemaker and experimenter in mutual hate and torture!"
>
> ⌘
>
> Venus. Color: red. Direction: east. Herald of the dawn and measurer of night.

influential figure in these debates, arguing against the tendency to treat critique as the only mode by which to write literary criticism and arguing for, instead, what she calls postcritique. She describes one version of what postcritique looks like in her manifesto *Uses of Literature*, which takes inspiration from Ludwig Wittgenstein and Bruno Latour in exploring how readers use texts, rather than trying to uncover latent meanings. It is with regard to Felski's work and the controversy it's stirred that my distinction between use and meaning in contemporary criticism refers. For a concise discussion of critique and postcritique and an example of postcritical reading, see Anker.

> Envious Ribald;
> Sin in his face and in his talk; he had no virtue in him.
> He is without understanding.
> He had no virtue in him. Mighty carnivorous teeth and a body withered like a rabbit.
> Deities return. Better get to know them.
> Venus of the Celestial Dragon with eight heads; each head hurls shafts of affliction down on mankind. Europeans call Venus 'Lucifer, the Bright One,' who fell from grace long ago. Venus resides in darkness until he rises as Morning Star. Dog-face partially blackened, a fish in his headdress, he swims up from the dark underworld.
> Error in translation of the Chumayel manuscript: 11 AHU was the year of the return of fair Quetzalcoatl. But the mention of the artificial white circle in the sky could only have meant the return of Death Dog and his eight brothers: plague, earthquake, drought, famine, incest, insanity, war, and betrayal." (571–2)

These passages are not nonsense, though they resist reading. Some refer to Maya or Aztec myths, separated from the contexts that make them meaningful, others have no apparent provenance. They cannot easily be read as stories, nor do they easily support political theorization. The almanac only becomes more difficult to read the more we learn about it. Over the centuries, it has become a pastiche of Laguna Pueblo prophecy, historical fragments that mimic the Maya *Books of Chilam Balam*, commentaries on the Maya codices, delusions, snippets of Western texts, and forgeries. The almanac remains open to revision and addition. Lecha records a story that Yoeme tells from her youth about Geronimo, which becomes "the first entry that had been written in English" (130).

The almanac comes to Lecha and Zeta in poor physical condition. "For hundreds of years, guardians of the almanac notebooks had made clumsy attempts to repair torn pages. Some sections had been splashed with wine, others with water or blood. Only fragments of the original pages remained" (569). As the quality of the almanac deteriorates, it becomes less and less legible: "the strange parchment got drier and more curled each season until someday the old almanac would reveal nothing more to an interpreter" (245). Further, "There was evidence that substantial portions of the original manuscript had been lost or condensed into odd narratives which operated like codes" (569). These "odd narratives" include the fragments I quoted above, which neither Lecha nor Zeta can make sense of. Much of what has been added to the almanac over time is untrustworthy, either because it originates in delusions or has been taken from Western texts or might be a forgery: "The great deal of what had accumulated with the almanac fragments had been debris gathered here and there by aged keepers of the almanac after they had gone crazy"; "Whole sections had been stolen from other books and from the proliferation of 'farmer's almanacs' published by patent-drug companies.... Not even the parchment pages or fragments of ancient paper could be trusted; they might have been clever forgeries, recopied, drawn, and colored painstakingly" (569–70).

One begins to get the sense that the point is that we are not supposed to be able to read the materially degraded, encoded, contaminated, and possibly forged almanac at the heart of the novel. Yet Lecha retains deferred hope that it holds the key to understanding the world. "Once the notebooks are transcribed, I will figure out how to use the old almanac. Then we will foresee the months and years to come—everything" (137). Still, Lecha does not say she will figure out how to *read* the almanac; rather, she says she will figure out how to *use* it.

Lecha's plan to use the almanac to foresee the future has a basis in the texts Silko took as her models. Silko leaves ample traces to lead attentive readers to these model texts. Readers encounter, for example, the following list, reproduced from the almanac:[15]

[15] Several hundred pages later, we find English translations of "Fragments from the Ancient Notebooks" (570). Among these is a passage that refers to the *Books of Chilam Balam*: "Error in translation of the Chumayel manuscript: 11 AHU was the year of the return of fair Quetzalcoatl. But the mention of the artificial white circle in the sky could only have meant the return of Death Dog and his eight brothers: plague, earthquake, famine, incest, insanity, war, and betrayal" (572). Intertextual references and a lack of context make this passage esoteric. Mention of "the Chumayel manuscript" refers to one of the *Books of Chilam Balam*—the *Book of Chumayel*—and "11 AHU" is itself a misspelling of 11 Ahau, the designation of a cyclical date, specifically that of 1539, which "initiated the cycle of the Spanish Empire" (*Ancient* xvii). "Death Dog" is a figure that pervades the novel, often named "Death-Eye Dog," and appears to be Silko's invention; it refers to the period of European colonization of the Americas. The passage, then, while still not entirely clear, presents a paradox: the year 11 Ahau, coupled with the description of an eclipse ("artificial white circle"), seems to signify the return both of Quetzalcoatl and of Death Dog, both of a Maya deity and of European colonization and its devastations, which should be mutually exclusive. The author of this passage simultaneously acknowledges the undecidability of the paradox and asserts that the correct translation would correlate 11 Ahau to Death Dog, thereby demonstrating that the Maya in fact predicted not the return of their god but the appearance of the Europeans. The arrival of the Europeans creates a

1. almanakh: Arabic.
2. almanac: A.D. 1267 English from the Arabic.
3. almanaque: A.D. 1505 Spanish from the Arabic.
4. a book of tables containing a calendar of months and days with astronomical data and calculations.
5. predicts or foretells the auspicious days, the ecclesiastical and other anniversaries.
6. short glyphic passages give the luck of the day.
7. Madrid
   Paris Codices
   Dresden

Initiates will recognize Madrid, Paris, and Dresden as the names of the three extant Maya codices that survived the purges of the Spanish Inquisition. At the heart of *Almanac of the Dead* is Silko's fantasy of this fourth codex that remains in indigenous hands.[16] The codices consist of "screenfold pages with glyphs and pictures" that contain, as the novel

crisis for the reading of the ancient text, which this passage longs to resolve. According to Bruce Love, the *Books of Chilam Balam* descend directly from the codices. "The same Maya intellectuals, Maya of noble descent who understood pre-Hispanic books, were the first to become literate in Spanish.... Among them were practicing subversives, believers in tradition who risked retaliation to pursue a form of cultural treason. They wrote—and therefore preserved forever—the 'sciences and histories' from the ancient hieroglyphic books. These books, written in the Mayan language using Spanish characters, are known today as the *Books of Chilam Balam*" (6). In other words, certain Maya responded to the destruction of their books by writing, as a subversive political act, more books: by taking the language taught to them by the colonizers and composing forbidden books. These new books continued to transform over time and became very different from the codices. Rather than a ritual handbook for a priest, the *Book of Tizimin*, one of the *Books of Chilam Balam*, "constitutes an outline history of Yucatan from the seventh century to the nineteenth"; this is not an almanac but a chronicle (*Ancient* xi). Silko's use of such a "secret history" engages *Almanac of the Dead* in a long-standing and ongoing tradition of resistance to European colonization through writing (*Ancient* xx).

[16] Silko upends the paradigm in which the peoples indigenous to the Americas practice oral traditions but cannot and do not write. Not only was the denial of indigenous writing central to early colonizers—as Sean Kicummah Teuton notes, "the Native American savage was defined precisely by his lack of true language and, more specifically, writing"—but it has shaped American Indian literary studies (1107). Kenneth Lincoln, in his generative study *Native American Renaissance*, defines the surge of Native American literature in the late 1960s and 1970s as "a written renewal of oral traditions translated into Western literary forms," and much of the subsequent criticism has followed suit (8). Craig Womack, writing in reference to pre-columbian Maya and Aztec books, challenges this paradigm, commenting that, "As rich as oral tradition is, we also have a vast, and vastly understudied, written tradition"; yet few scholars have taken up this challenge. Silko urges the history of indigenous writing to the foreground in *Almanac of the Dead.*

attests, "calendrical computations, divination and prophecy, prescriptions for rites and ceremonies, and history" (Love 5). Made from the inner bark of fig trees, they were written in Maya hieroglyphic script and pictures and used by Maya priests for religious and astrological purposes (Bricker and Bricker 111, 841). Each codex "was a sacred manual that conferred great status upon its owner. It empowered the Maya priest to see, as if through a crystal, the orderly workings of the universe" (Love 7).

The Maya *Books of Chilam Balam*, referenced in the allusion to the Chumayel manuscript above, serve as a second model for Silko's almanac.The *Books* "are by no means purely Mayan. They have been shaped by almost a thousand years of cultural confrontation" (*Ancient* xi). Because of this syncretism, "They are exasperatingly difficult to translate and interpret.... They are composed in archaic and elliptical language. Their chronology is obscured by esoteric numerological, astrological, and religious assumptions. The orthography of surviving texts leaves a great deal to be desired." (*Ancient* xi). As such, Munro S. Edmonson, the translator of one of the *Books*, concludes that "these texts are purposely obscure. They are not intended to make sense to others—and they don't" (xiv).

The third ancient text Silko draws from in *Almanac* is the most famous: the *Popol Vuh*. The editors of a recent volume comment, "A watershed event in Maya literary studies that brought Mayan Colonial literature to a lay public was [Dennis] Tedlock's translation of the *Popol Vuh* in 1985," which would have been available to Silko while she was writing *Almanac* (*Maya*). Tedlock writes about the *Popol Vuh* that it "tells the story of the emergence of light in the darkness, from primordial glimmers to brilliant dawns, and from rainstorms as black as night to days so clear the very ends of the earth can be seen" (15). It is a Maya creation narrative, one that mostly tells of mythical events, but which reaches into the present of its composition, or about 1554 (Tedlock 57). Like the *Books of Chilam Balam*, it is written in Mayan with a Latin alphabetic script. Silko appropriates narrative elements from the *Popol Vuh* for characters and plot developments in her novel. For instance, the *Popol Vuh* features two Hero Twins who descend into the underworld, trick the lords of the underworld into volunteering to be sacrificed on the premise that they will be resurrected, and then leave them dead. In *Almanac*, two leaders of the resistance are twin brothers, Maya, named

Tacho and El Feo. Tacho kills Menardo, one of the novel's lords of the underworld (510–11). Like the codices and the *Books of Chilam Balam*, the *Popol Vuh* gave access to the future. With it, the Maya knew "whether there would be death, or whether there would be famine, or whether quarrels would occur, they knew it for certain, since there was a place to see it, there was a book" (29).

Between the codices, the *Books of Chilam Balam*, and the *Popol Vuh*, Silko offers many models for how to use the almanac without having to read it like a literary critic. Its value might lie in its conferral of status upon those who possess it. It might function more like a manual than a narrative, instructing its users. It might endow those who possess it with prophetic gifts—as it does for Lecha. Its very illegibility—like the illegibility of the *Books of Chilam Balam*—might be its power. Again, Silko has indigenous history to draw on for this last point, and does. Indigenous peoples in the Americas have historically used esoteric text and cultural practices as anticolonial weapons that, in their illegibility, provoke violence from colonists. Two such precedents are especially important to *Almanac of the Dead*: Bishop Diego de Landa's burning of books, and the Wounded Knee massacre. Both illustrate the power of esoteric indigenous texts; Silko uses both to situate her political aims in *Almanac*.

The Devil's Falsehoods

Silko inscribes her novel in a long history of the relationship between literature and politics in the Americas. Central to that history, for Silko, is an event that took place on July 12, 1562, in the town of Maní in what we now call the Yucatán peninsula. On that day a Franciscan bishop named Diego de Landa "forcibly gathered" hundreds of the local Maya for an *auto de fé*, a punishment for heresy under the Spanish Inquisition (Chuchiak 613). As Bruce Love notes, "the cataclysmic onset of Spanish rule and the Franciscan zeal for religious conversion forced native religion underground. Possession and use of hieroglyphic books was punished by torture and death" (5). On July 12, 1562, however, before the gathered Maya, Bishop Landa punished not their bodies but their texts. He built "a large bonfire in the central plaza" and "ordered more than 20,000 idols and other ritual paraphernalia tossed into the fire. Along with the idols went forty Maya codices" (613–14). This was the most infamous burning of what *Almanac*'s Maya revolutionary Angelita La Escapía describes as "the great libraries of the Americas" (315).

"Books," Silko writes, "have been the focus of the struggle for the control of the Americas from the start" ("Books" 1873). In the introduction to her book of essays, *Yellow Woman and the Beauty of the Spirit*, Silko identifies Landa's book burning as the beginning of this struggle. For Silko, books governed the representation of indigenous peoples. The colonists needed "to be rid of all evidence that Native American cultures were intellectually equal to European cultures; they could then argue to the pope that these indigenous inhabitants were not fully human and that Europeans were therefore free to do with them and their land as they pleased" ("Introduction" 178). Silko charts the subsequent colonial function of books. After Landa, she writes, "Soon the only books of Native American life were written and made by non-Indians, who continued to portray indigenous people as subhumans. The United States government used books in their campaign of cultural genocide. Thus the representation or portrayal of Native Americans was politicized from the very beginning" (178).

But, for Silko, books can also be wielded as weapons against colonial powers—in fact, the colonial need to destroy indigenous books is evidence of their power. She begins her essay on the Maya codices by writing, "Books were and still are weapons in the ongoing struggle for the Americas" (1749). For centuries, colonizers relied on books to produce readings that devalued indigenous peoples and depicted them as destined to vanish. Conversely, indigenous writing maintained and reproduced indigenous lifeways. Silko calls books "weapons" and locates them at the heart of "the ongoing struggle for the Americas" because she recognizes that books are tools for maintaining lifeways that can subvert colonial control. Landa makes the power of indigenous texts especially clear, writing, "We found a great number of these books in Indian characters and because they contained nothing but superstition and the Devil's falsehoods we burned them all" (ibid.). Given that Landa could not read "Indian characters" he could not have known whether the books "contained nothing but superstition," but the fact of their alterity and the evidence of their dissemination compelled Landa to burn every one he could find.[17]

Paiute prophet Wovoka's Ghost Dance is especially important for *Almanac of the Dead*. In James Mooney's influential account, Wovoka:

> fell asleep in the daytime and was taken up to the other world. Here he saw God, with all the people who had died long ago engaged in their oldtime sports and occupations, all happy and forever young.... After showing him all, God told him he must go back and tell his people... that if they faithfully obeyed his instructions they would at last be reunited with their friends in this other world, where there would be no more death or sickness or old age. He was given the dance which he was commanded to bring back to his people. (772)

Wovoka's vision quickly spread among tribes in the western United States. But it was crushed with violence. In 1890, US troops massacred dancers at Wounded Knee, often noted as the end of the Indian Wars and the end of the Ghost Dance. The troops attested to feeling afraid of the dancers. The illegibility of Maya and Sioux texts and cultural practices frightened Landa and the US troops both. Silko writers her almanac into this history, carrying it into the present. Her character, Wilson Weasel Tail, a poet-lawyer, rewrites this history. "The truth is the Ghost Dance did not end with the murder of Big Foot and one hundred and forty-four Ghost Dance worshipers at Wounded Knee," he says. "The Ghost Dance has never ended" (724). On the contrary, the Ghost Dance persists as a battle cry for those "who cry

[17] Bruce Love, who has done important work with the Paris Codex, narrates the survival of Maya books as follows: "Maya books and the practice of writing them has survived in two forms. In their pre-Hispanic form—screenfold pages with glyphs and pictures—the books endured in the hands of Maya priests who refused to convert. Sometimes the priests clandestinely secluded the books within the very towns where Franciscans ruled, sometimes the books escaped with Maya people who fled to the hinterlands," such as in the case of Silko's imagined codex (5). Love continues, "Maya codices also survived by transforming.... The same Maya intellectuals, Maya of noble descent who understood pre-Hispanic books, were the first to become literate in Spanish.... Among them were practicing subversives, believers in tradition who risked brutal retaliation to pursue a form of cultural treason. They wrote—and therefore preserved forever—the 'scenes and histories' from the ancient hieroglyphic books. These books, written in the Mayan language using Spanish characters, are known today as the *Books of Chilam Balam*" (6).

out, who demand justice, and who call to the people to take back the Americas!" (ibid.).[18]

The Ghost Dance spread in popularity in the 1880s, which witnessed the nadir of American Indian population in the United States. It was a ripe time for an apocalyptic vision of defeating the conquerors and restoring the lives of the marginalized and the dead. If Wovoka's vision sounds familiar in the context of this monograph, it might be because he drew heavily on the Book of Revelation, which he was regularly exposed to as a child, growing up Christian. Like in Revelation, a prophet ascends to heaven, receives from God a revelation about imminent change, the end of empire, and the resurrection of the dead, and returns to disseminate the vision. In addition to bringing hope to Indians, Wovoka's syncretic vision served another purpose: it helped band together distinct tribes as Indians, an identity held in common and defined by shared resistance to colonization. It served the ends, in other words, of ethnogenesis, the creation of a people. Silko's *Almanac*'s almanac shares attributes with the Ghost Dance and the Book of Revelation: it envisions the end of empire and the resurrection of the dead. And it, maybe most revealingly for the novel, it aims to create a people.

Ethnogenesis

The almanac possesses the power of ethnogenesis. Though each member of the people from whom the almanac originated could die, still they know that, "if even part of their almanac survived, they as a people would return someday" (246). The theory that a text creates a people finds support in recent anthropological research on the Ghost Dance and on

[18] Mooney notes that Wovoka came after a series of Indian prophets with similar visions. There was a Delaware prophet "who preached a union of all the red tribes and a return to the old Indian life, which he declared to be the divine command, as revealed to him in a wonderful vision" (663). This vision instructed him to create "the great Book or Writing" which would show other Indians "the only way that was now left to them to regain what they had lost" (666). Some years later, the Yakima prophet Smohalla "added greatly to his reputation by predicting several eclipses. This he was enabled to do by the help of an almanac.... Smohalla had also a blank book containing mysterious characters, some of which resembled letters of the alphabet, and which he said were records of events and prophecies" (720). Smohalla used the authority gained from these writings and predictions to urge his followers to return to the practices of their indigenous past (719).

Yaqui Indians (such as Yoeme, Lecha, and Zeta). Gregory E. Smoak argues that, "the Ghost Dances were a prophetic expression of an American Indian identity that countered American attempts to assert a particular national identity and to impose that vision on American Indians" (198). In the late nineteenth century, under pressure of assimilation and extermination, tribes adopted the Ghost Dance, which helped to create a common group identity as Indians. When Wilson Weasel Tail insists that the Ghost Dance never ended, he is, in part, re-creating the common identity of Indians around the Ghost Dance as a text in resistance to ongoing colonialism (724–5). Kristin Erickson makes similar claims about how prophecy functions for Yaquis. To open *Almanac*, Silko writes, "Ancient prophecies foretold the arrival of Europeans in the America" (14). The Talking Tree story is one such prophecy that continues to be told among Yaquis (Erickson 24). Erickson observes that, "The narrative is doubly relevant in the present, as the prophecy of the arrival of the whites and the ensuing decision to *become* Yaquis mirrors and validates the continuing decision (in the face of tremendous pressure to change) to *be* Yaquis today" (38). The Ghost Dance and the Talking Tree prophecy are texts that serve to create and sustain group identities.

Almanac explores the limits of founding group identity in a text. *Almanac*'s almanac goes so far as to imagine a people's extinction and resurrection. It persists through the centuries, accumulating new texts, losing others, all while becoming less and less legible. The Ghost Dance and the Talking Tree prophecies present a clear vision for the people they create: you are one in resistance to European colonialism. But what kind of people does the almanac create with its baffling mix of apocalyptic storytelling and fragmented illegibility? This is another way of asking, what kind of people does Silko herself hope to create?

Literary critics have frequently addressed this question, and their answers align with their attention to the legible parts of the almanac. Elizabeth Cook-Lynn declares *Almanac*, "the foremost Indian novel in which we see the clear and unmistakable attempt to describe Indian nationalism in what [Silko] sees as modern terms" (90). But she ultimately believes *Almanac* fails in this nationalist approach, because it "does not take into account the specific kind of tribal/nation status of the original occupants of this continent" (93). Shari M. Huhndorf provides a cogent account of how *Almanac* works within nationalism while revising it through attention to an emerging transnationalism. She writes, "In showing how the tensions and continuities between indigenous nationalism and transnationalism inform cultural production since the 1980s, [*Almanac*] draw[s] attention to ongoing colonial endeavors and the particular challenges indigeneity presents to nation-states" (367). The novel imagines a transnational group identity that crosses ethnicities without erasing them, founded on resistance to colonialism and neoliberalism.[19] It is both product and enemy of its historical moment.

Yet scholars have not paid close enough attention to the novel's anxieties, uncertainties, and defensiveness. It is easy enough to find a signal in Silko's noise, to describe a plausible vision of the people she'd like to create with her novel. To do so requires neglecting the majority of the almanac, its illegibility, the tension in the novel between profiting on indigenous history and using it for political action, its multiple theories of how to effect change. The novel's almanac is either meaningful or meaningless, depending on one's selection and framing. The brilliance of the almanac resides in its dreamlike form, the way so many overdetermined dilemmas find themselves condensed in it—and, thus, it gives itself over to many modes of interpretation. What are the legacies of ancient indigenous forms for American Indians under neoliberalism? Is the novel meant to be an entertaining bestseller or propaganda for the revolution? Are there limits to storytelling—and reading for meaning, performing critique—as a political act under neoliberalism? Is an esoteric illegibility, in the tradition of the codices, *Chilam Balam*, and the *Ghost Dance* a better politics today? But if so, how could such a legible thriller as *Almanac of the Dead* do that work? I contend that the novel raises these questions without solving them because it cannot. Its initial premise—its vision of itself as a bestseller with revolutionary political aims—loads it down with intractable contradictions. The novel stages these contradictions through the figure of Lecha and the text of the almanac. Its genius is to condense the long history of colonialism in the Americas and the short history of neoliberalism into an epic thriller—for which it has no choice but to offer, in the end, an incoherent politics. It is a mistake to think a novel can resolve neoliberalism's

[19] For further exploration of this transnationalism, see Cherniavsky; Romero; and Shackleford.

contradictions. Instead, it can crystallize them, make from them rich and enchanting art. And it can, through the symptomatic readings of literary critics, crystallize an aporia for literary studies under neoliberalism, the question of critique or postcritique. Insofar as the terms of this debate are about political efficacy, a resolution is intractable. Where does that leave the novel? What does it do in the face of its own contradictions? It turns to apocalyptic form.

By turning to apocalypse, the political questions become, within the world of the novel, moot. Everything combusts. Apocalypse is the perfect form for *Almanac*. Apocalypse sublimates a paradox of political agency in the destruction of everything. Apocalypse wants the end of the world to be imminent and inevitable; it also wants to advocate individual actions. These two desires are in obvious tension. The tension is obviated by bloodthirsty locusts, four horsemen, and the descent of the New Jerusalem from heaven. Or, in this case, the imagined apotheosis of the social instability that accompanies neoliberalism.

The novel takes the rising inequality and dispossession that result from trade liberalization, deregulation, and privatization and fantasizes that they foment an apocalypse. "Rumors say United States troops will soon occupy Mexico to help protect U.S.-owned factories in Northern Mexico as well as the rich Mexico City politicians on the CIA payroll since prep school. There are shortages of cornmeal and rioting spreads. Rumors say the richest families have already opened bank accounts and purchased homes 'in the North'" (482). The unrest quickly spills into the United States. Menardo watches on TV as, "Without money or jobs even the U.S. was suffering crippling strikes as well as riots and looting.... Almost overnight, the people had discovered all their national treasuries were empty and now everywhere there were riots" (482). Across the last couple hundred pages of the novel, a traveling activist called the Barefoot Hopi advocates for the free flow of bodies across the borders of nation-states and prison walls (618–19), eco-terrorists dynamite the Glen Canyon Dam (727), Awa Gee, a Korean hacker, brings down what Silko, with her finger on the pulse of 1991, calls "'Arpanet, Internet, Milnet'" (686–8), Zeta readies the stockpile of weapons that she has gathered for decades for the arrival of the Army of Justice and Redistribution (740), and the earth itself, according to the Barefoot Hopi, is about to revolt: "All the riches ripped from the earth will be reclaimed by the oceans and mountains. Earthquakes and volcanic eruptions of enormous magnitude will devastate the accumulated wealth of the Pacific Rim. Entire coastal peninsulas will disappear under the sea; hundreds of thousands will die" (734).

Neoliberalism creates formal problems for the encounter between politics and aesthetics, problems that persistently recur, problems exemplified by *Almanac of the Dead*. How can a writer address the experience of helplessness ubiquitous today without immediately becoming coopted back into the machinery of neoliberalism? Apocalypse resolves the impossibility of escaping this dilemma. The novel takes us to the brink of the total collapse of European colonialism. It happens thanks to the work of activists and revolutionaries—and because the almanac said it would. It remains unclear—illegible—what will happen next.

5
Almost Magic

Early in David Foster Wallace's *Infinite Jest*, set in the near future, readers encounter a description from the perspective of a medical attaché serving on a Saudi legation to the United States: "of the idolatrous West's most famous and self-congratulating idol, the colossal Libertine Statue, wearing some type of enormous adult-design diaper" (33). To raise revenue, the novel's United States has chosen to subsidize time. Much of the novel takes place in the Year of the Depend Adult Undergarment. As a symbol of subsidization, the Statue of Liberty "holds aloft" the given year's product in place of her torch (367). Unsubtle, the image crystallizes the collapse of the political into the economic. Specifically, the light of liberty (the torch) has been supplanted by a commodity (an adult diaper). Freedom has become the freedom of capitalist consumption.

Infinite Jest, which Wallace mostly wrote from 1991 to 1994, satirizes the idea—popular at the time, and crystallized by Francis Fukuyama's *The End of History and the Last Man*—that the demise of the USSR and the end of the Cold War heralded the triumph of liberal democracy as a mode of governance and capitalism as a system of economics. At its most hyperbolic, such as in Fukuyama's formulation, advocates claimed that, with liberal democracy, the world had arrived happily at the end of history. *Infinite Jest* presents a world at the end of history, but for the opposite reason: here, liberal democracy has led the United States to the brink of apocalyptic implosion. It has engendered a nation doomed by its addictions to sports, drugs, and, above all, entertainment.

As the diapered "Libertine Statue" makes clear, *Infinite Jest* is not sanguine about the triumph of the market. To ensure readers get the point, the attaché notes that the Statue of Liberty in a diaper is "a hilariously apposite image" (33). Freedom has given way to a specific commodity that highlights how the United States, in its submission to the market, has succumbed to fatigue, old age, and incontinence. The

American Literature and the Long Downturn: Neoliberal Apocalypse. Dan Sinykin,
Oxford University Press (2020). © Daniel Sinykin.
DOI: 10.1093/oso/9780198852704.001.0001

Statue of Liberty's incontinence is "apposite" because the United States has become a nation of addicts, unable to control the desire to consume drugs and entertainment. By enshrining the commodity in place of freedom, the United States has given itself to the short-term pleasures of consumption. At the heart of the novel's satire is a film—called *Infinite Jest*—so entertaining that anyone who watches it becomes a vegetable, capable of doing nothing but watching the film until he dies. To further the joke, Wallace has the United States join with Canada and Mexico to become the Organization of North American Nations, or ONAN, a pun on the biblical figure who gives us the term onanism for masturbation. Across the novel, Québécois insurgents try to acquire the film to bring "O.N.A.N.'s self-destructing logic to its final conclusion" (725). In *Infinite Jest*, the United States's devotion to short-term pleasure makes it vulnerable to cataclysm.

Neoliberalism names the condition *Infinite Jest* satirizes, in which the freedom to consume subsumes political freedom. Milton Friedman, in his landmark collection of essays *Capitalism and Freedom*, argues that capitalism is "an indispensable means toward the achievement of political freedom" (8). His work defends the primacy of economic freedom, which aspires to a situation, as first presented by Michel Foucault and, later, by Wendy Brown, in which "all conduct is economic conduct; all spheres of existence are framed and measured by economic terms and metrics, even when those spheres are not directly monetized" (Brown 10). *Infinite Jest* is particularly interested in how neoliberalism transforms the *citizen* into the *consumer*, anticipating George W. Bush's requests that Americans respond to 9/11 with trips to Disney World, and by shopping, and through continuing business as usual.

Neoliberalism works hand in glove with financialization. US corporations managed the decreasing profitability of manufacturing by expanding their financial services. General Electric (GE), Sears, General Motors, and Ford "all created captive finance units that were originally intended to support consumer purchases of their products by offering installment financing but which eventually became financial behemoths that overshadowed the manufacturing or retailing activities of the parent firm" (Krippner 29). For the consumer (having supplanted the citizen), the increasing corporate dependence on finance entailed increasing debt. Finance became an engine for creating personal debt and harvesting profits from America's debtors. The discursive practices of neoliberalism facilitated the turn to finance. By making citizens into consumers and radically expanding the realm of the economic, neoliberalism encouraged the monetization, privatization, and financialization of everything.

The West's self-congratulation in the wake of the Cold War obscured the persistence of the long downturn and the structural limits to capitalism's growth. It appeared as if capitalism were the global victor, and not struggling. Finance and neoliberalism—having both achieved hegemonic status—assisted this obfuscation. The former enriched the elite while propping up the economy on shaky stilts, the latter enshrined human capital and veiled the precarious subject as an entrepreneur of the self.

With economic growth committed to creating debt, the consumer becomes *the addict*. This is the contention of *Infinite Jest*: citizen turned consumer turned addict. As noted in definitions that Wallace thought to include on *Infinite Jest*'s dedication page, but which were cut at the advice of his editor, the word "addict" comes from the Latin for "given over"; the definitions use variations on the words "bound" and "devoted." In *Infinite Jest*, "the addict" has given himself over to the short-term pleasure of consumption. *Infinite Jest* generalizes the figure of the addict to make it the characteristic subject of the American 1990s, proposing addiction as a general condition within the new debt economy.

Wallace envisions an unlikely escape route: Alcoholics Anonymous, especially through its use of cliché. He imagines AA as a potentially utopian community grounded in the countervailing logic of the gift economy. The use of cliché allows Wallace's characters to extricate themselves from their addictions, the forces that return them to the debt economy's spiraling demands for consumption. Yet cliché only serves, in the end, to shape subjects who become better suited for submitting to a debt economy that profits those bent toward inducing an American apocalypse in which citizens consume themselves into collective annihilation.

A Failed Entertainment

What Wallace hoped cliché would do for his characters—that it might extricate them from the debt economy's logic of addiction—he hoped the novel would do for its readers. He hoped the novel would break its readers from America's addiction to entertainment, and he designed the form of the novel to that end, deferring narrative coherence for more than two hundred pages, keeping the three main plots from ever fully coming together, and leaving the ending inconclusive. Each of these decisions aims to prevent the conventional satisfactions of narrative. His goal was that the novel be just entertaining enough to keep readers reading, but not so entertaining that it would be complicit with the culture it critiqued: it was meant to be the antidote to the venom of the debt economy. To this end, Wallace wanted to subtitle the novel "A Failed Entertainment," a subtitle that his editor, who fervidly marketed the book, rejected (Max 200).

His editor—Michael Pietsch, now CEO of the Hachette Book Group, one of the Big Five publishing conglomerates—in fact did the opposite of signaling that *Infinite Jest* would be a failed entertainment. With his colleagues at Little, Brown, and Company Pietsch orchestrated a hype campaign, sending a series of postcards to thousands of reviewers and booksellers promising, among other things, "infinite pleasure," which helped make the novel into an instant hit, and Wallace into a literary superstar. But the hype caused Wallace anxiety and he was ambivalent about the novel's success. Those readers who managed to read beyond the first two hundred frustrating pages often became cult fans. With bitter irony, the hype and success made *Infinite Jest* an object of obsession, even addiction. *Infinite Jest*'s success as a cult object and a widely heralded exemplar of (white male) genius made it not a failed entertainment, but a failure on its own terms, as a work of pedagogy. It is a moral and pedagogical novel.[1] It shares the disapproval of the United States expressed in the malapropism, "Libertine Statue." Wallace claimed his refusal to give the novel resolution was a tactic to resist the culture industry. In this, he failed. His refusal instead demonstrates his inability to reconcile a material problem (the long downturn) with a moral solution (let's eschew irony, adopt cliché, be earnest believers).

[1] Heather Houser argues that Wallace deploys disgust toward environmentalist ends, positioning disgust "against self-absorption and environmental, psychological, and social detachment in order to manage interaction between self and world through word" (165).

Infinite Jest tells three stories. One takes place at the elite Enfield Tennis Academy (ETA) and features the Incandenzas. The father and founder of ETA, James Incandenza, pursues a career in film that culminates with *Infinite Jest*. He kills himself soon after finishing it, several years before the novel's present. This plot's protagonist is James's middle son, Hal, a tennis prodigy who suffers from an addiction to marijuana as he copes with the pressures that accompany his talent. Hal attempts to come to terms with a world in which he is trained to become, as a tennis star, an embodied commodity, a "*Billboard Who Walks*" (676). For reasons never fully explained (and often debated in the scholarship), Hal ultimately succumbs to a condition that leaves him unintelligible and prone to seizure-like movements.

The second story takes place at Ennet House Drug and Alcohol Recovery House, a halfway house located down the hill from ETA. Recovering addict Don Gately is this plot's protagonist. He works as a counselor at Ennet House. From his post, the novel catalogs Ennet House's addicts. In a pivotal scene, Gately is shot while defending the house's residents; he spends the last few hundred pages in a hospital bed, struggling to refuse Demerol, the drug to which he is addicted, while experiencing flashbacks to his criminal life. Ennet House residents know ETA as a "snooty tennis prep school" for "blond gleaming tennis kids," while the kids at ETA know Ennet House as that "wretched halfway-house thing for wretched people" (197, 195, 633). These two institutions allow Wallace to portray the cultures of addiction from opposite sides of the class divide.

The third story makes clear that Wallace understands America's addiction crisis as rooted in economics. It tells of the race between US intelligence agencies and Québécois insurgent groups to acquire the master copy of the film *Infinite Jest*. Agents from both groups eventually converge on ETA and Ennet House. At the novel's horizon, hinted at in a brief aside, Hal Incandenza and Don Gately, under duress from Québécois insurgents, disinter James Incandenza's corpse to find the master copy, presumably leading to the film's dissemination and the apocalypse. Across the first half of the novel, two spies in pursuit of *Infinite Jest*—one Québécois, one from the United States—debate the film's implications. Their discussion lays bare the novel's theory about the relationship between the economy and addiction, presenting in the clearest terms the problem the novel imagines it needs to combat.

Can Such a U.S.A. Hope to Survive?

What conditions would have to obtain such that a nation could become apocalyptically threatened by the risk of indulging too much in an attractive commodity? Rémy Marathe of the Wheelchair Assassins, a Québécois insurgent group, and Hugh Steeply, an agent for the United States's Office of Unspecified Services discuss this question at length.

Marathe begins with a rhetorical question. "'Our attachments are our temple, what we worship, no? What we give ourselves to, what we invest with faith?'" (107). We should hear echoes of the etymology of "addiction" in Marathe's phrase "give ourselves to." He is setting up an argument on the grounds that actions reveal spiritual investments. "'What is this temple, thus, for U.S.A.s? What is it, when you fear you must protect them from themselves, if wicked Québecers conspire to bring [*Infinite Jest*] into their warm homes?'" (107–8). The United States only needs to prevent the dissemination of the film because Americans worship, above all, entertainment and pleasure. Implicit is a declension narrative, which, in reference to contemporaneous US culture, Frederic Jameson described in terms of "the success with which consumer America had overcome the Protestant ethic and was able to throw its savings (and future income) to the winds in exercising its new nature as the full-time professional shopper" (271). The Statue of Liberty's torch has become a commodity, with accompanying spiritual adjustments.

Later, Marathe returns to this argument, putting it in terms of appetite and drive, rather than worship and faith. "'This appetite to choose death by pleasure if it is available to choose—this *appetite* of your people unable to choose appetites, *this* is the death" (319). He implores Steeply (and Wallace implores the reader) to think "'about a U.S.A. where such a thing could be possible'" (318). In the first instance, Americans worship pleasure. In the second, Americans are beyond even the choice involved in worship, as Marathe's register shifts from the spiritual to the biological. The United States where *Infinite Jest* could be apocalyptic is a US where Americans have become infantilized by their incontinent drive for pleasure—the Libertine Statue in an adult diaper. Marathe insists that such a life, involuntarily given over to pleasure, is not life at all, but living death. *Infinite Jest* (the film) would only make literal the death

Americans already live. This serves both as motivation for Marathe's terrorism and as Wallace's *cri de cœer*. Marathe concludes, "'someone sometime let you [U.S.A.s] forget how to choose, and what'" (319). Wallace wants his readers to learn how to choose again.

Consider the moralism of this account. It places blame on individual consumers and that "someone" who let Americans "forget how to choose," which is to say, the state. Either way, the problem is moral; it is about behaving badly or irresponsibly. Such an account makes it possible to imagine that a novel—this novel—could help transform the moral landscape in America and alleviate the national illness. It also directs attention away from material conditions and how they ramify differentially along lines of class, race, and gender.

What do I mean by material conditions? A series of policies were put in place in the 1970s and 1980s that unleashed, in the United States, in the early to mid-1980s, an "endless expansion of credit"—with, as its corollary, an endless expansion of debt (Krippner 57, Brenner 158). This explosion of debt became necessary because of the earlier economic events that I have described in this book. In the late 1960s, the global economy began to suffer from the overproduction of commodities, which led to a global economic crisis. Unable to continue to grow through manufacturing, the United States turned to finance in an attempt to make up the difference. This allowed corporations a win-win: to transfer the onus for growth onto citizens-as-consumers, who financed their purchase of corporate commodities with corporate credit. By the early 1980s, the economy managed to avoid a serious depression only because the state deregulated the credit markets, basically pumping out enormous volumes of credit so that consumers could absorb "the surplus of supply" (Brenner xxiii). This created the conditions for the economy to become ever more dependent on expanding credit and debt. The policymakers who planned the deregulation in the late 1970s and early 1980s that made the unprecedented credit available expected that consumers' appetite for credit would reach a natural limit when the price became too high. But consumers, beginning in the 1980s, proved to have an insatiable appetite for credit—not least because inflation, wage stagnation, and rising wealth inequality meant that many of them needed credit to live, or, worse, they needed credit to pay off previous debt. In his history of debt in the United States, Louis Hyman writes, "the expansion of debt occurred because consumers were less and less able, on average, to pay back what they borrowed" (223). This suited industry fine. Expensive credit helped propel burgeoning financialization.

Why, in the heady post–Cold War years at the end of history, 1991–4, was Wallace worried that Americans would consume themselves into an abyss? Because they were. He spent a good portion of these years as an addict and a grad school dropout, living in Granada House in Brighton, outside of Boston, which became the basis for Ennet House. His life was precarious and those around him yet more so. He began to work out his vision of addiction and economics, what would become *Infinite Jest*. Seen from the perspective of capital, addiction serves as a mechanism to enrich the wealthy and impoverish the poor. Yet the novel's moral project depends on addressing the problem of addiction at the personal level of the addict, rather than the systemic level of capital.

Wallace understood the systemic basis of the moral problem. Marathe critiques liberalism for its economics. He tells Steeply, "'*utilitarienne*. Maximize pleasure, minimize displeasure: result: what is good. This is the U.S.A. of you" (423). Marathe gives voice to a dominant strand of neoliberalism, epitomized by Gary Becker. Becker argued that "extended utility functions"—calculations of how to maximize pleasure—are "the foundation of behavior" (5). His work extended "the definition of individual preferences to include personal habits, peer pressure, parental influences on the tastes of children, advertising, love and sympathy, and other neglected behavior" (4). In other words, he subsumed all the above within economic rationality, doing the work of neoliberalism as described by Foucault and Brown. Becker felt compelled to treat these preferences as economic because he did "not believe that any alternative approach—be it founded on 'cultural,' 'biological,' or 'psychological' forces—comes close to providing comparable insights and explanatory power" (ibid.). Within dashes, he dismisses the humanities, the hard sciences, and the non-economic social sciences. He won the Nobel Prize in Economics in 1992, when Wallace was in the middle of writing *Infinite Jest*. The prize recognized how Becker's thought had gained traction in the world. Marathe and Steeply stage a debate over what was then hegemonic economic policy and theory.

Marathe tries to convince Steeply that *Infinite Jest* reveals a contradiction in utilitarianism. He wants to know how Americans are supposed to calculate their "long-term overall pleasure," to which Steeply responds: *enlightened self-interest* (248). Steeply contends that the US education system teaches "'how to make knowledgeable choices about pleasure and delay and the kid's overall down-the-road maximal interests'" (429). Steeply offers the party line. He describes the Protestant work ethic. He describes rational actors who make choices on the basis of long-term happiness. This leads Marathe to point out what, given the context of their conversation, is obvious, namely: "'Why make a simple Entertainment, no matter how seducing its pleasures, a *samizdat* and forbidden in the first place if you do not fear so many U.S.A.s cannot make the enlightened choices?'" (430). Steeply's spy mission betrays his hypocrisy. He wouldn't need to stop Marathe from disseminating *Infinite Jest* if Americans could in fact calculate their long-term interest and make enlightened choices. Utilitarianism relies on the assumption that rational actors calculate their long-term best interest, yet the debt economy requires that consumers prioritize consumption for the short-term. With the rise of credit and the high interest rates of the late 1970s and 1980s, manufacturing was driven out and finance was encouraged. Finance took consumers' appetite for credit and made it the source of profits such that the spiraling of credit became necessary to the functioning of the economy (Krippner 57). The United States encouraged debt and consumption through the gratification of short-term pleasure, even as this contradicted dogma about rational actors and long-term planning. Steeply voices the dogma. Marathe says *Infinite Jest* proves it disingenuous.

According to Wallace, this is the contradiction that underlies the addiction crisis—that feels like the end of the world. Demand consumption through the immediate satisfaction of desires, then pathologize people as addicts when such consumption becomes culturally normative. Addicts fail to practice the Protestant work ethic that they have been asked to reject.

Marathe says that Americans do not know how to choose anything other than immediate gratification. Steeply says "'these are just the hazards of being free'" (320). Freedom is a keyword for Milton Friedman; it is the argument for capitalism. Marathe replies, "'Your freedom is the freedom-*from*: no one tells your precious individual U.S.A. selves what they must do'" (320). Freedom in the absence of moral guidance has made the United States vulnerable to infinite consumption. Marathe asks: "can such a U.S.A. hope to survive for a much longer time?" (318). *Infinite Jest* crystallizes this existential question in the body of the addict. Marathe's talk about abyssal appetites are literalized in these bodies. Their fates stand in, synechdochally, for the fate of "such a U.S.A." and the possibility of surviving the debt economy.

Everyone's an Addict

In an early section on Ennet House, the novel's narrator lists a number of "exotic new facts" that introduce the reader to recovery culture (200). One such fact is, "That gambling can be an abusable escape, too, and work, shopping, and shoplifting, and sex, and abstention, and masturbation, and food, and exercise, and meditation/prayer" (202). This "fact" was likely familiar to most of the novel's audience in 1996. 12-Step programs reached their peak of popularity during the 1980s and 1990s. Trysh Travis argues that, in these years, "virtually everyone in the U.S." could consider themselves some kind of addict (52). Under the debt economy, as citizens became consumers encouraged to satisfy their pleasures immediately, *excessive* pursuit of such pleasure became pathologized: an outcome of the economy's contradictory need for consumers who simultaneously prioritize the desire to consume commodities today *and* the ability to consume into the future. In a context where the immediate satisfaction of desires was increasingly encouraged, 12-Step culture and the discourse of addiction served to police which pleasures were legitimate. The characteristic figure, then, of both *Infinite Jest* and the American 1990s is "the addict."

One of *Infinite Jest's* addicts poses all addicts' problem: "how come I can't stop, if I want to, is the thing" (178). Two discourses dominated the response to this question in the 1980s and 1990s, as they do in *Infinite Jest*: that of economic rationality, and of disease. Both direct attention onto the individual and away from structural causes. Mind and body: economic rationality declares addiction perfectly rational; the discourse of addiction as disease naturalizes addiction in the body of the addict. Discussion of the addiction to entertainment in the novel tends to employ the terms of economic rationality. About *Infinite Jest*, for example, one terrorist theorizes, "There could be no index of diminishing satisfaction as in the econometrics of normal U.S.A. commodities" (727). In other words, consumers never get their fill of the film.

Gary Becker was the leading theorist of addiction as rational in the years leading to *Infinite Jest*. In the 1980s and 1990s, after watching his ideas of human capital and economic rationality become reality, Becker looked for an extreme test case that might challenge the fundamental rationality of *homo economicus*. In the dominant figure of "the addict" he found his challenge. He published an essay in 1988 titled, "A Rational Theory of Addiction," which begins: "Rational consumers maximize utility from stable preferences as they try to anticipate the future consequences of their choices. Addictions would seem to be the antithesis of rational behavior" (50). Yet, with his co-author, he writes, "we claim that addictions, even strong ones, are usually rational in the sense of involving forward-looking maximization" (50).

To maintain this thesis, Becker must perform sleights of hand, which, when pressed, reveal a rift in the rational actor. In the introduction to a collection of essays on addiction, published, like *Infinite Jest*, in 1996, Becker offers an anecdote. "A young man may drink heavily because he does not anticipate that he will become addicted" (9). If, unhappily, he becomes addicted, "He might decide to fight his addiction by joining Alcoholics Anonymous and in other ways; and, on the other hand, continuing to drink heavily could be a way of maximizing utility if his preferences 'shifted' greatly in favor of alcohol" (ibid.). Becker gives two possible futures for the young man. Either he fights his addiction or he embraces it. His choice depends on his preferences. Becker's scare-quoted *shift* marks the point at which the man can no longer imagine a future happy enough that it would be worth it to stop drinking. Continuing to drink outweighs the desire for an unaddicted future. But: he might need to stop drinking to be able to imagine a happy future. If he stops drinking, he might imagine a happier future, but he cannot imagine a happier future unless he stops drinking. Becker's theory of rationality cannot account for such subjunctive logic. Becker attempts to normalize addiction as an issue of rationality and preferences—addicts are unhappy and prioritize the present—oversimplifying desire, eliding the social construction of "the addict," and obscuring the figure's historical rise as a phenomenon of the debt economy.

Wallace engages neoliberal discourse about rational actors who extend market logics to all realms of life largely to critique it. He embraces instead the other prevailing discourse on addiction, that of disease. As a denizen of Ennet House asks, "'So this purports to be a disease, alcoholism? A disease like a cold? Or like cancer?'" (180).

Thinking of addiction as a disease gained traction in the twentieth century through the ideas and advocacy of Alcoholics Anonymous. The characters in *Infinite Jest* who cope best with their addiction adopt AA's 12-Step Program.[2] Wallace acknowledges AA's centrality to the novel on its copyright page where, after the standard disclaimers, we learn,

> Besides Closed Meetings for alcoholics only, Alcoholics Anonymous in Boston, Massachusetts also has Open Meetings, where pretty much anybody who's interested can come and listen, take notes, pester people with questions, etc. A lot of people at these Open Meetings spoke with me and were extremely patient and garrulous and generous and helpful. The best way I can think of to show my appreciation to these men and women is to decline to thank them by name. (x)

This is a way for Wallace to explain how he learned so much about recovery culture without being an addict (which he was and here dissimulates) and to credit himself for the lengthy research that went into the novel. In a note to his editor, he insisted on the importance of this passage: "The AA disclaimer is very important to me and is absolutely *required*" ("Infinite Jest Editorial").

Though hundreds of pages concern a halfway house governed by AA's 12-Step Program, scholars have yet to address the relationship between AA and *Infinite Jest* more than in passing. Scholars have hesitated in part because of AA's reputation. Wallace scholar Eric A. Thomas, for example, writes that "what's difficult for the critic is that AA is thoroughly anti-intellectual, not exactly susceptible to close reading and unpacking, given its adamant simplicity" (290). Trysh Travis, whose

[2] As Elizabeth Freudenthal observes, "Gately's mode of fighting addiction is the only one in the novel that actually works" (191).

book on recovery culture attempts to make it "a legitimate subject for sustained scholarly analysis," argues that prejudice against AA is endemic to social scientists and humanists, "whose lack of knowledge of and incuriosity about recovery is often so complete as to seem decidedly willful" (8). Wallace bucked this trend, thinking rigorously about addiction, recovery, and the philosophy of AA. His thoughts on the subject guide his treatment of the contemporary United States and his sense of its apocalyptic crisis.

Wallace saw AA as a gift economy, an idea he worked out in the margins of his copy of Lewis Hyde's *The Gift*, a book about the artist's discomfiture within a market economy. (Wallace is blurbed on the cover of the twenty-fifth anniversary edition, writing, "No one who is invested in any kind of art can read *The Gift* and remain unchanged.") He underlined Hyde's definition of capitalism as a system that "asks that we remove surplus wealth from circulation and lay it aside to produce more wealth" as opposed to gift economies that strive "to cease turning so much surplus into capital, that is, to treat most increase as a gift" (37). Gift economies were attractive to Wallace both as an addict and as a writer. He underlined the following passage on the artist's relationship to the market: "The costs and benefits of tasks . . . whose ends are easily quantified can be expressed through a market system. The costs and rewards of gift labors cannot. The cleric's larder will always be filled with gifts; artists will never 'make' money" (107). In the margin, Wallace wrote, "Artists take gifts; they don't 'make' money" (ibid.). He longed for an escape from the market. Gift economies defy the foundational requirement of capitalism—that it treat surplus as capital, an occasion to reproduce more capital, that, like a shark, it keep moving or die—offering Wallace, as a novelist and a member of AA, an alternative to neoliberalism and the debt economy.

In the margins of *The Gift*, beside a quote from Meister Eckhart, Wallace wrote, "AA's = those driven mad ~~by~~ w/fear by the paradigm of scarcity in a commodity/capitalist economy: require return to basically 1st-century communism of spirit" (127). Here Wallace makes plain his belief that addiction results from capitalism. The answer, then, is an alternative to capitalism. He turns to the earliest Christian communities as examples of gift economies, which he sees as predecessors of AA. If he identifies the structural conditions of addiction here, and the need for radical change, why does *Infinite Jest* limit itself to individual reformation?[3]

Believing in one's own utopian ambition does not make utopia exist. Artists can imagine that they receive gifts, not money, in exchange for their art, but the selling of *Infinite Jest* showed the falsehood of that fantasy. (We can see more clearly now why Wallace chafed at his publisher's marketing campaign for *Infinite Jest.*) Wallace maybe imagined that members of AA participate in a utopic enclave apart from capitalism. But the history of AA reveals a complicated relationship with the market and helps explain why *Infinite Jest* does not end with a "1st-century communism of spirit," but with an individual's battle to survive in a precarious world.

Founded in 1935, Alcoholic Anonymous's membership "skyrocketed after the Second World War, and exceeded 100,000 by 1950" (Travis 36). To position itself as critical of postwar corporate culture, "a significant portion of early AA literature devote[d] itself to denigrating the beliefs and practices dedicated to mass-producing the productive capitalist citizen" (65). Yet AA's philosophy proved a boon to the corporate culture it denigrated. The large corporations and bureaucracies that dominated the Fordist postwar economy demanded selves who effaced their agency. In this, corporations could not have found a better ally than AA.

In his testimonial about his life as an alcoholic and his salvation through AA, Bill W., the organization's founder, writes that, to be cured of the disease, "a price had to be paid. It meant destruction of self-centeredness. I must turn in all things to the Father of Light" (14). This surrender of agency accompanied a mandate to work. Bill W. writes of the addict, "if he did not work, he would surely drink again, and if he drank he would surely die" (15). Working, then, is a matter of life or death. The Big Book itself—AA's bible—describes the Higher Power to

[3] Wallace might have been inspired to turn to individual reformation from *The Gift* itself. Lee Konstantinou argues that "Hyde's dispositional Third Way (stripped of Bourdieu's sense of the social determination of disposition or habitus) promotes an ethos, an ethic of generosity, meant to neutralize the calculating disposition. There may be 'a constant tension between the gift sphere to which his work pertains and the market sphere which is his context,' but 'there is little to be gained by a wholesale attack on the market'" ("Lewis" 132). As Konstantinou makes clear, "If writers and critics wish art to be more than a commodity, they will need to address the defining political and economic institutions within which the commoditized arts of the present get made"—changing one's attitude is not enough (145). And this is how Wallace and Hyde fail.

whom all addicts must submit in such a way as to train addicts, however unintentionally, to submit to the postwar economy: "We had a new Employer. Being all powerful, He provided what we needed, if we kept close to Him and performed His work well" (63). Economic leaders quickly recognized AA's potential and played an active role in its postwar expansion. "In a 1946 speech that was heavily publicized within the business community, [biostatistician E. M.] Jellinek... noted that 29.7 million work days were lost each year to alcoholism" (44). R. Brinkley Smithers, "heir to the IBM fortune," listened to Jellinek and began a "campaign aimed at getting business and industry leaders to 'Save the man, save the investment!'" (ibid.). In this slogan we hear what will soon become Gary Becker's concept of human capital. AA became a mechanism for human capital's appreciation.

If AA's discourse facilitated, against its ostensible aims, the production of good workers, its institutional structure became increasingly integrated with the state and medical and insurance agencies—what one of the early legislators in support of this growth would later call an "alcohol and drug industrial complex" (qtd in Travis 46). By the mid-1980s, decreasing profits "meant that converting under-utilized facilities into specialized alcohol treatment wards became an attractive option for many hospitals" (48). Such is the case with Ennet House, which "leases a former physicians' dormitory in the Enfield Marine Public Health Hospital Complex" (135). The hospital building, "stripped of equipment and copper wire, defunct," remains "solvent" by leasing to Ennet House and other "state-related health agencies and services" (194). By the time Wallace hoped to find in AA a community grounded in a gift economy, it had become discursively ("Save the man, save the investment!") and materially (integrating with the health care industry through government subsidy) complicit with capitalism. It had also become immensely popular. AA and 12-Step Programs reached their peak in the late 1980s and 1990s. As one of *Infinite Jest*'s footnotes claims, "At the zenith of the self-help-group movement in the [Before Subsidization] mid-1990s, there were estimated to be over 600 wholly distinct Step-based fellowships in the U.S.A." (996).

Infinite Jest betrays greater ambivalence about the utopian possibilities of AA than does Wallace's marginalia in Hyde's book. Rather than develop a vision of AA as a community apart from the market, Wallace, in his novel, turns to AA's rhetorical dependence on cliché as an avenue for personal salvation. An analysis of cliché—an exploration of how cliché resists meaning—demonstrates how and why *Infinite Jest* elevates the figure as a tactic of resistance against neoliberalism and makes it the trick ("almost magic") to the transition from a capitalist economy to gift economy, from the addict to the believer.

Buy These Poor Yutzes Some Time

> One day at a time.
> Easy does it.
> First things first.
> Ask for help.
> It works if you work it.
> Grow or go.
> Keep coming back.
> Turn it over.
> Fake it till you make it.
> Getting in touch with your feelings.
> Abiding in the present.

The above list is a small selection of AA clichés from *Infinite Jest*. To break addiction's spiral of consumption, Wallace's characters turn to cliché. Many of them find this turn counterintuitive, frustrating, even insulting. As one says, indignantly, "'So then at forty-six years of age I came here to learn to live by clichés.... To turn my will and life over to the care of clichés'" (270). In response, Don Gately, leading man, hero, an alumnus who works as staff at Ennet House, thinks, if only he can "buy these poor yutzes some time, some thin pie-slice of abstinent time, till they can start to get a whiff of what's true and deep, almost magic, under the shallow surface" (271). Why turn to the much-maligned figure of cliché to fight addiction? What about cliché is "true and deep, almost magic"?

Elsewhere, Gately provides a definition of cliché in relation to addiction, contending that "clichés are (a) soothing, and (b) remind you of common sense, and (c) license the universal assent that drowns out silence; and (4) silence is deadly, pure Spider-food, if you've got the Disease" (278).[4] In each of Gately's cases, clichés induce an affect or behavior, they sooth or remind or license; in none of these cases do they mean. Eric Partridge offers a more standard definition in his *A Dictionary of Clichés*, where he describes cliché as a phrase "that has become so hackneyed that careful speakers and scrupulous writers shrink from it because they feel that its use is an insult to the intelligence of their audience or public: 'a coin so battered by use as to be defaced'" (xi). As a defaced coin no longer holds exchange value, a cliché no longer produces meaning. Cliché is a word or phrase that, through repeated use, has had its meaning effaced. No longer circulating as meaningful, cliché becomes instead a figure that functions through its meaningless use. As such, it is a figure that offers the characters of *Infinite Jest* the possibility of transferring from imbrication in the logic of the debt economy to that of the gift economy.

As a subject of the debt economy, "the addict" is trapped in a spiral of consumption, with a felt need to return with ever more haste to the realms of economic circulation, to shopping malls or drug dealers or visual entertainment. (The figure of "the addict," recall, serves to pathologize the increase of consumer debt, transferring blame from an unjust system to immoral individuals.) Embracing cliché, internalizing its logic, trains addicts in a logic that departs from circulation, that, in its advocacy of meaningless use, disciplines addicts to stop asking for more (meaning, pleasure).

In *Infinite Jest*, cliché is the cure offered by Ennet House and Alcoholics Anonymous. Don Gately, for example, thinks to himself, "You just have to Ask For Help and like Turn It Over, the loss and pain, to Keep Coming, show up, pray, Ask For Help. Gately rubs his eyes. Simple advice like this does seem like a lot of clichés" (273(). The capitalization

[4] Academics have written little on cliché. As Marshall McLuhan comments, cheekily, "The banishing of the cliché from serious attention was the natural gesture of literary specialists" (55). Though the editors of a recent collection of essays on Wallace recognize "the impassioned defense the author under scrutiny here mounted of cliché," it has yet to be taken up as a topic for sustained analysis. To the contrary, one of the few academic essays that addresses Wallace's use of cliché treats it as scandal: "No one who champions a work so original and thought-dense can possibly endorse Ennet's beliefs about living with clichés" (Letzler 319). This critic rightly notices the peculiar tension in *Infinite Jest* between its extensive vocabulary and inventive style on the one hand and its celebration of cliché on the other, yet his tone of outrage brings us no closer to learning what makes cliché almost magic.

signals phrases that Gately treats as clichés. Clichés are an unlikely cure, as Gately's dismissal acknowledges. And yet, they work. Gately considers an addict indignant about having to learn to live by clichés, and decides that "the thing is that the clichéd directives are a lot more deep and hard to actually *do*. To try and live by instead of just say" (ibid.).[5] In a long AA scene, Gately remembers his own process learning to live by cliché, narrating how:

> you sweep floors and scrub out ashtrays and fill stained steel urns with hideous coffee, and you keep getting ritually down on your big knees every morning and night asking for help from a sky that still seems a burnished shield against all who would ask aid of it—how can you pray to a "God" you believe only morons believe in, still?—but the old guys say it doesn't yet matter what you believe or don't believe, Just Do It they say, and like a shock-trained organism without any kind of independent human will you do exactly like you're told. (350)

To escape addiction and live by cliché requires the quotidian institutional work of showing up, doing chores, listening to testimonials, all of which works to create a subject who responds "like a shock-trained organism" to cliché.[6]

This biological rhetoric resonates with an argument made by Anton Zijderveld, whose *On Clichés* is the only book-length study on cliché in English. He writes, "clichés are able to trigger speech and behavior in a

[5] N. Katherine Hayles, reading *Infinite Jest* from an ecological perspective, writes in a similar vein, "If the problem originates in the presumption of autonomy that is the founding principle for the liberal humanist self, then nothing less than a reconceptualization of subjectivity can offer a solution" (692).

[6] Cliché thus functions in *Infinite Jest* to invoke what Amy Hungerford has called "postmodern belief," or "belief without meaning" (49). Hungerford argues that a similar dynamic exists in Don DeLillo's work, in which words in general become the occasion for a ritual of belief without meaning. She traces the ritual quality of utterance in DeLillo to his Catholic background. Wallace, who dabbled in Catholicism himself, saw DeLillo as a literary mentor and borrowed from him extensively in writing *Infinite Jest*, which we might see as a source for the ritual quality of how recovering addicts use cliché in the novel. Hungerford, for her part, has pointedly *not* read *Infinite Jest*. She notes, in *Making Literature Now*, that Wallace treated women badly in life, and that he imagined his relationship to readers similarly: i.e. *fuck the reader*. Since we have limited time, and every book we choose to read is at the exclusion of others, then why refuse to read any number of novels in favor of *Infinite Jest*, a book, in her accounting, founded on misogyny? Why join in the lionization of a novel whose reputation of white male genius was created from the outset by a clever marketing campaign on the part of its publisher?

kind of behavioristic stimulus-response mechanism" (13). Gately, the novel's example of the ideal recovering addict, exemplifies this model of recovery. Despite his doubts, "he takes one of AA's very rare specific suggestions and hits the knees in the AM and asks for Help and then hits the knees again at bedtime and says Thank You, whether he believes he's talking to Anything/-body or not, and he somehow gets through that day clean" (443). Performing rituals, regardless of belief, Gately stays clean: behavior provokes response. Cliché saves.

Yet living by cliché requires a *kind* of belief, which keeps "the addict" coming back to AA. This is belief that Lee Konstantinou[7] writes is not "toward some aspect of the world but [is] rather the ethos of belief in and of itself" (90). Konstantinou argues that Wallace creates an "ethical countertype" to the "incredulous ironist" through this kind of a belief, a subject he calls "the believer" (85). Wallace's reception has often been guided by Wallace's own writing about his goals and ambitions. Above all, writers have focused on the end of his essay "E Unibus Plurum," where he calls for "single-entendre principles," a refusal of irony in favor of sincerity and emotional vulnerability.[8] One objective of this chapter is to ask how the sincerity required of the believer, the recovering addict, bowing before cliché, fails to extricate the addict from the debt economy that is at the root of his addiction.

Infinite Jest's adoption of cliché creates new problems. Its embrace of cliché is ambivalent. Gately recognizes that Boston AA's axiom, *check your head at the door*, "is almost classically authoritarian, maybe even proto-Fascist" (374). Gately has a suspicion, that is, of the purposes to which others could put the obedient recovering addicts, trained by cliché to stop thinking and to submit to a Higher Power. Cliché might help "the addict" and create "the believer," but at what cost? The novel is especially productive in the tension between invention and cliché, between "the addict" and "the believer"—a tension that manifests in its form. *Infinite*

7 Konstantinou is the author of an exemplary neoliberal apocalyptic novel, *Pop Apocalypse*, which manages to unite the concerns spread throughout this book: racism, evangelicalism, rapture, human capital, and commodified entertainment. Published in 2009, just after the financial crisis, it synthesizes the cultural implications of forty years of economic downturn.

8 See Konstantinou, *Cool Characters*; Stephen J. Burn, *David Foster Wallace's* Infinite Jest; and Adam Kelly, "Dialectic of Sincerity." David P. Rando challenges this trend in "David Foster Wallace and Lovelessness," arguing that scholars have relied too heavily on Wallace's own categories, thus obscuring how, for instance, affectlessness plays a large role in his writing.

Jest's celebration of cliché rubs against its own famously manic, inventive prose. The terseness of cliché with its injunction to depart from thought is countermanded by *Infinite Jest*'s heady expansiveness. Those qualities that make the novel an addictive commodity eschew cliché.

The novel spends much of its last 173 pages playing out the drama between "the addict" and "the believer," manic style and cliché, the debt economy and AA, as Don Gately lies in a hospital bed, hovering between his present and his past. Through this drama, the novel wrestles with its own contradictions, against which it finally gives up, and lies down.

Everything Unendurable Was in the Head

Don Gately is in debt. He is "paying off restitution schedules in three different district courts" (277). To keep most of his criminal cases "Closed Without Finding," he is "making biweekly reparation payments out of the pathetic paycheck" he earns (463). Debt, along with the culture of AA, compels Gately to work and places him in peonage to the state. Gately is only one of *Infinite Jest*'s myriad addicts, recovering to become believers, who have been captured into peonage. In the 1990s, debt penetrates AA's utopian community, preventing its autonomy from the market.

Maybe because of this peonage, believers in the novel imagine AA as a system of figural debt. "Sobriety in Boston is regarded as less a gift than a sort of cosmic loan. You can't pay the loan back, but you can pay it *forward*, by spreading the message that despite all appearances AA works" (344). What does it mean, here, that AA works? It works, for one, by "the coupling of economics and ethics, work and work on the self": through a shift of discursive registers, paying a loan (economics) becomes paying it forward (ethics) (Lazzarato 75). The loan, in this instance, is metaphorical, yet the move from *gift* to *loan* to *pay it forward* illustrates how Boston AA, in the novel, takes Wallace's old notion of AA as a gift economy and recodes it first as a debt economy, and then, finally, as a moral economy. In *The Financialization of Daily Life*, Randy Martin notes the usefulness of AA's best-known cliché for debtors: "To feel free of obligation and to reduce unsecured debt, one must repeat the following: 'one day at a time'" (95). AA works, in *Infinite Jest*, by creating the believer who believes in the power, "despite all appearances," of cliché, who displaces the addict, but who, in the process, becomes a perpetual and unquestioning debtor.[9] During the postwar years of the large corporation, members of AA could easily imagine their Higher Power as an omnipotent Employer who, if they worked well, would take care of them. Under the debt economy, the Higher Power becomes the omnipotent Creditor.

The production of well-disciplined debtors occurs in the context of neoliberalism, in which, "to become human capital or an entrepreneur of the self means assuming the costs as well as the risks of a flexible and financialized economy, costs and risks which are not only—far from it—those of innovation, but also and especially those of precariousness, poverty, unemployment, a failing health system, housing shortages" (Lazzarato 51). The neoliberal state increasingly shifts responsibilities away from the state and onto individuals. We can see the boom of recovery culture in the late 1980s and 1990s as the localization of care, through self-help discourse and small communities like AA.

Infinite Jest teems with the debt economy's castoffs, its precarious subjects, characters who float in and out of shelters like Ennet House and whose lives are always endangered. The novel lingers on Poor Tony Krause, a transgender heroin addict who suffers a series of misadventures, describing at length his squalid heroin withdrawal while living in an "Empire Displacement Co. dumpster" (in case the narrative of imperialism turning Krause into trash weren't yet obvious) and, later, in "an obscure Armenian Foundation Library men's room" stall (301). Wallace describes Krause's suffering in grisly detail. "He weighed fifty kilos and his skin was the color of summer squash. He had terrible shivering-attacks and also perspired. He had a sty that scraped one eyeball as pink as a bunny's. His nose ran like twin spigots and the output had a yellow-green tinge he didn't think looked promising at *all*. There was an uncomely dry-rot smell about him that even he could

9 Several scholarly studies have, in recent years, shown how "fiction taught economic subjects to accept the uncertainties of an economy dependent on credit" thus "making possible the faith and credulity on which the modern economy depended" (McClanahan, "Dead Pledges"). Most of these have focused on eighteenth- and nineteenth-century novels, tracing the emergence of the subject of finance capitalism. I am thinking of Deirdre Lynch, *The Economy of Character*; Catherine Gallagher, *Nobody's Story*; and Mary Poovey, *Genres of the Credit Economy*.

smell" (ibid.). His condition gets worse from there. In the end, Marathe's *Assassins des Fauteuils Rollents* apprehend Krause and use him as a test-subject, making him view *Infinite Jest*, which will, we know, kill him (845). The novel offers up Poor Tony Krause as an exemplar of the precarious subject's disposability.

Don Gately, at the center of *Infinite Jest*'s long, anticlimactic denouement, bears the weight of determining whether cliché can extricate addicts from the suffering inflicted by the debt economy. The novel's judgment depends on his fate. Can brave Gately, through the power of cliché, resist Demerol, his drug of choice, as he lies in a hospital bed in intense pain? This is the question that dominates the greater part of the novel's final 173 pages. He teeters between clichés in the present and flashbacks from his past as an addict.

He has been hospitalized after being shot while in the process of protecting Ennet House's residents from attack. Now, in bed, he "lies there pinwheel-eyed from pain and efforts to Abide via memory" (918). He finds his greatest strength in the notion that "everything unendurable was in the head, was the head not Abiding in the Present" (861). The phrase "everything unendurable was in the head" encapsulates the problems and the promise of AA. It gives addicts the agency to resist their addiction. Yet it erases the material conditions at the root of that addiction. If everything unendurable is in the head, then everything unendurable—poverty, immiseration, debt—is not the product of an unjust system. But the force of Gately's pain pushes him to a moment of doubt. He asks, "what if God is really the cruel and vengeful figurant Boston AA swears up and down He isn't, and He gets you straight just so you can feel all the more keenly every bevel and edge of the special punishments He's got lined up for you?" (895). What if the Higher Power, the Employer, the Creditor, has other purposes for you than absolving you of your addiction? What if those other purposes are cruel, vengeful? What if the narrative of AA isn't *one day at a time* but *one day at a time Whoever controls this mess will make life harder and harder?*

Infinite Jest leaves the reader with this question. We do not learn whether Gately resists his addiction. We know that his condition worsens, that "the poor son of a bitch was burning down" (973). He relives, through the scene that ends the novel, a near-fatal drug binge that leads to the torture and death of his partner-in-crime, Gene Fackelmann. Gately and Fackelmann worked together as, of all things, debt collectors. Fackelmann takes advantage of confusion over a bet that leaves him with piles of ill-gotten funds, which he uses to purchase an inordinate quantity of drugs, on which he and Gately binge. When the money's rightful owner discovers what his debt collector has done, he sends lackeys to torture and kill Fackelmann, lackeys who inject the already-bingeing Gately with enough drugs to make him black out. The novel's last line finds Gately after he wakes up: "he was flat on his back on the beach in the freezing sand, and it was raining out of a low sky, and the tide was way out" (981). The image of Gately supine and small on the beach against a dark and sweeping landscape illustrates, above all, his precarity.

You Get to Decide

So. How does *Infinite Jest* answer Marathe's question: "can such a U.S. A. hope to survive for a much longer time?" (318). Can a United States that replaces citizens with consumers, worships commodities, and has an apparently bottomless appetite for debt survive? Can the United States of the Libertine Statue in an adult diaper survive? The novel itself doesn't seem to know. Like Gately, it teeters. It teeters between endorsing a personal, moral solution—everything unendurable is in the head, single-entendre principles—to a systemic problem and, otherwise, resigning in the face of that system's cruel inevitability. The hidden ending it buries in a sentence in the novel's first pages—in which Hal Incandenza and Don Gately disinter the master copy of *Infinite Jest*, apparently on behalf of Québécois terrorists—suggests resignation, apocalypse. Yet by leaving us, in the end, with Gately in his hospital bed, Gately on the beach, the novel suggests at least the possibility of endurance through cliché, through Abiding, through the conscious choice to persist.

That *Infinite Jest* endorses survival through the will to attend to clichés is an interpretation that has gained a large following, thanks not only to "E Unibus Plurum" and Wallace's interviews, but especially thanks to his widely read 2005 Kenyon College commencement speech, packaged and marketed after his death as a little book, *This is Water*. In that speech, he insisted that the most important thing, and "the only thing that's capital-T True is that you get to decide how you're gonna try to see" the world (np). He opposed suffering from participation in "the rat race" with embracing that "how we construct meaning" is "a matter of personal, intentional choice" (np.) He returns repeatedly to "clichés" in the speech—"the mind being an excellent servant but a terrible master"; a "liberal arts education is . . . about quote teaching you how to think"—arguing that they express "a great and terrible truth": that we have "the choice of what to think about," that, and here he echoes Marathe, we "get to decide what to worship" (np).

How we construct meaning might be a personal choice, and we might get to decide how we see the world (though as a reader of critical theory, especially Ludwig Wittgenstein and Jacques Derrida, Wallace knows better), but our choice to make meaning or see the world as we wish doesn't change the conditions that make life precarious for most Americans in the debt economy. Worse, Wallace misleads his audience into thinking that the problem with Americans is that they choose to worship money and power—that, to take a page from *Infinite Jest*, Americans are addicted to consumption—in a context where "personal debt was no longer a private choice, but a structural imperative" (Hyman 282). The idea that Americans worship money moralizes, as does the very notion of addiction. These framings suggest that Americans are behaving badly in their consumption habits. And yet, as Louis Hyman argues in his history of debt in the United States, "instead of seeing extravagant spenders in debt, we should see underpaid workers trying to keep up" (282). These workers go into debt for the "ability to rent and to buy housing, to afford an education, to shop for clothes and food, to commute to work, and even to receive medical care—that is, the basic materials of daily life" (281). Wallace wants to believe that the solution to our precarity during the long downturn is a change in attitude: "you get to decide," "everything unendurable was in the head." Like AA in *Infinite Jest*, this position turns an economic problem into a moral one. Nothing could be more neoliberal.

Infinite Jest's ambivalence, its teetering, its refusal to decide between sincerity and apocalypse makes it more interesting than Wallace's commencement speech. And yet, its recoding of the debt economy as being about addiction to drugs and entertainment makes it a moral and conservative novel. Wallace struggled much more in *Infinite Jest* than in *This is Water* to reconcile the debt economy with his moral vision. He couldn't. But the tension between the two is what drives the novel's manic searching prose, its aspirations toward endlessness, infinity.

Conclusion

Giovanni Arrighi ends *The Long Twentieth Century* with a vision of "capitalism burning up humanity 'in the horrors (or glories) of... escalating violence'" (Chakrabarty 200). This is a tidy summary of the worldview shared by the texts studied in this book. Thirteen years later, in *Adam Smith in Beijing*, Arrighi is less worried about whether capitalism will lead to apocalyptic violence than he is about how much capitalism the earth itself can take. My mostly chronological account has brought us to the end of the twentieth century. Regarding neoliberal apocalypticism in the twenty-first century, Arrighi proves a reliable weathervane.

Naomi Klein believes we've had the worst timing. Climate change became a crisis just as neoliberalism, which she also calls "deregulated capitalism" and "market fundamentalism," made the necessary responses "politically heretical" (19). Rather than taking measures to resist climate change, the United States has allowed the crisis to become existential. When a crisis feels existential, we are tempted to narrate it as apocalyptic. Klein invokes apocalypse as a threat we might still escape. In *This Changes Everything* she declares, "our economic system and our planetary system are now at war" (21). She consecrates what has become a widely held belief: that solutions to climate change are incompatible with free market capitalism. She argues that we have no time to reform capitalism, "no gradual, incremental options are now available"; our only option now is to "change pretty much everything about our economy" (22). If we do not embrace revolution, we face global chaos, bloodshed, starvation, death. If we do not act soon, we will lose our agency to an inexorable destiny: "once we allow temperatures to climb past a certain point, where the mercury stops is not in our control" (13). This is the rhetoric James Baldwin used in *The Fire Next Time*. Reform failed to eradicate racism; the choice now is revolution or apocalypse. This form

American Literature and the Long Downturn: Neoliberal Apocalypse. Dan Sinykin,
Oxford University Press (2020). © Daniel Sinykin.
DOI: 10.1093/oso/9780198852704.001.0001

retains a sliver of hope. It is not quite yet properly apocalyptic. Apocalypse is the threat. Apocalypse is at the horizon. This is a jeremiad.

Others think the end is here. In *Learning to Die in the Anthropocene*, Roy Scranton writes, "we're fucked" (16). The present is the future: "droughts and hurricanes, refugees and border guards, war for oil, water, gas, and food" (82). We have no way out, "the problem is too big" (68). Like Baldwin in *No Name in the Street*, Scranton is apocalyptic. He invokes the history of apocalypticism to insist that this time is different. This is "not the latest version of a hoary fable of annihilation" (17). This time the end is a fact. Baldwin and Scranton see the task as the same. With no way out, we must remake humanity for after the end of civilization. Baldwin: we need "to forge a new morality, to create the principles on which a new world will be built" (407). Scranton: "we're going to need new myths and new stories, a new conceptual understanding of reality" (19). Scranton gets more specific than Baldwin, advocating "slowness, attention to detail, argumentative rigor, careful reading, and meditative reflection" (108). For Scranton, as for Baldwin, Manson, McCarthy, Silko, and Wallace, capitalism has created the conditions that will destroy it.

If Klein's jeremiad feels fantastical and Scranton's apocalypse seductive, this is at least in part because of how each relates to a triumphal neoliberalism. Central to neoliberalism is its thesis, which it coercively enforces, that there is no alternative to free market capitalism. The finality of neoliberalism, its demotion of any other politics to impossibility, invites feelings of claustrophobia, impotence, and hopelessness—apocalyptic feelings.

There is, this is to say, a fundamental continuity between the apocalypticism charted in this book and that evoked by climate change. Climate change would not be the existential crisis that it is were it not for the particular context of neoliberalism and the long downturn, which accelerate global warming while preemptively eliminating solutions. In *The Collapse of Western Civilization*, Erik M. Conway and Naomi Oreskes narrate the apocalyptic encounter between neoliberalism and climate change. The authors describe their short book as a hybrid of history and science fiction. It is written from the perspective of "a future historian looking back on a past that is our present and (possible) future" (ix). The historian's animating dilemma is to wonder how we knew what we did and yet failed to act. Her thesis is that we failed because of our "denial and self-deception, rooted in an ideological fixation on 'free markets'" (ibid.). After presenting the history—the ineffectual or harmful policies of the first decades of the twenty-first century, the breakdown of social order in the 2050s, mass migration, black death, humankind's near extinction—the narrator delivers an extended account of neoliberalism, including readings of canonical works by Friedrich von Hayek and Milton Friedman. Neoliberalism, she writes, embraced liberalism's thesis that "societal needs were served most efficiently in a free market economic system" and made it *neo* by adding that this was "the *only* manner of doing so that did not threaten personal freedom" (38). This ideology enabled techno-optimists to believe the market would solve climate change, but led to a situation in which "the development neoliberals most dreaded—centralized government and loss of personal choice—was rendered essential by the very policies that they had put in place" (49). The book's message to the present, its attempt at persuasion, is the irony of this *reductio ad absurdum*.

We have already been here. We have, for decades, been grappling with how best to narrate life under existential threats that have, at their irreparable core, capitalism. We have, for decades, turned to apocalypse as the story to tell to assuage our hopelessness. If by now we find these stories unmoving, maybe it is because they are too familiar. How many times can we be told *this is the end* before we stop believing? Scranton's appeal to the facticity of *this* apocalypse does not distinguish his story: each makes this appeal. And yet we keep compulsively narrating the end.

But climate change introduces a difference. Dilapidated housing, abject poverty, financial crises, and debt enact themselves on bodies in felt ways. These are legible crises. Climate change, many argue, is not. It is too big, too temporally extended, too abstract. It is an exemplary instance of what Rob Nixon famously calls "slow violence": "a violence that occurs gradually and out of sight, a violence of delayed destruction that is dispersed across time and space, an attritional violence that is typically not viewed as violence at all" (2). Slow violence presents "formidable representational obstacles that can hinder our efforts to mobilize and act decisively" (ibid.). Think of the absurdity of pointing to a hot day as proof of climate change. Linking individual hurricanes and droughts to climate change can give the misleading sense that climate change is expressible in that instance. In a period characterized by the fact that humans are affecting the geological record (the Anthropocene), we cannot, as Ian Baucom puts it, "ever experience ourselves as a geophysical force—though we now know that this is one of the modes of our collective existence" (153). We grasp for evidence perceptible by our frail human sensoria. How do we represent a phenomenon that is beyond the scale of our experience?

The problem of representation is an opportunity for literature. Nixon thinks so, at any rate, writing that "imaginative writing can help make the unapparent appear, making it accessible and tangible" (15). As of 2005, writers had little to say about climate change, prompting the prominent environmentalist Bill McKibben to ask, "Where are the books? The poems? The plays? The goddamn operas?" (np).[1] Like Nixon, he argued that we need writers to provide visions of a world where it is possible to confront climate change. Against the representational challenges, he asked, "can we register it in our imaginations, the most sensitive of all our devices?" (np).

Writers accepted the challenge. Since 2005, we have seen the emergence of a genre devoted to climate change, called climate fiction, or cli-fi.[2] Frequently cited as belonging to the genre are novels by Margaret Atwood, Paolo Bacigalupi, Barbara Kingsolver, Cormac McCarthy, and Kim Stanley Robinson. They confront whether fiction, as a form, provides traction on the hard problem of representing climate change.

Fiction offers the power of the subjunctive. It shows us how the world might otherwise be. For some, like literary critic Ed Finn, this is enough. Finn argues that cli-fi can "show us what it might look like to literally inhabit our ideas" (np). Further, it can take "numbing debates" over the data of climate change and "put them into gripping, visceral context" (np). He concludes hopefully that, "perhaps the single best tool we have to combat wicked problems and complex systems is narrative—the ambiguity, complexity, and specificity of stories that can capture an

[1] Caroline Edwards provides an extensive survey of one subset of cli-fi—flood fictions—in "All Aboard for Ararat!"

[2] Environmentalists have long found apocalypse a useful form. In *Ecocriticism*, 101–13, Greg Garrard charts this history, focusing on Rachel Carson's *Silent Spring*, Paul Ehrlich's *The Population Bomb*, the poetry of Robinson Jeffers, and the radical environmentalist organization, Earth First!

entire era through the eye, and the heart, of a single character" (np). But if the challenge of climate change is that it is incomprehensible from the perspective of a single human, then ambiguity, complexity, and specificity, no matter how visceral, are not enough to overcome the limits of a mind. Fiction might give us virtual access to an alternative organization of human life, but does it bring us any closer to a true experience of climate change?

Amitav Ghosh attempts to answer this question in *The Great Derangement*. Like McKibben and Finn, Ghosh believes the great power of fiction in the face of climate change is its ability "to approach the world in a subjunctive mode, to conceive of it as *if* it were other" (xx). Unlike them, he worries that dominant conventions of contemporary literature present obstacles to its ambitions (7). He takes his cue from Dipesh Chakrabarty, who teaches at the University of Chicago, where Ghosh's book began as a series of lectures in 2015. Chakrabarty's 2009 essay, "The Climate of History: Four Theses," has been influential for climate change debates in the humanities. He argues that climate change requires that we revise our fundamental understanding of "the human" and "history"—we need now to think simultaneously in the registers of capitalism, imperialism, and the species as geological. We have considerable practice with the former two modes, but the third is new, and difficult, because, with regard to climate change, "we experience specific effects of the crisis but not the whole phenomenon" (221). "To call human beings geological agents" he writes, "is to scale up our imagination of the human" (206). Ghosh, with Chakrabarty in the audience, attends to the problem scaling up representation for literature.

He identifies three ways that climate change resists representation in contemporary literary fiction, captured in three keywords: *improbability*, *nonhuman*, and *collective*. He contends that the novel has, from its beginnings, been bound up with probability, that both express "the same kind of experience" (16). Conventions of literary fiction prohibit outlandish coincidences and deus ex machina conclusions. Events should bear the imprimatur of good sense. This literary commitment to the probable, Ghosh writes, is what "makes a certain kind of narrative a recognizably modern novel" (23). But climate change rejects probability. "[G]lobal warming defies both literary fiction and contemporary common sense: the weather events of this time have a very high degree of improbability" (26). In addition to its attachment to probability, the literary novel functions at the scale of the human. It relates its narratives, in Finn's words, "through the eye, and the heart, of a single character"—or sometimes more—but, at any rate, at human scale. Ghosh writes that climate change introduces scales "long ago expelled from the territory of the novel—forces of unthinkable magnitude that create unbearably intimate connections over vast gaps in time and space" (63). As a corollary, the novel is individualistic. Ghosh writes, "at exactly the time when it has become clear that global warming is in every sense a collective predicament, humanity finds itself in the thrall of a dominant culture in which the idea of the collective has been exiled from politics, economics, and literature alike" (80). To represent climate change, the novel must be able to engage the improbable, the nonhuman, and the collective, but its formal conventions conscript it to the probable, the human, and the individual. Thus, for Ghosh, "the irony of the 'realist' novel: the very gestures with which it conjures up reality are actually a concealment of the real" (23).

The qualifier "realist" indicates a flaw in Ghosh's argument. What constitutes the "realist" novel has been up for debate among scholars in the twenty-first century, but Ghosh acts as if there were consensus. He at times calls realist novels "modern," "literary," or simply "novels." This category excludes science fiction, a genre that engages improbability, the nonhuman, and the collective. For Ghosh, as soon as a novel speaks in cli-fi terms, it is by definition no longer realist. He also sees genres hierarchically. Attempts to break realist conventions "relegate" a work to "the genre of science fiction"—it is "banished" to the "outhouses" of "science fiction and fantasy" (7, 66). He is committed to repairing realist fiction because the Anthropocene "resists science fiction: it is precisely not an imagined 'other' world apart from ours" (72). We need realist fiction that can respectably address the realness of climate change in our world now. He prophesies that "new, hybrid forms will emerge and the act of reading itself will change once again" (84).

Ghosh's depiction of a contemporary literary field sharply divided between well-regarded literary fiction and trashier genre fiction bears little resemblance to reality. We spy its anachronism in Ghosh's use of John Updike, who peaked decades ago and is dead, as an authority on the norms of literary fiction. Kate Marshall points out, in a sharp review of

The Great Derangement, that science fiction and fantasy authors (Margaret Atwood, Samuel Delany, Ursula K. Le Guin, Kim Stanley Robinson) have achieved literary respectability, and that a "marked engagement with genre" has become "a commonplace feature" of contemporary literary fiction (i.e. Kazuo Ishiguro, Cormac McCarthy, George Saunders, Colson Whitehead) (np). Leif Sorensen has argued that, within this milieu, and against Ghosh's claims, women of color novelists including Octavia Butler, Nnedi Okorafor, and Leslie Marmon Silko have successfully become "vernacular theorists of the entanglement of human and nonhuman agencies, actions, energies, and scales" (524). Sarah Chihaya, meanwhile, has pointed to A. S. Byatt's list-making in *Ragnarök* as offering "a new, necessarily doubled chronotope for the work of art in the age of environmental destruction, a work that imaginatively positions itself simultaneously in the midst of ongoing planetary crisis and at, or even after, its end" (577). Ghosh's hoped-for literary future is already here. But Ghosh, with his anachronistic sense of literary norms, cannot manage to recognize it for what it is.

Marshall's principal criticism is that Ghosh is preoccupied with the representation of climate change at the level of plot and setting: "to argue that it's only this kind of direct fictional representation that can provide the kind of engagement with the material complexity of our current era is both dangerous and not a little depressing" (np). I take Marshall to mean that representations of climate change must register subtler and more pervasive quotidian modes of comprehension that manifest through form as much as content.[3] Over the course of several recent essays, Marshall has shown how contemporary fiction has been responsive to the Anthropocene in ways that go beyond what Ghosh manages to imagine. She identifies a set of apparently realist novels (Rachel Kushner's *The Flamethrowers*, Ken Kalfus's *Equilateral*, Don DeLillo's *Point Omega*) that situate themselves in geological time through the reflexive staging of "the production of art on Pleistocene desert sands" (524). Most important to Marshall is her discovery of nonhuman narration across "a range of recent novels," including McCarthy's *Blood Meridian*, Marilynne Robinson's *Housekeeping*, Michael Cunningham's *Specimen Days*,

[3] For an account of the forms of ecological catastrophe in American poetry, see *Remainders* by Margaret Ronda.

and Colson Whitehead's *Zone One* (645). It makes sense, then, that she finds Ghosh interesting when he "points to the Anthropocene itself as the one knowing critic of our time, registering the issues persistently at hand" (np). An "uncanniness attends" nonhuman narration, which breaks "the assumptions lying behind narrative interiority from within," offering precisely what Ghosh asks for—the improbable, the nonhuman, the collective—though, looking for more obvious signs, he fails to see what Marshall shows us is ubiquitous (ibid.). Her intervention is necessary: cli-fi is more capacious than we think; we cannot look for the Anthropocene in only the most on-the-nose novels.

It remains a temptation to fit climate change to apocalyptic form. To fully treat the varieties of cli-fi apocalypticism, I would need another book. Let me close by positing that, in addition to introducing a representational challenge to literature, climate change has provided an opportunity for neoliberal apocalypticism to open itself to utopia. With capitalism as referent, apocalypticists had difficulty imagining another world. Neoliberalism coerced them into imaginative constraints. But climate change has coincided with—and, maybe, given its geological scale, abetted—the loosening of neoliberalism's chains. Gerry Canavan describes a politics common to apocalyptic cli-fi. "The utopian potentiality implied—and, often, made possible—by apocalyptic critique is the necessary critical move to rescue us from a diagnosis of the world situation that would otherwise appear utterly hopeless" (16). Hopelessness transforms dialectically into hope.[4]

Consider Ben Lerner's *10:04*. It takes on the representational challenges of climate change and brings apocalypse toward a utopian horizon. Lerner announces his project in the first pages. The protagonist, whose name is Ben, recalls what he told his agent when she asked him how he would write the book that would become *10:04*. In retrospect, he feels he "should have said": "I'll project myself into several futures simultaneously"; "I'll work my way from irony to sincerity in the sinking city, a would-be Whitman of the vulnerable grid" (4). His description of New York as a "sinking city" and a "vulnerable grid" make clear that this

[4] Rebecca Evans names this form—when apocalypse opens onto utopia, when it "threatens, but does not resolve neatly in a cathartic finality"—"*open* apocalypse" (502–3). She argues that the form of open apocalypse evades the apocalyptic risk of fatalism and "produces a new and politically salient form of historical consciousness" (503). See also *Utopia and the Contemporary British Novel* by Caroline Edwards.

is apocalyptic cli-fi. What's more, the novel begins with Hurricane Irene in 2011 and ends with Hurricane Sandy in 2012. In between, Ben worries about a medical condition, mentors a Latino boy, considers fathering a child with his best friend, and spends time in Marfa, Texas, on a writing fellowship.

Though describing two improbable climate events, the novel, per Ghosh's requirement, is decidedly realist. It is convincing not least because it nabs the hurricanes from real life. It signals its attention to a second of Ghosh's requirements, the collective, through Walt Whitman. Whitman, Lerner tells us, "has to be nobody in particular in order to be a democratic everyman, has to empty himself out so that his poetry can be a textual commons for the future into which he projects himself" (168). This is the Whitman of "Song of Myself" ("what I assume you shall assume, / For every atom belonging to me as good belongs to you") and, especially, of "Crossing Brooklyn Ferry" ("It avails not, time nor place—distance avails not, / I am with you"). A textual commons, a literary text that could create through its own existence the space for community, is Lerner's objective. He writes, "I resolved to be one of the artists who momentarily made bad forms of collectivity figures of its possibility" (108). Aware of his privilege as a white man in Brooklyn, Lerner tries to account for the erasure of capitalism and imperialism entailed in projecting himself as the model for collectivity by discussing his privilege as a white man in Brooklyn (during Occupy Wall Street, at Park Slope Coop). His success is debatable. How he expects to accomplish the lofty goal of creating a textual commons is unclear. The most likely contender for his utopian method is—as Marshall teaches us to see—his formal experimentation. His Whitmanian projection into the future is paired with a messianic epigraph from Walter Benjamin, which ends with a line about "the world to come" that becomes the novel's reprise: "Everything will be as it is now, just a little different" (ix). Lerner iterates what here is a temporal doubling of worlds, just a little different, with recourse to genre. If *10:04* is about anything, Lerner writes, it is the "crossing of reality and fiction" (57). His protagonist is the Ben who is writing *10:04.* His setting is New York City in 2011 and 2012, detailed with verisimilitude. We can't know where fact ends and imagination begins, the novel is "neither fiction nor nonfiction, but a flickering between them" (194). This flickering activates, for Lerner, "the utopian glimmer of fiction" (54). It is how he aims to shake loose from his tendency "to figure the global apocalyptically" (14). It is an enactment, formally, of the subjunctive, an invocation of the future where everything will be as it is now, just a little different. It is a mystical fantasy of escape from the fatalism of our certain end. What else best instantiates that escape than a child to come? In the final pages, Ben and his best friend walk through the city in the dark of Sandy, and she is pregnant, and the unborn baby is a Benjaminian messiah, a utopian hope projected into the future against the apocalyptic present.

* * *

Climate change, I wrote, is unique in its illegibility. It is too big, too temporally extended, too conceptually abstract. These are the same characteristics that Fredric Jameson famously claimed for capitalism in the late twentieth century and that created a crisis for representation. If capitalism cannot be represented, then—because it is inextricable from reality—all representations are false. Jameson argued that writers responded with postmodernism. Pastiche and metafiction are formal strategies to deal with the inaccessibility of history. Cognitive mapping is Jameson's term for how we model an incomprehensible world, how we bend and deform it into legibility. Apocalypse is a bid for control amid chaos. It is a grasp for certainty in a world that has become incomprehensible. It is an outcry when the problem is too big.

The major texts I have studied in this book each stage a crisis of representation. Baldwin, in one of his most gregarious texts, turns in the end to silence. McCarthy, in his enigmatic epilogue, posits the typewriter ("escapement," "pallet") as that which civilizes the world by enclosing its chaos, a chaos that it cannot, ultimately, control, and that will undo everything. Silko's almanac's power is its illegibility. For Wallace, cliché enables a fantasy about breaking from signification. Writing and death, order and chaos, meaning and nothingness.

The long downturn created widespread immiseration, anxiety, and fear. For many, it came to feel like the end of the world. It also created a crisis for representation. It became unclear how any individual connected to the whole. But Jameson, who cared little for contemporary American literary fiction, missed how so many writers responded to the incomprehensibility of capitalism by grasping for the certainty of apocalypse.

* * *

I have wondered why *I* wrote a book about apocalypse. I feel the hopelessness at the heart of the form. I feel helpless in response to the suffering of the long downturn and neoliberalism. I struggle to comprehend the extent of my complicity as I live everyday embodying it. Against this condition, apocalypse strives for certainty, but the failures of neoliberal apocalypticism, not the certainty, are what move me. When I began, I saw Baldwin, McCarthy, Silko, and Wallace as irreproachable artists. It was my job to channel them, to clarify their intent, to understand. I came to understand their fallibility, that the beauty of their texts is not in their boldest visions of what may come, but in their desperate attempt to make sense of life now. They ask, consciously or not, the question that Roy Scranton takes as most urgent, "how do we make meaningful decisions in the shadow of our inevitable end?" (20). Scranton ends with an allusion to W. H. Auden's poem, "September 1, 1939." The poem's speaker is sitting at a bar in New York City as Germany invades Poland, starting World War II. Against the terror of that moment, he says, "we must love one another or die." He says that all he has is his voice, and that all he is, like all of us, is Eros and dust, and that all we can do is speak and hope that our speech shines like "ironic points of light" that will "show an affirming flame." "The only practical question remaining" Scranton writes with his final line, "is whether we, existing as we are, will be that light" (117).

I don't know about the light. I know that experience, these last decades, has many reaching for certainty. But this is a yearning for something that isn't there. I lean on different lines from Auden's poem:

> Faces along the bar
> Cling to their average day:
> The lights must never go out,
> The music must always play,
> All the conventions conspire
> To make this fort assume
> The furniture of home;
> Lest we should see where we are,
> Lost in a haunted wood,
> Children afraid of the night
> Who have never been happy or good.

Works Cited

Aes-Nihil, John, Nick Bougas, Adam Parfey, Boyd Rice, Jimmi Rocket, Nikolas Schreck, and Jack Stevenson, eds. *The Manson File*. Feral House, 2011.

Alcoholics Anonymous: The Story of How Many Thousands of Men and Women Have Recovered from Alcoholism. 3rd edn. Alcoholics Anonymous World Services, Inc., 1976.

Anam, Nasia. "The Migrant as Colonist: Dystopia and Apocalypse in the Literature of Mass Migration." *ASAP/Journal*, vol. 3.3, 2018, pp. 653–77.

Anker, Elizabeth. "Postcritical Reading, the Lyric, and Ali Smith's *How to be Both*. *diacritics*, vol. 45.4, 2017, pp. 16–42.

Argüello, Ana Rosa Suárez. "El Interesa Expansionista Norteamericano en Sonora, 1848–1861." *Estudios de Historia Moderna y Contemporánea de México*, vol. 11, 1988, pp. 123–48.

Argüello, Ana Rosa Suárez. *La Batalla por Tehuantepec: El peso de los intereses privados en la relación México-Estados Unidos, 1848–1854*. Mexico: Secretaría de Relaciones Exteriores, 2003.

Arnold, Ellen L., ed. *Conversations with Leslie Marmon Silko*. University of Mississippi Press, 2000.

Arrighi, Giovanni. *The Long Twentieth Century: Money, Power, and the Origin of Our Times*. Verso, 1994.

Auden, W. H. "September 1, 1939." https://www.poets.org/poetsorg/poem/september-1-1939.

Bahng, Aimee. *Migrant Futures: Decolonizing Speculation in Financial Times*. Duke University Press, 2018.

Baldwin, James. "Encounter on the Seine: Black Meets Brown." *Collected Essays*. Edited by Toni Morrison. Library of America, 1998, pp. 85–90.

Baldwin, James. "Fifth Avenue, Uptown." *Collected Essays*. Edited by Toni Morrison. Library of America, 1998, pp. 170–9.

Baldwin, James. *The Fire Next Time*. *Collected Essays*. Edited by Toni Morrison. Library of America, 1998, pp. 291–348.

Baldwin, James. *No Name in the Street*. *Collected Essays*. Edited by Toni Morrison. Library of America, 1998, pp. 349–476.

Baldwin, James. "Notes on the House of Bondage." *Collected Essays*. Edited by Toni Morrison. Library of America, 1998, pp. 799–807.

Baldwin, James. "Open Letter to the Born Again." *Collected Essays*. Edited by Toni Morrison. Library of America, 1998, pp. 784–7.

Baldwin, James. "A Report from Occupied Territory." *Collected Essays*. Edited by Toni Morrison. Library of America, 1998, pp. 728–38.

Baldwin, James. "Stranger in the Village." *Collected Essays*. Edited by Toni Morrison. Library of America, 1998, pp. 117–29.

Baldwin, James. "The International War Crimes Tribunal." *The Cross of Redemption: Uncollected Writings*. Edited by Randall Kenan. Vintage, 2010, pp. 82–7.

Baldwin, James. "What Price Freedom?" *The Cross of Redemption: Uncollected Writings*. Edited by Randall Kenan. Vintage. 2010, pp. 82–7.

Baldwin, James. "The White Problem." *The Cross of Redemption: Uncollected Writings*. Edited by Randall Kenan. Vintage. 2010, pp. 88–97.

Balfour, Lawrie. *The Evidence of Things Not Said: James Baldwin and the Promise of American Democracy*. Cornell University Press, 2001.

Barkun, Michael. *Disaster and the Millennium*. 1974. Syracuse University Press, 2015.

Barkun, Michael. "Racist Apocalypse: Millennialism on the Far Right." *American Studies*, vol. 31.2, 1990, pp. 121–40.

Bartlett, John Russell. *Personal Narrative of Explorations & Incidents in Texas, New Mexico, California, Sonora, and Chihuahua: Connected with the United States and Mexican Boundary Commission, During the Years 1850, '51, '52, and '53.* Kindle edn, D. Appleton & Co., 1854.

Baucom, Ian. *Specters of the Atlantic: Finance Capital, Slavery, and the Philosophy of History*. Duke University Press, 2005.

The Beatles. "Blackbird." *The Beatles*. Apple, 1968.

The Beatles. "Helter Skelter." *The Beatles*. Apple, 1968.

Becker, Gary. *Accounting for Tastes*. Harvard University Press, 1996.

Beebee, Thomas O. *Millennial Literatures of the Americas, 1492–2002*. Oxford University Press, 2008.

Bercovitch, Sacvan. *The American Jeremiad*. 1978. The University of Wisconsin Press, 2012.

Berger, J. M. "The Turner Legacy: The Stories Origins and Enduring Impact of White Nationalism's Deadly Bible." *International Centre for Counter-Terrorism Research Paper*. https://icct.nl/wp-content/uploads/2016/09/ICCT-Berger-The-Turner-Legacy-September2016-2.pdf.

Berger, James. *After the End: Representations of Post-Apocalypse*. University of Minnesota Press, 1999.

Berlant, Lauren. *Cruel Optimism*. Duke University Press, 2011.

Bernes, Jasper. *The Work of Art in the Age of Deindustrialization*. Stanford University Press, 2017.

Bernstein, Lee. "Prison Writers and the Black Arts Movement." *New Thoughts on the Black Arts Movement*. Edited by Lisa Gail Collins and Margo Natalie Crawford. Rutgers University Press, 2006.

Best, Stephen and SharonMarcus. "Surface Reading: An Introduction." *Representations*, vol. 108.1, 2009, pp. 1–21.

Birkerts, Sven. "Apocalypse Now: *Almanac of the Dead* by Leslie Marmon Silko." *The New Republic*, vol. 205.19, 1991, pp. 39–41.

Birmingham, Kevin. "'History's Ass Pocket': The Sources of Baldwinian Diaspora." *James Baldwin: American and Beyond*. Edited by Cora Kaplan and Bill Schwarz. University of Michigan Press, 2011, pp. 141–58.

Bloom, Harold. "Introduction." *Blood Meridian: Or the Evening Redness in the West*. The Modern Library, 2001, pp. v–xiii.

Boyer, Paul. *When Time Shall Be No More: Prophecy Belief in Modern American Culture*. Reprint edn, Belknap Press, 1994.

Boyer, Paul. "Bible Prophecy Belief in Contemporary American Culture." *Anglican and Episcopal History*, 67.4, 1998, 448–66.
Brenner, Robert. *The Economics of Global Turbulence: The Advanced Capitalist Economies from Long Boom to Long Downturn, 1945–2005*. Verso, 2006.
Breu, Christopher. *Insistence of the Material: Literature in the Age of Biopolitics*. University of Minnesota Press, 2014.
Bricker, Harvey M. and Victoria Reifler Bricker. *Astronomy in the Maya Codices*. American Philadelphia Society, 2011.
Brier, Evan. A Novel Marketplace: Mass Culture, the Book Trade, and Postwar American Fiction. University of Pennsylvania Press, 2010.
Brigham, Ann. "Productions of Geographic Scale and Capitalist-Colonialist Enterprise in Leslie Marmon Silko's *Almanac of the Dead. Modern Fiction Studies*, vol. 50.2, 2004, pp. 303–31.
Brouillette, Sarah. *Literature and the Creative Economy*. Stanford University Press, 2014.
Brouillette, Sarah. "Neoliberalism and the Demise of the Literary." *Neoliberalism and Contemporary Literary Culture*. Edited by Mitchum Huehls and Rachel Greenwald Smith. John Hopkins University Press, 2017, pp. 277–90.
Brouillette, Sarah. *UNESCO and the Fate of the Literary*. Stanford University Press, 2019.
Brown, Wendy. *Undoing the Demos: Neoliberalism's Stealth Revolution*. Zone Books, 2015.
Burgin, Angus. *The Great Persuasion: Reinventing Free Markets since the Depression*. Harvard University Press, 2015.
Burn, Stephen. *David Foster Wallace's* Infinite Jest: *A Reader's Guide*. Continuum, 2003.
Burn, Stephen J., ed. *Conversations with David Foster Wallace*. University of Mississippi Press, 2012.
Campbell, Neil. "Liberty beyond Its Proper Bounds: Cormac McCarthy's History of the West in *Blood Meridian*," *Myth, Legend, Dust: Critical Responses to Cormac McCarthy*. Edited by Rick Wallach. Manchester University Press, 2014, pp. 217–26.
Canavan, Gerry. "Introduction: If This Goes On." *Green Planets: Ecology and Science Fiction*. Edited by Gerry Canavan and Kim Stanley Robinson. Wesleyan University Press, 2014, pp. 1–24.
Chakrabarty, Dipesh. "The Climate of History: Four Theses." *Critical Inquiry*, vol. 35.2, 2009, pp. 197–222.
Chamberlain, Samuel. *My Confession: Recollections of a Rogue*. Edited by William H. Goetzmann. Texas State Historical Association, 1996.
Chapman, Jennie. *Plotting Apocalypse*. University Press of Mississippi, 2013.
Cherniavsky, Eva. "Tribalism, Globalism, and Eskimo Television in Leslie Marmon Silko's *Almanac of the Dead*." *Angelaki: Journal of Theoretical Humanities*, vol. 6.1, 2001, pp. 111–26.
Chihara, Michelle and Matt Seybold, eds. *The Routledge Companion to Literature and Economics*. Routledge, 2018.
Chihara, Michelle and Matt Seybold. "Introduction." *The Routledge Companion to Literature and Economics*. Routledge, 2018.
Chihaya, Sarah. "What is Missing: Cataloguing the End." *ASAP/Journal*, vol. 3.3, 2018, pp. 571–93.

Chuchiak, John F. "*In Servitio Dei*: Fray Diego de Landa, the Franciscan Order, and the Return of Extirpation of Idolatry in the Colonial Diocese of Yucatán, 1573–1579." *Americas*, vol. 61.4, 2005, pp. 611–46.

Cleaver, Eldridge. *Soul on Ice*. Dell Publishing Co., 1968.

Clover, Joshua. "Autumn of the System: Poetry and Financial Capital." *Journal of Narrative Theory*, vol. 41.1, 2011, pp. 34–52.

Clover, Joshua. *Riot. Strike. Riot.: The New Era of Uprisings*. Verso, 2016.

Clover, Joshua and Julianna Spahr. *#Misanthropocene: 24 Theses*. Commune Editions, 2014.

Clune, Michael W. *American Literature and the Free Market, 1945–2000*. Reprint edn, Cambridge University Press, 2015.

Cohen, Samuel and Lee Konstantinou. "Introduction: Zoologists, Elephants, and Editors." *The Legacy of David Foster Wallace*. Edited by Samuel Cohen and Lee Konstantinou. University of Iowa Press, 2012, pp. xi–xxv.

Cohn, Norman. *The Pursuit of the Millennium: Revolutionary Millenarians and Mystical Anarchists of the Middle Ages*. Revised edn, Oxford University Press, 1970.

Collier, George Allen and Elizabeth Lowery Quaratiello. *Basta!: Land and the Zapatista Rebellion in Chiapas*. Food First Books, 2005.

Collins, John J. *The Apocalyptic Imagination: An Introduction to Jewish Apocalyptic Literature*. 2nd edn, Eerdmans, 1998.

Collins, John J. *Apocalypse, Prophecy, and Pseudepigraphy: On Jewish Apocalyptic Literature*. Eerdmans, 2015.

Collins, John J. "Introduction: Toward the Morphology of a Genre." *Semeia*, vol. 14, 1979, pp. 4–18.

Conversations with Ishmael Reed. Edited by Bruce Dick. University of Mississippi Press, 1995.

Conway, Erik M. and Naomi Oreskes. *The Collapse of Western Civilization*. Columbia University Press, 2014.

Coogan, Michael, David Marc Zvi Brettler, Carol A. Newsom, and Pheme Perkins, eds. *The New Oxford Annotated Bible*. Oxford University Press, 2010.

Cook-Lynn, Elizabeth. *Why I Can't Read Wallace Stegner and Other Essays: A Tribal Voice*. University of Wisconsin Press, 1996.

DeLay, Brian. "Independent Indians and the U.S.–Mexican War." *American Historical Review*, vol. 12.1, 1997, pp. 35–68.

DeLay, Brian. *War of a Thousand Deserts: Indian Raids and the U.S.–Mexican War*. Kindle edn, Yale University Press, 2008.

DeLillo, Don. *White Noise*. Viking Penguin, 1985.

Derrida, Jacques. "No Apocalypse, Not Now: (Full Speed Ahead, Seven Missiles, Seven Missives)." Translated by Philip Lewis and Catherine Porter. *Diacritics*, vol. 14.2, 1984, pp. 20–31.

Dewey, Joseph. *In a Dark Time: The Apocalyptic Temper in the American Novel of the Nuclear Age*. Purdue University Press, 1990.

Dickstein, Morris. *Leopards in the Temple: The Transformation of American Fiction, 1945–1970*. Harvard University Press, 2002.

Didion, Joan. "The White Album." *The White Album*. Simon and Schuster, 1979.

Donnelly, Daria. "Old and New Notebooks: *Almanac of the Dead* as Revolutionary Entertainment." *Leslie Marmon Silko: A Collection of Critical Essays*. University of New Mexico Press, 1999.

Du Bois, W. E. B. *The Souls of Black Folk*. 1903. Penguin Books, 1996.

Eaton, Mark. "Dis(re)membered Bodies: Cormac McCarthy's Border Fiction." *Modern Fiction Studies*, vol. 49.1, 2003, pp. 155–80.

Edmonson, Munro S., trans. *The Ancient Future of the Itza: The Book of Chilam Balam of Tizimin*. University of Texas Press, 1982.

Edwards, Caroline. "All Aboard for Ararat!: Islands in Contemporary Apocalyptic Flood Fiction." *ASAP/Journal*, 2019, vol. 4.1.

Edwards, Caroline. *Utopia and the Contemporary British Novel*. Cambridge University Press, 2019.

English, James. *The Economy of Prestige: Prizes, Awards, and the Circulation of Cultural Value*. Harvard University Press, 2008.

Erickson, Kristin. *Yaqui Homeland and Homeplace: The Everyday Production of Ethnic Identity*. University of Arizona Press, 2008.

Evans, Rebecca M. "The Best of Times, the Worst of Times, the End of Times?: The Uses and Abuses of Environmental Apocalypse." *ASAP/Journal*, vol. 3.3, 2018, pp. 501–22.

Feher, Michel. "On Credit, Self-esteem, and Sharing: An Introduction to the Neoliberal Condition." Cornell University. Public Lecture. October 24, 2013.

Felski, Rita. *Uses of Literature*. Wiley-Blackwell, 2008.

Field, Douglas. *Historical Guide to James Baldwin*. Oxford University Press, 2009.

Finn, Ed. "Imagining Climate: How Science Fiction Holds Up a Mirror to Our Future." *Medium*. https://medium.com/@zonal/imagining-climate-40d8f20d62f.

Fischer, Edward F. and R. McKenna, eds. *Maya Cultural Activism in Guatemala*. University of Texas Press, 1996.

Fisher, Mark. *Capitalist Realism: Is There No Alternative?* Zero Books, 2009.

Fluck, Winfried. "The Nineteenth-Century Historical Novel." *The Cambridge History of the American Novel*. Edited by Leonard Cassuto, Clare Virginia Eby, and Benjamin Reiss. Cambridge University Press, 2011, pp. 117–34.

Ford, III, James Edward. "When Disaster Strikes: On the Apocalyptic Tone of Hip Hop." *ASAP/Journal*, vol. 3.3, 2018, pp. 595–622.

Ford, Nick Aaron. "The Evolution of James Baldwin as Essayist." In *James Baldwin: A Critical Evaluation*. Edited by Therman B. O'Daniel. Howard University Press, 1997, pp. 85–104.

Foucault, Michel. "What is an Author?" *The Foucault Reader*. Edited by Paul Rabinow. Pantheon Books, 1984.

Foucault, Michel. *The Birth of Biopolitics*. Picador, 2010.

Francis, Consuela. *The Critical Reception of James Baldwin*. Camden House, 2016.

Freedman, Jonathan. "Anti-Semitism without Jews: *Left Behind*, the Christian Right, and the Conversion of the Jews." *Antisemitism and Philosemitism in the Twentieth and Twenty-First Centuries: Representing Jews, Jewishness, and Modern Culture*. Edited by Phyllis Lassner and Lara Trubowitz. University of Delaware Press, 2008.

Freudenthal, Elizabeth. "Anti-interiority: Compulsiveness, Objectification, and Identity in *Infinite Jest*." *New Literary History*, vol. 41.1, 2010, pp. 191–211.

Friedman, Milton. *Capitalism and Freedom: Fortieth Anniversary Edition*. University of Chicago Press, 2002.

Fukuyama, Francis. *The End of History and the Last Man*. Free Press, 1992.

Gaines, Kevin. "Exile and the Private Life of James Baldwin, George Lamming, and the First World Congress of Negro Writers and Artists." *James Baldwin: American and Beyond*. Edited by Cora Kaplan and Bill Schwarz. The University of Michigan Press, 2011, 173–87.

Gallagher, Catherine. *Nobody's Story: The Vanishing Acts of Women Writers in the Marketplace, 1670–1820*. University of California Press, 1994.

Gallagher, Catherine. *The Body Economic: Life, Death, and Sensation in Political Economy and the Victorian Novel*. Princeton University Press, 2008.

Garrard, Greg. *Ecocriticism*. Routledge, 2004.

Ghosh, Amitav. *The Great Derangement*. The University of Chicago Press, 2016.

Giles, Paul. *The Global Remapping of American Literature*. Princeton University Press, 2011.

Giles, Paul. "All Swallowed Up: David Foster Wallace and American Literature." *The Legacy of David Foster Wallace*. Edited by Samuel Cohen and Lee Konstantinou. University of Iowa Press, 2012, pp. 3–22.

Gitlin, Todd. *The Sixties: Years of Hope, Days of Rage*. Bantam, 1993.

Gladstone, Jason and Daniel Worden. "Introduction." *Postmodern/Postwar and After: Rethinking American Literature*. University of Iowa Press, 2016, pp. 1–24.

Gladstone, Jason, Andrew Hoberek, and Daniel Worden, eds. *Postmodern/Postwar and After: Rethinking American Literature*. University of Iowa Press, 2016.

Glass, Loren. *Counterculture Colophon: Grove Press, The Evergreen Review, and the Incorporation of the Avant-Garde*. Stanford University Press, 2013.

Glick, Reuven and Kevin J. Lansing. "U.S. Household Deleveraging and Future Consumption Growth." FRSBF Economic Letter May 15, 2009.

Gordon, Robert J. *The Rise and Fall of American Growth: The U.S. Standard of Living since the Civil War*. Princeton University Press, 2017.

Goux, Jean-Joseph. *Symbolic Economies: After Marx and Freud*. Cornell University Press, 1990.

Graham, Billy. *World Aflame*. Doubleday, 1965.

Grausam, Daniel. *On Endings: American Postmodern Fiction and the Cold War*. University of Virginia Press, 2011.

Greenberg, James B. "The Impact of Neoliberal Policies on Rural Producers in Oaxaca, Mexico." *Neoliberalism and Commodity Production in Mexico*. Edited by Thomas Weaver. University of Colorado Press, 2012.

Guinn, Jeff. *Manson: The Life and Times of Charles Manson*. Simon & Schuster, 2014.

Gutjahr, Paul C. "No Longer Left Behind: Amazon.com, Reader Response, and the Changing Fortunes of the Christian Novel in America." *Book History*, vol. 5, 2002, pp. 209–36.

Haines, Christian P. "Financialisation." *The Routledge Companion to Literature and Economics*. Routledge, 2018.

Hardy, Clarence. *James Baldwin's God: Sex, Hope, and Crisis in Black Holiness Culture*. The University of Tennessee Press, 2003.

Harvey, David. *A Brief History of Neoliberalism*. Oxford University Press, 2005.

Hayek, Friedrich. *The Road to Serfdom*. University of Chicago Press, 2007.

Hayles, N. Katherine. "The Illusion of Autonomy and the Fact of Recursivity: Virtual Ecologies, Entertainment, and *Infinite Jest*." *New Literary History*, vol. 30.3, 1999, pp. 675–97.

Hicks, Heather. *The Post-Apocalyptic Novel in the Twenty-First Century: Modernity beyond Salvage*. Palgrave Macmillan, 2016.

Hicks, Heather. "'Smoke Follows Beauty': The Femme Fatale and the Logic of Apocalyptic Affiliation in Claire Vaye Watkins's *Gold Fame Citrus.*" *ASAP/Journal*, vol. 3.3, 2018, pp. 623–51.

Hoberek, Andrew. "Introduction: After Postmodernism." *Twentieth Century Literature*, vol. 53.3, 2007, pp. 233–47.

Hoberek, Andrew. "The Novel after David Foster Wallace." *A Companion to David Foster Wallace Studies.* Edited by Marshall Boswell and Stephen J. Burn. Palgrave Macmillan, 2013, pp. 211–28.

Hoberek, Andrew. "Postmodernism and Modernization." *Twentieth Century Literature*, vol. 57.3/4, 2011, pp. 341–53.

Hoberek, Andrew. *The Twilight of the Middle Class: Post–World War II American Fiction and White-Collar Work.* Princeton University Press, 2005.

Horsman, Reginald. *Race and Manifest Destiny: The Origins of American Racial Anglo-Saxonism.* Harvard University Press, 1981.

Houser, Heather. *Ecosickness in Contemporary U.S. Fiction: Environment and Affect.* Columbia University Press, 2014.

Howard-Pitney, David. *The African American Jeremiad.* Temple University Press, 1990.

Howe, Daniel Walker. *What Hath God Wrought: The Transformation of America 1815–1848.* Oxford University Press, 2007.

Hu-DeHart, Evelyn. *Yaqui Resistance and Survival: The Struggle for Land and Autonomy, 1821–1910.* University of Wisconsin Press, 1984.

Huehls, Mitchum. *After Critique: Twenty-First Century Fiction in a Neoliberal Age.* Oxford University Press, 2016.

Huehls, Mitchum and Rachel Greenwald Smith, eds. *Neoliberalism and Contemporary Literary Culture.* Johns Hopkins University Press, 2017.

Huhndorf, Shari M. "Picture Revolution: Transnationalism, American Studies, and the Politics of Contemporary Native Culture." *American Quarterly*, vol. 61.2, 2009, pp. 359–81.

Hungerford, Amy. "On the Period Formerly Known as the Contemporary." *American Literary History*, vol. 20.1-2, 2008, pp. 410–419.

Hungerford, Amy. *Postmodern Belief: American Literature and Religion since 1960.* Kindle edn, Princeton University Press, 1960.

Hungerford, Amy. *Making Literature Now.* Stanford University Press, 2016.

Hurley, Jessica. "Impossible Futures: Fictions of Risk in the *Longue Durée.*" *American Literature*, vol. 89.4, 2017, pp. 761–89.

Hurley, Jessica. *Infrastructures of Apocalypse.* University of Minnesota Press, 2020.

Hurley, Jessica and Dan Sinykin. "Apocalypse: Introduction." *ASAP/Journal*, vol. 3.3, 2018, pp. 451–66.

Hyde, Emily and Sarah Wasserman. "The Contemporary." *Literature Compass*, vol. 14.9, 2017.

Hyman, Louis. *Debtor Nation.* Princeton University Press, 2012.

Isenberg, Andrew. *The Destruction of the Bison: An Environmental History, 1750–1920.* Cambridge University Press, 2000.

Jack Van Impe Ministries, "The Walking Bible." June 20, 2017, https://www.jvim.com/about/scripture-memorization. Accessed June 20, 2017.

Jacobson, Matthew Frye. *Roots Too: White Ethnic Revival in Post-Civil Rights America.* Harvard University Press, 2006.

Jameson, Fredric. *Postmodernism: Or, the Cultural Logic of Late Capitalism*. Duke University Press, 1991.

Jarman, Michelle. "Exploring the World of the Different in Leslie Marmon Silko's *Almanac of the Dead*." *MELUS*, vol. 31.3, 2006, pp. 147–68.

Jarrett, Robert L. *Cormac McCarthy*. Twayne Publishers, 1997.

Jenkins, Jerry B. and Tim LaHaye, *Left Behind*. Tyndale House Publishers, 1995.

Johnson Frykholm, Amy. *Rapture Culture:* Left Behind *in Evangelical America*. Oxford University Press, 2004.

Jones, Leroi. *Blues People*. 1963. HarperCollins, 2002.

Jones, Leroi. *Home*. 1966. AkashiClassics, 2009.

Kaplan, Cora and Bill Schwarz, eds. *James Baldwin: American and Beyond*. University of Michigan Press, 2011.

Katanski, Amelia V. *Learning to Write "Indian": The Boarding-School Experience and American Indian Literature*. University of Oklahoma Press, 2005.

Kelly, Adam. "Dialectic of Sincerity." *Post45*, 2014.

Kermode, Frank. *The Sense of an Ending: Studies in the Theory of Fiction*. 2nd edn, Oxford University Press, 2000.

Ketterer, David. *New Worlds for Old: The Apocalyptic Imagination, Science Fiction, and American Literature*. Anchor Press, 1974.

King, Jr, Martin Luther. "Remaining Awake through a Great Revolution." *A Testament of Hope: The Essential Writings and Speeches of Martin Luther King, Jr*. Edited by James M. Washington. HarperCollins, 1991, pp. 268–78.

Klein, Naomi. *This Changes Everything: Capitalism vs. the Climate*. Simon & Schuster, 2015.

Konstantinou, Lee. "No Bull: David Foster Wallace and Postironic Belief." *The Legacy of David Foster Wallace*. Edited by Samuel Cohen and Lee Konstantinou. University of Iowa Press, 2012, pp. 83–112.

Konstantinou, Lee. "Lews Hyde's Double Economy." *ASAP/Journal*, vol. 1.1, 2016, pp. 123–45.

Konstantinou, Lee. *Cool Characters: Irony and American Fiction*. Harvard University Press, 2016.

Konstantinou, Lee. *Pop Apocalypse: A Possible Satire*. Harper Perennial, 2009.

Kornbluh, Anna. *Realizing Capital: Financial and Psychic Economies in Victorian Form*. Fordham University Press, 2014.

Krippner, Greta R. *Capitalizing on Crisis: The Political Origins of the Rise of Finance*. Harvard University Press, 2011.

La Berge, Leigh Claire. *Scandals and Abstraction: Financial Fiction of the Long 1980s*. Oxford University Press, 2014.

La Berge, Leigh Claire and Alison Shonkwiler, eds. *Reading Capitalist Realism*. University of Iowa Press, 2014.

La Berge, Leigh Claire and Quinn Slobodian. "Reading for Neoliberalism, Reading Like Neoliberals." *American Literary History*, vol. 29.3, 2017, pp. 602–14.

de Landa, Diego. *The Maya: Diego de Landa's Account of the Affairs of Yucatán*. Edited and translated by A. R. Pagden. J. P. O'Hara, 1975.

Lange, Charles H. "Western Anasazi." *Handbook of North American Indians*, Vol. 9: *Southwest*. Edited by Alfonso Ortiz. Smithsonian Institution, 1978, pp. 108–30.

Lardas, John. *The Bop Apocalypse: The Religious Visions of Kerouac, Ginsburg, and Burroughs*. University of Illinois Press, 2001.

Lazzarato, Maurizio. *The Making of the Indebted Man: An Essay on The Neoliberal Condition*. Semiotext(e), 2012.

Leeming, David. *James Baldwin: A Biography*. Knopf, 1994.

Leigh, David J. *Apocalyptic Patterns in Twentieth-Century Fiction*. University of Notre Dame Press, 2008.

Lerner, Ben. *10:04*. Picador, 2015.

Letzler, David. "Encyclopedic Novels and the Cruft of Fiction: *Infinite Jest's* Endnotes." *Studies in the Novel*, vol. 44.3, 2012, pp. 304–24.

Levine, Caroline. *Forms: Whole Rhythm, Hierarchy, Network*. Reprint edn, Princeton University Press, 2017.

Levine, Lawrence W. *Black Culture and Black Consciousness: Afro-American Folk Thought from Slavery to Freedom*. 1977. Oxford University Press, 2007.

Lewicki, Zbigniew. *The Bang and the Whimper: Apocalypse and Entropy in American Literature*. Praeger, 1984.

Lincoln, Kenneth. *Native American Renaissance*. University of California Press, 1983.

Lindsey, Hal. *The Late Great Planet Earth*. Zondervan, 1970.

Lopenzina, Drew. *Red Ink: Native Americans Picking up the Pen in the Colonial Period*. State University of New York Press, 2012.

Love, Bruce. *The Paris Codex: Handbook for a Maya Priest*. University of Texas Press, 1994.

Lustig, Nora. *Mexico: The Remaking of an Economy*. Brookings Institution Press, 1998.

Lynch, Deidre. *The Economy of Character: Novels, Market Culture, and the Business of Inner Meaning*. University of Chicago Press, 1998.

Maltby, Paul. *Christian Fundamentalism and the Culture of Disenchantment*. The University of Virginia Press, 2013.

Mani, Lakshmi. *The Apocalyptic Vision in Nineteenth Century American Fiction: A Study of Cooper, Hawthorne, and Melville*. University Press of America, 1981.

Marable, Manning. *Race, Reform, and Rebellion: The Second Reconstruction and Beyond in Black America, 1945–2006*. 1984. University Press of Mississippi, 2007.

Marshall, Kate. "The Old Weird." *Modernism/Modernity*, vol. 23.3, 2016, pp. 631–49.

Marshall, Kate. "The Readers of the Future Have Become Shitty Literary Critics." *boundary2*, February 26, 2018. https://www.boundary2.org/2018/02/kate-marshall-the-readers-of-the-future-have-become-shitty-literary-critics/.

Marshall, Kate. "What Are the Novels of the Anthropocene? American Fiction in Geological Time." *American Literary History*, vol. 27.3, 2015, pp. 523–38.

Martin, Randy. *The Financialization of Everyday Life*. Temple University Press, 2002.

Martin, Theodore. *Contemporary Drift: Genre, Historicism, and the Problem of the Present*. Columbia University Press, 2017.

Max, D. T. *Every Love Story is a Ghost Story: A Life of David Foster Wallace*. Penguin Books, 2013.

May, John R. *Toward a New Earth: Apocalypse in the American Novel*. University of Notre Dame Press, 1974.

McBride, Dwight A., ed. *James Baldwin Now*. NYU Press, 1999.

McCann, Sean. *A Pinnacle of Feeling: American Literature and Presidential Government*. Princeton University Press, 2008.

McCarthy, Cormac. *Blood Meridian: Or, The Evening Redness in the West*. 1985. New York: The Modern Library, 2001.

McCarthy, Cormac. "Early Draft Fragments." Box 38. Folder 3. Cormac McCarthy Papers, Southwestern Writers Collection, The Wittliff Collections. Texas State University–San Marcos.

McCarthy, Cormac. "Holograph notes." Box 35. Folder 4. Cormac McCarthy Papers, Southwestern Writers Collection, The Wittliff Collections. Texas State University–San Marcos.

McCarthy, Cormac. "Photocopy spiral notebook pages with notes." Box 35. Folder 5. Cormac McCarthy Papers, Southwestern Writers Collection, The Wittliff Collections. Texas State University–San Marcos.

McClanahan, Annie. *Dead Pledges: Debt, Crisis, and Twenty-First-Century Culture*. Stanford University Press, 2016.

McClanahan, Annie. "Dead Pledges: Debt, Horror, and the Credit Crisis." *Post45* 05/07/12. www.post45.research.yale.edu.

McClanahan, Annie. "Serious Crises: Rethinking the Neoliberal Subject." *boundary2*, vol. 46.1, 2019, 103–132.

McDonald, Andrew. *The Turner Diaries*. Barricade Books, 1996.

McGinn, Bernard. *Apocalyptic Spirituality: Treatises and Letters of Lactantius, Adso of Montier-en-Der, Joachim of Fiore, the Franciscan Spirituals, Savonarola*. Paulist Press, 1979.

McGurl, Mark. *The Program Era: Postwar Fiction and the Rise of Creative Writing*. Harvard University Press, 2011.

McInerney, Jay. *Bright Lights, Big City*. Vintage Contemporaries, 1984.

McKibben, Bill. "What the Warming World Needs Now is Art, Sweet Art." *Grist*, April 22, 2005. https://grist.org/article/mckibben-imagine/.

McLuhan, Marshall and Wilfred Watson. *From Cliché to Archetype*. Viking, 1970.

Michaels, Walter Benn. *The Gold Standard and the Logic of Naturalism: American Literature at the Turn of the Century*. University of California Press, 1988.

Michaels, Walter Benn. "Model Minorities and the Minority Model—the Neoliberal Novel." *The Cambridge History of the American Novel*. Edited by Leonard Cassuto. Cambridge University Press, 2011, pp. 1016–30.

Michaels, Walter Benn. "Real Toads." *The Imaginary and Its Worlds: American Studies after the Transnational Turn*. Edited by Laura Bieger, Ramón Saldívar, and Johannes Voelz. Dartmouth College Press, 2013, pp. 177–91.

Miller, D. Quentin, ed. *Re-Viewing James Baldwin*. Temple University Press, 2000.

Miller, D. Quentin. *A Criminal Power: James Baldwin and the Law*. The Ohio State University Press, 2012.

Montgomery, Maxine Lavon. *The Apocalypse in African-American Fiction*. University of Florida Press, 1996.

Mooney, James. *The Ghost-Dance Religion and the Sioux Outbreak of 1890*. University of Nebraska Press, 1991.

Morrison, Toni. *Playing in the Dark*. Vintage, 1993.

Musto, David. *The American Disease: Origins of Narcotic Control*. Kindle edn, Oxford University Press, 1999.

Nixon, Richard. "Special Message to the Congress on Drug Abuse Prevention and Control." http://www.presidency.ucsb.edu/ws/?pid=3048.

Nixon, Rob. *Slow Violence and the Environmentalism of the Poor*. Harvard University Press, 2013.

Ngai, Sianne. "Merely Interesting." *Critical Inquiry*, vol. 34.4, 2008, pp. 777–817.

Olmsted, Jane. "The Uses of Blood in Leslie Marmon Silko's *Almanac of the Dead*." *Contemporary Literature*, vol. 40.3, 1999, pp. 464–90.

O'Meally, Robert G. "The Vernacular Tradition, Part 2." *The Norton Anthology of African American Literature*, Vol. 2. Edited by Henry Louis Gates, Jr, and Valerie Smith. W. W. Norton & Company, Inc., 2014, pp. 3–11.

Osteen, Mark and Martha Woodmansee, eds. *The New Economic Criticism: Studies at the Interface of Literature and Economics*. Routledge, 1999.

Owens, Louis. *Other Destinies: Understanding the American Indian Novel*. University of Oklahoma Press, 1992.

Oxford English Dictionary. Oxford University Press, 2012.

Parrish, Timothy. *From the Civil War to the Apocalypse: Postmodern History and American Fiction*. University of Massachusetts Press, 2008.

Partridge, Eric. *A Dictionary of Clichés*. Routledge and Kegan Paul, 1950.

"Pat Robertson Controversies." *Wikipedia*. https://en.wikipedia.org/wiki/Pat_Robertson_controversies. Accessed June 21, 2017.

Piketty, Thomas. *Capital in the Twenty-First Century*. Translated by Arthur Goldhammer. Belknap Press, 2017.

Poovey, Mary. *Genres of the Credit Economy: Mediating Value in Eighteenth- and Nineteenth-Century Britain*. University of Chicago Press, 2008.

Quashie, Kevin. *The Sovereignty of Quiet: Beyond Resistance in Black Culture*. Rutgers University Press, 2012.

Radway, Janice A. *A Feeling for Books: The Book-of-the-Month Club, Literary Taste, and Middle-Class Desire*. The University of North Carolina Press, 1997.

Rainwater, Catherine. *Dreams of Fiery Stars: The Transformations of Native American Fiction*. University of Pennsylvania Press, 1999.

Rando, David P. "David Foster Wallace and Lovelessness." *Twentieth-Century Literature*, vol. 59.4, 2013, pp. 575–95.

Reed, T. V. "Toxic Colonialism, Environmental Justice, and Native Resistance in Silko's *Almanac of the Dead*." *MELUS*, vol. 34.2, 2009, pp. 25–42.

Reinecke, Yvonne. "Overturning the (New World) Order: Of Space, Time, Writing, and Prophecy in Leslie Marmon Silko's *Almanac of the Dead*." *Studies in American Indian Literature*, vol. 10.3, 1998, pp. 65–83.

Rippy, J. Fred. "The Indians of the Southwest in the Diplomacy of the United States and Mexico, 1848–1853." *The Hispanic American Historical Review*, vol. 2.3, 1919, pp. 363–96.

Robertson, Pat. *The End of the Age*. W Publishing Group, 1995.

Robinson, Douglas. *American Apocalypses: The Image of the End of the World in American Literature*. The Johns Hopkins University Press, 1985.

Rodgers, Daniel T. *Age of Fracture*. Belknap Press, 2011.

Roediger, David. *The Wages of Whiteness: Race and the Making of the American Working Class*. Verso, 1991.

Romero, Channette. "Envisioning a 'Network of Tribal Coalitions': Leslie Marmon Silko's *Almanac of the Dead*." *American Indian Quarterly*, vol. 26.4, 2003, pp. 623–40.

Ronda, Margaret. *Remainders: American Poetry at Nature's End*. Stanford University Press, 2018.

Ronda, Margaret. "The Social Forms of Speculative Poetics." *Post45: Contemporaries*, April 8, 2019.

Rosen, Elizabeth K. *Apocalyptic Transformation: Apocalypse and the Postmodern Imagination*. Lexington Books, 2008.

Roth, Philip. *American Pastoral*. Vintage, 1998.

Roth, Philip. *The Human Stain*. Vintage, 2001.

Roth, Philip. *The Dying Animal*. Vintage, 2002.

Ruxton, George Frederick Augustus. *Adventures in Mexico and the Rocky Mountain*. 1848. Kindle edn, J. Murray, 1961.

Sachs, Jeffrey D. "Introduction." *Developing Country Debt and the World Economy*. Edited by Jeffrey D. Sachs. University of Chicago Press, 1989.

Said, Edward. *Culture and Imperialism*. Vintage, 1994.

Schaeffer, Francis A. *How Shall We Then Live?* Crossway Books, 2005.

Schryer, Stephen. *Maximum Feasible Participation: American Literature and the War on Poverty*. Stanford University Press, 2018.

Scott, Lynn Orilla. *James Baldwin's Later Fiction*. Michigan State University Press, 2002.

Scranton, Roy. *Learning to Die in the Anthropocene*. City Lights Publishers, 2015.

Sepich, John. *Notes on* Blood Meridian. University of Texas Press, 2008.

Shackleford, Laura. "Counter-Networks in a Network Society: Leslie Marmon Silko's *Almanac of the Dead*." *Postmodern Culture*, vol. 16.3, 2006.

Shell, Marc. *The Economy of Literature*. Johns Hopkins University Press, 1993.

Shell, Marc. *Money, Language, and Thought: Literary and Philosophic Economies from the Medieval to the Modern Era*. Johns Hopkins University Press, 1993.

Shulman, George. "Baldwin, Prophecy, and Politics." *James Baldwin: American and Beyond*. Edited by Cora Kaplan and Bill Schwarz. University of Michigan Press, 2011, pp. 106–25.

Silko, Leslie Marmon. *Almanac of the Dead*. Penguin Books, 1992.

Silko, Leslie Marmon. *Yellow Woman and a Beauty of the Spirit: Essays on Native American Life Today*. Kindle edn, Simon & Schuster, 1996.

Sinykin, Dan. "Trump and the End Times." *The Los Angeles Review of Books*. May 9, 2016, https://lareviewofbooks.org/article/trump-end-times. Accessed June 21, 2017.

Slobodian, Quinn. *Globalists: The End of Empire and the Birth of Neoliberalism*. Harvard University Press, 2018.

Smethurst, James. *The Black Arts Movement: Literary Nationalism in the 1960s and 1970s*. University of North Carolina Press, 2005.

Smith, Caleb. *Prisons and the American Imagination*. Yale University Press, 2009.

Smith, Rachel Greenwald. *Affect and American Literature in the Age of Neoliberalism*. Cambridge University Press, 2015.

Smith, Ralph A. "John Joel Glanton, Lord of the Scalp Range." *Smoke Signals*, vol. 6, 1962, pp. 9–15.

Smith, Ralph A. "The Scalp Hunt in Chihuahua, 1849." *New Mexico Historical Review*, vol. 40.2, 1965, pp. 16–40.

Smoak, Gregory E. *Ghost Dances and Identity: Prophetic Religion and American Indian Ethnogenesis in the Nineteenth Century*. University of California Press, 2006.

Sorensen, Leif. "The Apocalypse is a Nonhuman Story." *ASAP/Journal*, vol. 3.3, 2018, pp. 523–46.

Spurgeon, Sara. "The Sacred Hunter and the Eucharist of the Wilderness: Mythic Reconstructions in *Blood Meridian*." *Cormac McCarthy: New Directions*. Edited by James D. Lilley, 2002, pp. 75–102.

Stout, Joseph. *Schemers & Dreamers: Filibustering in Mexico, 1848–1921*. Texas Christian University Press, 2002.

Streeck, Wolfgang. *How Will Capitalism End?: Essays on a Failing System*. Verso, 2016.

Stuart, Lyle. "Introduction by the Publisher." *The Turner Diaries*. Barricade Books, 1996.

Sutton, Matthew Avery. *American Apocalypse: A History of Modern Evangelicalism*. Harvard University Press, 2014.

Szalay, Michael. *Hip Figures: A Literary History of the Democratic Party*. Stanford University Press, 2012.

Tedlock, Dennis. "Introduction." *The Popol Vuh: the Mayan Book of the Dawn of Life*. Translated by Dennis Tedlock. Simon & Schuster, 1996.

Teuton, Sean Kicummah. "The Native American Tradition." *The Cambridge History of the American Novel*. Edited by Leonard Cassuto. Cambridge University Press, 2011.

Thomas, Eric A. "'Psychotic Depression' and Suicide in David Foster Wallace's *Infinite Jest*." *Critique: Studies in Contemporary Fiction*, vol. 54.3, 2013, pp. 276–91.

Thornton, Russell. *American Indian Holocaust and Survival: A Population History since 1492*. University of Oklahoma Press, 1987.

Tillett, Rebecca. "The Price of 'Free' Trade: NAFTA and the Economies of Border Crossing in George Rabasa's *The Floating Kingdom* and Leslie Marmon Silko's *Almanac of the Dead*." *Comparative American Studies*, vol. 6.4, 2008, pp. 329–43.

Travis, Trysh. *The Language of the Heart: A Cultural History of the Recovery Movement from Alcoholics Anonymous to Oprah Winfrey*. The University of North Carolina Press, 2009.

Vermes, Geza. "Introduction." *The Complete Dead Sea Scrolls in English*. Edited by Geza Vermes. Penguin, 2011, pp. 1–90.

Wall, Cheryl A. "Stranger at Home: James Baldwin on What It Means to Be an American," *James Baldwin: American and Beyond*. Edited by Cora Kaplan and Bill Schwarz. University of Michigan Press, 2011, pp. 35–52.

Wallace, David Foster. *Infinite Jest*. Little, Brown, and Company, 1996.

Wallace, David Foster. "Fictional Futures and the Conspicuously Young." *Both Flesh and Not: Essays*. Little, Brown, and Company, 2012.

Watkins, Mel. "The Fire Next Time This Time." *Critical Essays on James Baldwin*. Edited by Fred L. Standley and Nancy V. Burt. G. K. Hall & Co., 1988, pp. 232–7.

Weber, David. *The Mexican Frontier: 1821–1846: The American Southwest under Mexico*. University of New Mexico Press, 1982.

Widiss, Benjamin Leigh. *Obscure Invitations: The Persistence of the Author in Twentieth-Century American Literature*. Stanford University Press, 2011.

Wilkens, Matthew. *Revolution: The Event in Postwar Fiction*. Johns Hopkins University Press, 2016.

Wilkens, Matthew. "The Perpetual Fifties of American Fiction." *Neoliberalism and Contemporary Literary Culture*. Edited by Mitchum Huehls and Rachel Greenwald Smith. John Hopkins University Press, 2017, pp. 181–202.

Wilson, Robert Anderson. *Mexico and Its Religion: With Incidents of Travel in That Country during Parts of Years 1851–52–53–54*. Kindle edn, Harper & Bros., 1855.

Wilson, William Julius. 1978. *The Declining Significance of Race: Blacks and Changing American Institutions*. The University of Chicago Press, 2012.

Wittgenstein, Ludwig. *Philosophical Investigations: The German Text, with a Revised English Translation*. Translated by G. E. M. Anscombe. 50th Anniversary Commemorative edn, Wiley-Blackwell, 1991.

Womack, Craig. *Red on Red: Native American Literary Separatism*. University of Minnesota Press, 1999.

Woubshet, Dagmawi. *The Calendar of Loss: Race, Sexuality, and Mourning in the Early Era of AIDS*. Johns Hopkins University Press, 2015.

Zaborowska, Magdalena J. *James Baldwin's Turkish Decade*. Duke University Press, 2008.

Zamora, Lois Parkinson. *Writing the Apocalypse: Historical Vision in Contemporary U.S. and Latin American Fiction*. Cambridge University Press, 1993.

Zijderveld, Anton. *On Clichés: The Supersedure of Meaning by Function in Modernity*. Routledge and Kegan Paul, 1979.

Index

For the benefit of digital users, indexed terms that span two pages (e.g., 52–53) may, on occasion, appear on only one of those pages.

The manufacturer's authorised representative in the EU for product safety is Oxford University Press España S.A. of el Parque Empresarial San Fernando de Henares, Avenida de Castilla, 2 – 28830 Madrid (www.oup.es/en or product.safety@oup.com). OUP España S.A. also acts as importer into Spain of products made by the manufacturer.

www.ingramcontent.com/pod-product-compliance
Lightning Source LLC
LaVergne TN
LVHW010320220926
848484LV00004BB/809
* 9 7 8 0 1 9 8 8 5 2 7 0 4 *